# The Philosophy of Religious Language

B

*To Carrie, who reminds me of what is most important.*

# The Philosophy of Religious Language

Sign, Symbol, and Story

*Dan R. Stiver*

Copyright © Dan R. Stiver, 1996

The right of Dan R. Stiver to be identified as author of this work has been
asserted in accordance with the Copyright, Designs and Patents Act 1988.

First published 1996
2  4  6  8  10  9  7  5  3  1

Blackwell Publishers Inc.
238 Main Street
Cambridge, Massachusetts 02142, USA

Blackwell Publishers Ltd
108 Cowley Road
Oxford OX4 1JF
UK

*Library of Congress Cataloging-in-Publication Data*
Stiver, Dan R.
    The philosophy of religious language: sign, symbol, and story / Dan R. Stiver.
        p.      cm.
    Includes bibliographical references and index.
    ISBN 1-55786-581-7 (alk. paper). – ISBN 1-55786-582-5 (pbk.: alk. paper)
    1. Language and languages–Religious aspects.   2. Religion–Philosophy.
    I. Title.
    BL65.L2S74   1996
    210′.14–dc20                                                        95-17446
                                                                              CIP

*British Library Cataloguing in Publication Data*

A CIP catalogue record for this book is available from the British Library.

Typeset in 11½ on 13½ pt Bembo
by Best-set Typesetter Ltd., Hong Kong
Printed in Great Britain by Hartnolls Ltd, Bodmin, Cornwall.

This book is printed on acid-free paper

# Contents

Preface     ix
Acknowledgments     xiii

1   Introduction     1

    The Linguistic Turn in Philosophy     4

    The Linguistic Turn in Religion     6

    Philosophical Foundations     8

2   Historical Approaches to Religious
    Language     14

    Three Traditional Ways     15
      *The negative way*     16
      *The univocal way*     20
      *The analogical way*     23

    The Universals Controversy     29

    Literal and Allegorical Exegesis     31

3   The Falsification Challenge     37

    The Early Wittgenstein     37

    Logical Positivism     42

    The Falsification Challenge     47

**4   Language  Games**                                    **59**

The  Later  Wittgenstein                                59

Religious  Language  as  Noncognitive                   67
*Wittgenstein on religion*                              67
*Wittgensteinian fideism*                               69

Religious  Language  as  Cognitive                      72
*John  Wisdom*                                          73
*Ian  T.  Ramsey*                                       74
*Ian  Crombie*                                          78

Speech–act  Theory                                      79
*Austin*                                                80
*McClendon and Smith*                                   82

**5   Hermeneutical  Philosophy**                          **87**

From  Regional  to  General  Hermeneutics               87

Ontological  Hermeneutics                               90

Critical  Hermeneutics                                  96

Ricœur  and  Critical  Hermeneutics                     100

Reader-response  Theory                                 107

**6   Metaphor,  Symbol,  and  Analogy**                   **112**

Metaphor  as  Ornamental                                113

Metaphor  as  Cognitive                                 114

Symbol  and  Analogy                                    122

Metaphor  in  Exegesis                                  127

Metaphor  in  Theology                                  129

**7   Narrative  Theology**                                **134**

The  Chicago  School                                    135

The Yale School                                    139

*Hans Frei*                                         140
*George Lindbeck*                                   145
*Ronald Thiemann*                                   150

The California School                              154

*James Wm McClendon Jr*                            154
*Michael Goldberg*                                 155
*Terrence Tilley*                                  159

**8  Structuralism and Poststructuralism          163**

Structuralism                                      163

*De Saussure's influence on Structuralism*         163
*Structuralist thinkers*                           166
*Critique*                                         171

Structuralism in Religious Studies                173

*Ricœur*                                           174
*Thiselton*                                        175
*Patte*                                            177
*Crossan and Via*                                  178

Poststructuralism                                  180

*Derrida*                                          181
*Foucault*                                         184
*Critique*                                         186

Poststructuralism in Religious Studies            188

**9  Conclusion: A Changing Paradigm              193**

Reducing the Contrasts                             194

A Changing Paradigm                                197

Religious Language and Truth                       201

*Contents*

**Notes**      206

**Recommended Reading**      246

**Index**      251

# Preface

When I began teaching an introductory course in the philosophy of religion in 1984, my colleague, Richard B. Cunningham, and I both required students to study a text devoted to the issue of the philosophy of religious language. The linguistic turn in philosophy had not only altered the philosophical terrain, it had in turn impacted all other areas of theological studies. We felt, therefore, that this issue required special attention. What made the need for such a text even more pressing was the fact that many of the introductory books in the philosophy of religion ignored linguistic issues altogether.

At the time the best text on the philosophy of religious language in my opinion was Frederick Ferré's *Language, Logic, and God*, despite its 1961 date of publication. It dealt concisely with the important currents in Anglo-American philosophy of language as they impinged on "God-talk" as well as bringing in some developments in continental theology. On the other hand, a profusion of movements had come to prominence since the 1960s. Increasingly important in religious and theological studies, they were clamoring for attention. It is difficult to understand developments in theology and biblical studies in the last half of this century in isolation from developments in hermeneutical philosophy, philosophies of metaphor, philosophies of narrative, structuralism, and poststructuralism. When Ferré's book went out of print for a time, I searched for another book that had its strengths but was more up to date – but I was unsuccessful.

More recent books similarly focused on Anglo-American

analytic philosophy but for the most part neglected other movements. Some books treated the newer movements, but approached them from other perspectives such as literary criticism or the sociology of knowledge. Excellent book-length treatments of single movements could be found. Still, I was unsuccessful in locating anything close to being adequate as a survey in the philosophy of religious language – thus the inspiration for this work.

After beginning the project, I realized why such books were few and far between. The task was to cover the important areas that the other books had covered as well as treating the new developments. Touching on the various dimensions of the philosophy of language and the implications for religious language in these different movements, all within a concise study, proved to be a daunting enterprise.

First of all, it was difficult to treat all of the movements in the area of language. I brought in issues in semantic theory and in literary criticism tangentially as they were significant in other areas, but I certainly did not give them full treatment. It was also difficult to explore all the ramifications of the particular areas that I did treat. That is why there are full-length studies of metaphor, narrative, and so on. Likewise, it was difficult adequately to treat all the implications for religious language, for example, of hermeneutical philosophy and of structuralism. The choice of themes and examples is further shaped by my own limitations of expertise. A similar type book is that by Anthony C. Thiselton published in 1992; his focus is not particularly on philosophy, but he explores many of this same issues, especially in relation to biblical studies. This is a remarkably erudite book, and I highly recommend it. His text and notes, however, come to 619 pages, which illustrates the difficulty of an introductory treatment.

In light of these difficulties, I have tried to introduce the most significant developments in the philosophy of language for understanding the philosophy of religious language. This is a map that gives the main features of the terrain, but is no substitute for on-site exploration. As an aid to such further investigation, I have offered two kinds of guide. At the end of the book is a short list of recommended additional reading that delves more deeply into the main subjects of the chapter. In addition, I have provided fuller notes than I had originally planned for this introductory work. The text is therefore oriented to those coming to these topics for the first time; for the more advanced, it is hoped that the notes will offer further explanation and suggestions for inquiry.

One difficulty in particular needs some explanation. Given the limits of space, I was not sure whether to provide a separate chapter on feminist philosophy and its impact on biblical studies. The problem is that feminist concerns arise in virtually every other area treated, leading to recapitulation of the issues in every chapter; moreover, there is great diversity among feminist thinkers. What I ended up doing, therefore, was dealing with some of these issues as they arose in contexts such as ideology critique, metaphor, and poststructuralism. This was still an uneasy compromise; feminist issues in religious language could well have deserved separate treatment. A similar question could be raised concerning other liberationist perspectives in theological studies. I hope that relevant material is supplied here; but the philosophy of language has not been self-consciously central in their critiques.

Trying to cover such a broad landscape leaves me in debt to many other "shoulders." I have been dependent upon teachers and colleagues in other specialties in philosophical and religious studies. One factor that led me to think a study like this possible was all the full-length studies of the particular topics, which suggested that the discussion was mature enough to be ready for summary. In the end, the reader will have to evaluate the validity of that judgment; but even the attempt at an introductory work would not have been possible without all the previous efforts.

Of especial importance is my colleague Richard Cunningham, who led me through doctoral studies of many of these issues and who has encouraged my work in this area as a colleague. Several graduate students in philosophy have been partners in exploration along the way and have contributed both by their formal and informal contributions. Particularly I would name Charles

Hawkins, Tim Maddox, Greg Johnson, Bill Becker, Mike Robinson, John Meadors, and Perry Hildreth. Greg and Nancy Johnson read almost the entire manuscript and Charles Hawkins read what they did not, offering helpful criticism. Charles Scalise, former colleague now at Fuller Theological Seminary, and Amy Plantinga Pauw of Presbyterian Theological Seminary, read and discussed with me the basic idea as well as some specific chapters. Charles and Pamela Scalise especially have been fellow-learners of religious and theological issues over the past ten years. As friends and colleagues, we have shared innumerable conversations that have altered my perspectives in ways I can hardly specify.

I cannot omit my context of a theological seminary, where all of these issues are continually raised in the classroom and with colleagues in a multitude of contexts. Hermeneutics, exegesis, preaching, theology, all are a part of the atmosphere, providing a constantly heated crucible for testing the implications of philosophical ideas. Not the least important part of this context has been living through a tumultuous period of theological struggle where issues of religious language have been fraught not only with theoretical but with political and career significance. Few have wanted to listen to a philosopher's crumbs of advice, but the philosophical issues discussed in this work have nevertheless been for us issues of anguish as well as of illumination. The Southern Baptist Theological Seminary has been the occasion of sorrow over these years but also of great joy. It has provided me with the opportunity to teach students who care about these issues. It also provided a sabbatical at the University of Tübingen during the academic year 1990–1, where I wrote the first draft of the manuscript. Several classes have endured the testing of this material along the way, and many thanks is due them for their encouragement and feedback.

Finally, this work is dedicated to my daughter, Carrie, who is now eleven and who has struggled for time in competition with this work. She has been my greatest teacher, however, on the importance of these issues. She has helped me see what Augustine saw, namely, that despite all the difficulties with respect to religious language, we cannot be silent.

# Acknowledgments

The author and publisher would like to thank the following for permission to reprint material included in this volume:

Selected extracts in Chapter 3 are reprinted with the permission of Simon & Schuster, Inc., from *New Essays in Philosophical Thought,* edited by Anthony Flew and Alasdair MacIntyre. Copyright © 1955 by SCM Press Ltd., renewed 1983 by Anthony Flew and Alasdair MacIntyre.

Other extracts in Chapter 3 are from *Theology Today,* 17 (1960), pp. 18–19. Reprinted by permission of the Editors of *Theology Today.*

# 1

# *Introduction*

When future philosophers assess this century's major philosophical emphasis, it surely will be claimed as the century of the linguistic turn.[1] Whereas other eras have been dominated by interest in metaphysical speculation, the nature of reason, or major philosophical–political ideologies, a preoccupation with language has emerged again and again in the twentieth century. Given the symbiotic relationship of philosophy and religion, this philosophical fascination with language has profoundly impacted the understanding of religious language in the twentieth century. This is the story I wish to tell.

Religion has always had a concern for language that has outstripped that of the philosophical tradition, due in large part to the common conviction that the primary subject of religious language is a mystery that is expressed only with difficulty. In the fifth century, Augustine, a theologian-philosopher who wrote more than most about the divine mystery, was struggling to plumb the nature of the Christian doctrine of the Trinity, the belief that God is both one and yet the three persons of Father, Son, and Holy Spirit. In his frustration, he wondered whether he should say anything at all. After considering this option, the answer came to him, "But the formula three persons has been coined, not in order to give a complete explanation by means of it, but in order that we might not be obliged to remain silent."[2]

Such ambivalence between confidence and fearfulness toward the power of words runs through the religious traditions. On the one hand, in the Genesis creation story, God spoke the world

1

into existence, and then Adam named the animals, representing the power of human language to construct a meaningful world through language. The prophets spoke the word of the Lord, and in the New Testament, Christians saw Jesus Christ as the Word of God through whom God created and saves the world (John 1: 1–3). The religions of Judaism, Christianity, and Islam all developed into textual religions centered around the written word through which salvation and healing are mediated.

On the other hand, religion is full of disputes about words. The mystical tradition that characterizes many Eastern religions and much of the Western tradition often claims that words have no descriptive power at all, a position that we will examine in chapter 2. For mystics, the way to God is through transcendence of words. Yet their works about this unnameable experience abound with evocative imagery, which if it does not describe at least elicits these same experiences. Christianity has fought strenuously about words. Is Jesus Christ the same as God or similar to God? Are the stories in the Bible literal or symbolic? Or both? What does grace mean and what do works mean? Lives and careers have often been on the line, depending on whether a person has been characterized as Pelagian, Arminian, Calvinist, liberal, conservative, critical, inerrantist, mainline, or evangelical. These words have had power even when their meaning has been sharply disputed. In the nineteenth century, Søren Kierkegaard was appealing to indirect communication as the best way to convey religious and philosophical truth at the same time that North American fundamentalists were claiming that the Bible is an encyclopedia of literal facts, plain for all eyes to see.[3] In our time, people sometimes wonder if religious words mean anything at all. While some celebrate the new-found liberating power of the Gospel, others with great anguish long to find meaning in the religious symbols but cannot. The American theologian Langdon Gilkey characterizes the contemporary situation as follows: "The doubts which the world has long known about the articles of belief are now recognized by the Church to be her own doubts, and the world's problems with her theological language are the theologian's problems."[4] If Augustine could have known what would happen in the following centuries of the history of Christianity, even he might have wondered if it really was better to speak rather than remain silent!

Yet more is being said and written about religion than ever before. Human beings are *homo loquens*, the speaking animal, as much as they are *homo sapiens*, the thinking animal. The French philosopher Maurice Merleau-Ponty said that humans are condemned to meaning.[5] He might well have said that we are condemned to language. A fascinating example of the indispensable power of language to create a world is found in the autobiography of Helen Keller, who was struck deaf and blind at the age of two. With the help of her teacher, Annie Sullivan, she was lured into the world of symbolic communication (language does not have to be verbal or written). After a stormy childhood incident in which she took a doll, which had been a gift, and trampled it underfoot, her teacher took her outside:

> Some one was drawing water and my teacher placed my hand under the spout. As the cool stream gushed over one hand she spelled into the other the word water, first slowly, then rapidly. I stood still, my whole attention fixed upon the motions of her fingers. Suddenly I felt a misty consciousness as of something forgotten – a thrill of returning thought; and somehow the mystery of language was revealed to me. I knew that "w-a-t-e-r" meant the wonderful cool something that was flowing over my hand. That living word awakened my soul, gave it light, hope, joy, set it free!
>
> I left the well-house eager to learn. Everything had a name, and each name gave birth to a new thought. As we returned to the house every object which I touched seemed to quiver with life.[6]

Such creative power of language has been both lauded and questioned in the twentieth century. We have seen both the intricate detail of symbolic logic and the expansiveness of grand ideologies. We have seen at the same time a profusion of critical

3

analysis and a level of propaganda that the world has never known. For good or ill, perhaps never before has language been so much the center of attention. The French philosopher Paul Ricœur says of our situation:

> The same epoch holds in reserve both the possibility of emptying language by radically formalizing it and the possibility of filling it anew by reminding itself of the fullest meanings, the most pregnant ones, the ones which are most bound by the presence of the sacred to man.
>
> It is not regret for the sunken Atlantides that animates us, but hope for a re-creation of language. Beyond the desert of criticism, we wish to be called again.[7]

Our task is therefore two-fold. The first is to identify significant currents of thought on language in philosophy; the second is to trace the way they have flowed through various aspects of religious reflection. We will begin with historical background, dealing with the philosophical background in this chapter and the religious background in the second. Then we will consider the various innovative movements in philosophy in the twentieth century that have significantly affected the philosophy of religious language.

## The Linguistic Turn in Philosophy

The major philosophical movement in the English-speaking world in the first half of this century, logical positivism, was a reappropriation of David Hume in the light of new logical tools and, not least, a new concern for the philosophical significance of language. This movement was quickly followed by linguistic analysis, which rejected the formalism and absorption in logic of logical positivism and turned to the everyday use of language. On the continent, phenomenology and existentialism merged into philosophical hermeneutics, with the understanding that for human beings it is truer to say that language speaks us than that we speak language. The French schools of structuralism and poststructuralism, or deconstruction, which emerged in the sixties are explicitly concerned with understanding everything to do with the human as being "structured" like a language. The powerful feminist critique of patriarchy centers on the ideology critique of patriarchal language.

In Mark Johnson's collection of essays on the philosophy of metaphor, he humorously reports that if books on metaphor continue to proliferate at their present rate, by the middle of the next century there will be more books on metaphor than there are people.[8] This is not to mention the pervasive influence of new appropriations of narrative and story in philosophy, theology, and many other disciplines. It is perhaps not surprising that in a century where probably more has been said and written to more people than at any other time in history, there has been a preoccupation, if not obsession, with language.

This phenomenon is all the more striking when we consider that the dominant philosophical attitude towards language as a matter of serious concern to philosophers, in the West anyway, has been either neglect or downright contempt. Issues of language had long been relegated to rhetoric or poetics, in other words to the less "scientific" areas, which from the philosophical perspective do not concern themselves with accurately understanding reality. What has been of most concern for the longest period of the West's history has been metaphysics, the attempt to understand the nature and structure of reality. The modern period, however, has seen a general "turn to the subject," as it has been called, and with that shift a correlative concentration on epistemology, the question of how and with what justification we know reality. The logic of that shift is preeminently exemplified in the thought of Immanuel Kant: we must first understand knowing before we can be confident about what we know. The extension to issues of language that has arisen in this century smoothly follows from the fecund realization that we cannot understand knowing or thought apart from the language in which it is expressed. As John Sturrock says, "Language is no longer the simple, transparent medium of thought it was once accepted as being. We prefer now to equate language with thought; and instead of looking through it, at reality, we look at it, in an attempt to understand how we first of all acquire it and then use it."[9] Or as Jonathan Culler says, speaking of the North American philosopher C.S. Peirce's stress on signs and symbols, "It is not that we have objects on the one hand and thoughts or meanings on the other; it is, rather, that we have signs everywhere."[10] Therefore, to put it perhaps too simply, we must understand speaking in order to understand knowing, and perhaps in the end we can return to the issue of understanding reality or being. It is true, however, that the long road back has appeared too treacherous to many thinkers, so that in the meantime the purpose of philosophy has often taken a permanent detour from metaphysics in the grand style to more chastened and limited enterprises of analyzing language.

Given this connection with epistemology, the discussions in the following chapters will often deal with the truth or cognitivity of language. A movement like logical positivism deals with religion by rejecting its attempt to make truth claims. In response, some affirm the usefulness of religious language but concede that it is noncognitive. Many thinkers explore the multitudinous ways that religious language can be meaningful, but a constant question is how it depicts reality and how it can be justified. In this sense, despite the way in which these movements strike out in new directions, they do not escape their philosophical past.

## The Linguistic Turn in Religion

The emerging skepticism about many traditional uses of language at the beginning of this century led to a burgeoning concern of philosophers with language and religion, for the relationship between the two has been deep and pervasive. Despite the disciplinary divorce between philosophy and theology since the outset of the modern period, there at least have been "visitation rights." Consequently, the split has not led to a complete break in the relationship, although the influence tends to be one way, flowing from philosophy to theology. In its turn, however, as we shall see, philosophy itself has been not only deeply affected by science, but has been threatened with the very demise of its task by science. If philosophers have occasionally called for the end of religion on one flank, it is often in the face of being overrun by science on another flank. The impact of science, however, has not been only negative. In a more positive vein, for example, the recent attention that philosophers of science have paid to the pervasive influence of the metaphor has attracted philosophers and theologians alike (see chapter 6).

In the light of the intricate connections between philosophy and religious reflection, we would expect the turn to language to have had its impact – and such a supposition is justified. We cannot comprehend the twists and turns of philosophy of religion and theology in this century aside from issues such as the falsification challenge, demythologization, hermeneutical philosophy, the parables as metaphors, narrative theology, structuralism, the feminist critique of patriarchy, and deconstruction. With the increasing specialization of disciplines, the influence of a philosophical movement may be felt at one point more in biblical studies, at another in theology, and at another in history. For example, the falsification challenge engaged philosophical theology, structuralism engaged biblical studies, and the philosophy of narrative has influenced theology, biblical studies, and historiography more widely.

Despite the fact that this century is marked above all by linguisticality, there is also a historical foundation for contemporary understanding of religious language. Medieval debates about the univocal way or the analogical way, or between realism and nominalism, or between the merits of four-fold exegesis and the *sensus literalis* (the literal sense) continue to inform and provide the backdrop for contemporary understanding. This is not to mention the significant emphasis of mystical traditions upon the noncognitive use of religious language. These are the issues of specifically religious language with which we will deal in chapter 2.

## Philosophical Foundations

General philosophy of language also is rooted in tradition. Despite the twentieth-century turn to language, ours is not the first century to grapple with language. Certain views, philosophies, if you will, of language developed quite early and exerted a remarkable influence through the centuries. The basic approach to language rooted in Plato and Aristotle continued to be the dominant paradigm up until the twentieth century – and continues to be very significant.

In the fifth century before the Christian era the fledgling development of philosophy in the Greek city state of Athens was already threatened by a modern-sounding skepticism concerning language.[11] After the part metaphysical, part natural-scientific theories of the "pre-Socratics," who boldly announced the basic nature of reality, for example, as water (Thales), air (Anaximenes), or fire (Heraclitus), the problems raised threatened to leave philosophy stillborn. The conflicting views – particularly the standoff between the views of Parmenides that movement is an illusion and of Heraclitus that rest is an illusion – led some to an early disenchantment with speculative philosophy.

Socrates, in fact, after initial enthusiasm in his younger days for such natural-metaphysical speculation, sharply turned his back on it and towards a more ethical concern, the question of how one should live. In the meantime, however, in part due to the blind alleys reached by the earlier philosophers, the Sophist movement had spread throughout Greece. We encounter some of its more radical representatives in Plato's dialogues, where the search for rational truth is abandoned for political expediency. These teachers taught political survival skills to young aristocrats in exchange for money. These proto-Machiavellians had as their premise that if there was such a thing as truth, it was based on power. Those who have the most power determine what is true and just.[12] As a result, they taught how to gain power, primarily through linguistic skills. This was the beginning of the pejorative connotation of rhetoric – as sophistry – and the split between rhetoric and philosophy.[13] This kind of rhetoric had little to do with truth but much to do with demagoguery.

Socrates criticized this movement, but he was often considered part of it. And it is true that some of his arguments, as reflected in Plato's accounts, do not represent always a sincere search for truth, but a desire to trick his opponent. Nevertheless, in the main Socrates has a positive confidence in the ability to discern some ethical truth by which to live – and die – even if he was as irritating as a gadfly in critically examining the flaws in how to express it. As revealed in Plato's early dialogues, few could match the artistry with which Socrates could employ dialogical question and answer to plumb the hidden problems and possibilities behind ordinary language – of course, often without coming to any final conclusion about the real truth of the matter. That could wait for another day.

Beyond Socrates' critical approach, we find in his student Plato, and in Plato's student Aristotle, a return to and perhaps the establishment of philosophical speculation proper. In Plato we find the foundation of the prevailing paradigmatic approach to language in the West. Language is a reflection of what is more ultimate, namely, eternal "forms" or concepts or ideas. Perhaps influenced by the more mystical Pythagorean philosophy, Plato places an emphasis on direct "seeing" over speaking, speaking over writing, and direct speech over figurative speech – this last despite the fact that Plato himself was one of the greatest artisans of figurative speech. Notoriously, however, in his ideal republic he placed strict limits upon the poets, who could only inadequately represent reality and inflame dangerous emotions, in favor of a cooler, literal, nonfigurative language. Reality itself is only a shadow or imitation of the real ideational world, according to Plato, and artistic imitation can only be an imitation of an imitation.[14]

In *Cratylus*, Plato asks:

> Let us suppose that to any extent you please you can learn things through the medium of names, and suppose also that you can learn them from the things themselves – which is likely to be the

9

nobler and clearer way; to learn of the image, whether the image and the truth of which the image is the expression have been rightly conceived, or to learn of the truth whether the truth and the image of it have been duly executed?[15]

This passage suggests the secondary nature of language for the grasp of reality. Plato has even more disdain for the capacity of the written word to capture what can be expressed in dialogue and perceived in the soul. The distance of writing from the immediacy of living dialogue gives rise to the following criticism by Socrates in the dialogue *Phaedrus*: "He would be a very simple person . . . who should leave in writing or receive in writing any art under the idea that the written word would be intelligible or certain; or who deemed that writing was at all better than knowledge and recollection of the same matters."[16] A similar view is offered in Plato's letter regarding one student's attempt to share in writing the gist of Plato's teaching. Plato writes, "No man of intelligence will venture to express his philosophical views in language, especially not in language that is unchangeable, which is true of that which is set down in written characters."[17]

Aristotle, while being more positive about language and less other worldly, also reflected the split between straightforward prosaic language and figurative language. Poetics and rhetoric belong to "practical philosophy," not to scientific, metaphysical philosophy proper. While crucial for life, and analyzed with rare acuity, practical philosophy is not nourishing wisdom *per se*; it is not what the wise person contemplates. Nevertheless, in Aristotle many have seen a forerunner of that practical and sensible attention to the "uses" of ordinary language that was recaptured in modern Oxford "ordinary language philosophy" (not surprisingly by those who cut their eye teeth on Aristotle above all), and neglected in the metaphysical elaborations of later philosophers. In the end, however, Aristotle contributed to the idea of language as an instrument for thought and to the idea of the superiority of univocal or literal language over the symbolic (see chapter 6 for more discussion on this point).

As a last note on Greek beginnings, after the fall of Athens and any grounds for the kind of confidence exhibited by Plato and Aristotle, the Skeptical School emerged. In what was considered to be a return to Socrates they denied the human capacity to grasp reality at all, understood words as mere practical devices furthering human life, and exhibited an ethical life-style based on these modest metaphysical claims.

The philosophical paradigm rooted in Greek philosophy that has predominated in philosophical thought until modern times has three components. First, meaning lies in individual words. Second, the meaning of words is primarily literal or univocal, which implies that figurative language must be translated into literal language in order for it to be understood. Last, language is instrumental for thought. The first point implies a kind of verbal atomism, often promoting a neglect of the wider context of words and of their actual use. The second promotes the relegation of figurative language for the most part to secondary status, significant at best not for cognitive purposes but for persuasive (rhetoric) or aesthetic (poetic) purposes. A corollary of Aristotle's approach thus was that the meaning of figurative language can be grasped only if it can be transposed or reduced to literal language. This approach has been called the substitutionary theory of symbolic language because it is based upon the idea that one can "substitute" a literal term for the figurative. Often, figurative language was regarded with a Platonic suspicion, in the medieval period as well in the modern. As we shall see, biblical language was an important exception, but the obvious significance of poetic language in Scripture could be justified as a special case – for it had a very trustworthy author – God. The third point recognizes the priority of thought. The idea was that thinking is in some ways a separate process from speaking, as evidenced by the common experience of seeking for the right word to express a thought. The effect also was to make language, philosophically speaking, secondary and less significant.[18]

Two additional assumptions closely related to epistemology, the theory of knowledge, affect the understanding of language. Clarity is a virtue when it comes to the expression of knowledge.

11

In other words, the clearer we are, the better. Plato's allegory of the cave compared knowledge to seeing things in the clear light of the sun, representing a common appeal to ocular metaphors for knowledge.[19] René Descartes in the seventeenth century argued that a sign of knowing something is that it is "clear and distinct."[20] As we shall see in chapter 4, Ludwig Wittgenstein advanced a similar criterion in his early philosophy: "Everything that can be thought at all can be thought clearly. Everything that can be put into words can be put clearly."[21]

The second additional assumption is that certainty is similarly a virtue; the more certain, the better. Plato argued that "opinion," where we are uncertain, is an entirely different faculty than knowledge.[22] Aristotle sensitively explored a category of practical wisdom (*phronesis*), which can never be completely rule governed. On the other hand, he privileged the realm of certain and demonstrable knowledge as the realm of knowledge *per se*.[23] Hence Thomas Aquinas, working out the implications of an Aristotelian philosophy for Christian theology in the thirteenth century, sharply distinguished between knowledge, which is self-evident or can be demonstrated with certainty, and faith, which is a species of opinion that nevertheless allows firm assurance due to its reliance on God's authority.[24] In the modern period, the requirement of certainty moved to rigorous scientific methodology and verification, with enormous implications for religion (see chapter 3).[25]

Looking at religious language in light of these five assumptions, it is evident that it does not fit. Religious language tends to be shrouded in imprecision and mystery. It can hardly be verified and is profuse with symbol and imagery. The characteristic response has been to segregate religious language as the language of faith from the language of reason in various ways such as reason preceding faith (Aquinas) or faith preceding reason (Augustine).

Virtually every philosophical movement we will trace in the ensuing chapters rejects this paradigm. The exceptions are in chapter 2, which is a historical survey of the different perspectives on religious language before the twentieth century, and chapter 3, which delineates one of the most vigorous reaffirmations of the traditional paradigm – now in a linguistic mode – and its concomitant aggressive challenge to the cognitivity of religious language. The remaining chapters look at quite new directions whose impact is still being realized. Chapter 4 treats the turn toward ordinary language and Ludwig Wittgenstein's conception of "language games." Chapter 5 turns to the continental tradition of hermeneutical philosophy. Chapter 6 focuses on the philosophy of metaphor and chapter 7 on narrative. Chapter 8 draws together the French movements of structuralism and post-structuralism; their effect is to open up novel ways to treat the cognitivity of religious language. These movements characteristically question what John Austin termed "the descriptive fallacy," that the primary purpose of language is to depict reality (see chapter 4). Thus they explore other uses and functions of language that open up a new appreciation of the various complex uses of language in religion, to wit, to pray, to worship, to confess, to praise, etc. More radically, however, they explore new ways in which religious language is cognitive. Religious language in their perspective may appropriately convey meaning by and not despite its imprecision (chapters 4 and 8), its immersion in communities of tradition (chapter 5), its heavy reliance on metaphor (chapter 6), and its largely narrative shape (chapter 7). We will return in the last chapter to consideration of the cumulative effect of these movements toward a new paradigm for religious language.

# 2

# *Historical Approaches to Religious Language*

The twentieth-century turn to language has opened up many new directions for the understanding of religious language, but it certainly has not been the first century to grapple with the issue. As Augustine's lament – that he spoke only in order not to be silent – over language about the Trinity indicates, religious thinkers have long been perplexed about how to stretch and elongate words from one context to fit another, very different reality.[1] What we will seek in this chapter are the basic results of these earlier wrestlings with the difficulty of using our "human, all too human" language to speak of what is transcendent.[2] What we will find are some well-traveled paths that will provide entry into the thicket of problems raised by the twentieth-century philosophy of language for religious language. Three basic options that we still face in religious language have already been clarified for us by the theological tradition, so we will examine them in some detail.

More briefly, we will then look at other historical discussions that impinge upon our concerns. A significant medieval debate centered around the basis of "universals," common nouns like person or goodness. Are they rooted in some reality in things, or in something beyond things (perhaps ideas in God's mind?), or are they simply pragmatic human constructions? In the early Christian church, debate centered on whether the Scripture should be interpreted literally or allegorically, raising the whole issue of the exegesis, or interpretation, of sacred texts. Are there distinctive matters pertaining to Scripture, for example, as opposed to religious language in general? These questions about universals and the exegesis of sacred texts are still with us. It may be that the twentieth century offers no better answers than the previous centuries; on the other hand, these lingering questions certainly were a part of the ferment that has led to new resources – and perhaps new answers.

## Three Traditional Ways

In the medieval period we find the clearest expression of the three options that traditionally have provided the only choices for religious language. In the thirteenth century, Thomas Aquinas (1224/5–74) argued that religious language is *analogical*, that is, it conveys truth but not literal truth. In the same century, John Duns Scotus (1264–1308) contended that Thomas's view was incoherent. In fact, he emphasized that only two options are possible, univocal and equivocal language. For example, the word "bat" can mean two very different things, a baseball bat or a flying mammal. If we do not know to which it refers, the use is equivocal. If we do know to which it refers, it is literally, or univocally, one or the other. No other option exists. What is interesting in this difference of opinion is that neither thinker took seriously the alternative of equivocal language. They assumed that since religious language, particularly Scripture, is in fact meaningful, it must be either univocal or analogical. They neglected, however, an important trajectory in Christian history, namely, that religious language is noncognitive. This view is a minority voice in Christian thought but is perhaps the majority view in Eastern thought. More specifically, all words must be denied or negated in order to understand Ultimate Reality truly, hence this option is often designated as "the negative way" (*via negativa*).

Contemporaneously with Aquinas and Scotus this view was being presented by perhaps the most famous preacher of the time, the German mystic Meister Eckhart (1260–1327), and also by the great Jewish philosopher, Moses Maimonides

15

(1135–1204). This tradition sees language as valuable only in the sense of being evocative of an experience of the divine or the ultimate. Such a view has again come to prominence in the twentieth century. We shall begin by considering this rather low-profile negative option of the West, then the univocal option, and finally Thomas's analogical view.

## *The negative way*

The assertion that all religious language is equivocal, and must be negated, may strike us as being skeptical and belonging rather to unbelief than to belief. What is perhaps surprising at first glance is that this view is often held by those who are most emphatic about the reality and vividness of an experience of God. This is a characteristic view of the mystical tradition that, according to some, cuts across different world religions.[3] In the West the view is rooted in Platonic thought. As we have seen, however, Plato's thought itself is influenced by Eastern ideas mediated by the Pythagorean School. Neo-Platonism emphasized that aspect of Plato's thought that stressed the transcendence of the One (or the Good), and the way the One is beyond all categorical language or thought. In the third century Plotinus (CE 204–70) portrayed a mystical view of God and a mystical approach to God. The One is beyond all knowing and saying. The One however emanates forth into mind, which further emanates into soul. Emanation continues downward, we can say, into matter. The result is a hierarchy or chain of being. In Plotinus' monistic thought, there is no separate reality of evil *per se* as in dualism, but evil is the result of coming ever closer to pure matter, being the farthest remove from pure spirit.

The spiritual ascent to the One then lies in an imageless or "apophatic" type of meditation.[4] One quiets oneself, getting rid of the "lowest" and moving to the "higher," that is, one quiets first the body, then the images of the mind, then the words and thoughts of the mind, opening up the possibility of the unmediated encounter with the One, "the flight from the alone to the alone," as Plotinus called it.[5] What is usually emphasized is that this experience is ineffable and indescrib-able yet intensely real, the most real experience one can have. Such a mystical practice, whether rooted in the pervasive influ-ence of the neo-Platonism of Plotinus or not, is widely repre-sented in the medieval spirituality tradition, for example, in Meister Eckhart and in the anonymous author of *The Cloud of Unknowing.*

Neo-Platonism became the primary philosophical foundation for the early church, in significant ways influencing Augustine, who in turn was the key intellectual figure in the Western church until Aquinas. The other great source of spiritual thought, however, was a Christian theologian much more influenced by Plotinus than was Augustine, Pseudo-Dionysius the Areopagite, whose writings virtually carried the weight of Scripture until the Reformation.

The reason for his authority is that later Christians believed him to be the Dionysius mentioned in Acts in the context of Paul's sermon in Athens (Acts 17: 34). So they regarded him as a disciple of Paul and virtually an eye witness of the early church. It was not until the fifteenth century that such authenticity was severely questioned.[6] In any case, Pseudo-Dionysius suggested that there are different approaches to God. In *The Divine Names* he shows how the names of God do not literally describe God but point to God as the cause of all things. On the other hand, he appears to subordinate this affirmative way to the negative way. He argues that "the higher we ascend the more our lan-guage becomes restricted" until finally we arrive at "a complete absence of discourse and intelligibility."[7] The way we must fol-low to this highest point is the *via negativa,* which means that all terms must be denied of God. A striking example, which will be quoted at length in order to convey the flavor of this approach, is in his *Mystical Theology:*

> Once more, ascending yet higher we maintain that It is not soul, or mind, or endowed with the faculty of imagination, conjecture, reason, or understanding; nor is It any act of reason or under-standing; nor can It be described by the reason or perceived by

the understanding, since It is not number, or order, or greatness, or littleness, or equality, or inequality, and since It is not immovable nor in motion, or at rest, and has no power, and is not power or light, and does not live, and is not life; nor is It personal essence, or eternity, or time; nor can It be grasped by the understanding, since It is not knowledge or truth; nor is It kingship or wisdom; nor is It one, nor is It unity, nor is It Godhead or goodness; nor is It a Spirit, as we understand the term, since It is not sonship or Fatherhood; nor is It any other thing such as we or any other being can have knowledge of; nor does It belong to the category of non-existence or to that of existence; nor do existent beings know It as it actually is, nor does It know them as they actually are; nor can the reason attain to It to name It or to know It; nor is It darkness, nor is It light, or error; or truth; nor can any affirmation or negation apply to It; for while applying affirmation or negations to those orders of being that come next to It, we apply not unto It either affirmation or negation, inasmuch as It transcends all affirmation by being the perfect and unique Cause of all things, and transcends all negation by the pre-eminence of Its simple and absolute nature – free from every limitation and beyond them all.[8]

Several observations about this characteristic passage can be made. First, it relies on a common method of the negative way. One moves beyond words and concepts by denying them, which is to lead, not to skepticism or unbelief, but precisely to the truth, to the insight and actual experience that God is beyond all such words. This represents a reliance on language, but it is reliance on a functional or evocative sense only. No cognitive or descriptive content is allowed. We will see that even Thomas finds the *via negativa* an important first step to understanding religious language, while not seeing it as more than partial. Second, we must note the remarkable thoroughness with which he carries through the method. Not only the negative terms are denied – evil, falsehood, unreality – but the positive terms – goodness, truth, reality – also are negated, even to the point of denying fatherhood and sonship to God – an astonishing step for a Christian theologian. Third, we should note that the rigor of this passage undercuts any approach involving cognitive meaning. Fourth, despite the thoroughness, at the end the author lapses into unusually straightforward assertion. When he deals with the question of why we should approach God in this way, he alludes to common rational explanations of God's relation to the world.

What happens to Dionysius here points to a perplexing inconsistency on the part of most proponents of the equivocal way.[9] It is very difficult to speak and write about what one has experienced, in short, to communicate meaningfully about it, without supposing that one can indeed communicate about it, which is what they want to deny. In fact, mystical writings are very extensive and often very illuminating. Perhaps the only consistent response would simply to be silent and not say or write anything.

A similar approach in the Western tradition was the twelfth-century work of the Jewish philosopher Moses Maimonides, who also influenced Aquinas. He writes in *The Guide for the Perplexed*:

> There is a great danger in applying positive attributes to God. For it has been shown that every perfection we could imagine, even if existing in God . . . would in reality not be of the same kind as that imagined by us, but would only be called by the same name, according to our explanation; it would in fact amount to a negation.[10]

He contends that the best that can be done is simply to deny any attribute applied; the result will be that "you have undoubtedly come one step nearer to the knowledge of God."[11] Some would argue that such a purely negative approach simply fails; it never says enough to make a difference.[12] And even if it did, Maimonides inconsistently, like Pseudo-Dionysius, calls upon affirmations of God at other points in his thought such as God's simplicity and God's understanding.[13]

Another example from the Eastern mystical tradition that especially underscores the "instrumental" use of religious language is the Zen Buddhist *koan*, a seemingly nonsensical riddle that is to be the means to *satori*, or Enlightenment. A well-known *koan* is "What is the sound of one hand clapping?"[14] A disciple may puzzle over such a riddle for months or even years, and when the disciple comes to the end of all rational approaches, precipitated perhaps by a slap or blow by the Master at the opportune time, *satori* occurs. The nonsense is the point. This usage exemplifies very well how language can be valuable in the negative way, but as a means, not as a description. Nevertheless, even Zen Buddhists speak of what is supposedly unspeakable, if only to distinguish their vision of ultimate reality from a more typically Western one.

This contradiction or difficult challenge that lies at the heart of the negative way appears almost insuperable, especially if it arises in the context of a Western religion centered on a written revelation from God. Thus Aquinas and Scotus assumed that the equivocal option is ruled out because God has indeed communicated to us about the divine nature. On the other hand, this approach is a reminder, especially to the univocal way, that language is notoriously unstable when applied to God. We are stretching it to its breaking point – and perhaps beyond. It is a warning against the idolatry of language. Even religions centered on writing and speaking can see how language functions to protect the transcendence of God. An obvious example in the Jewish tradition was the earlier refusal to speak or write the name of God, with the result that today we still are not sure of what that name was.

## The univocal way

John Duns Scotus argued that the choice is between univocal language and equivocal language. Since it is clear that meaningful revelation has been given, religious language must consequently be either univocal or based on univocal language. What did he mean by univocal language? Scotus replies, "I call that a univocal concept whose unity suffices for contradiction when it is affirmed and denied of the same things. It also suffices as a syllogistic middle term."[15] For example, in the syllogism – All humans are mortal; Socrates is human; therefore, Socrates is mortal – "human" is used univocally as the middle term. Scotus recognized that there is much figurative language in Scripture, but the implication is that we would not know what such language meant apart from being able to translate it into literal language.

Scotus has been followed by modern theologians also. It is not surprising to find perhaps the most significant evangelical theologian, Carl Henry, making the same point as Scotus. He argues against the third way of analogy: "The logical difficulty with the theory of analogical prediction [sic; predication] lies in its futile attempt to explore a middle road between univocity and equivocacy. Only univocal assertions protect us from equivocacy; only univocal knowledge is, therefore, genuine and authentic knowledge."[16] Further, he writes, "Unless we have some literal truth about God, no similarity between man and God can in fact be predicated. . . . The alternative to univocal knowledge of God is equivocation and skepticism."[17] Scotus could not have expressed it better. What is curious is that within a short space Henry goes on to write, "Of course God is epistemologically transcendent; of course human beings do not have exhaustive knowledge of him." This concession appears to take back with one hand what he gave with the other. One can see in this tension Henry's awareness of doing justice to the transcendence of God, yet at the risk of self-contradiction, which was one of the dangers of the equivocal way.

What may be more surprising is to find someone at the other end of the theological spectrum, such as Paul Tillich, making the same point. Tillich is usually recognized for opening up the significance of symbolic language in expressing what cannot be expressed in any other way (see chapter 6). He has also been claimed for the equivocal way, making him representative of all three options.[18] Nevertheless, it is quite clear in Tillich's systematic theology that he expresses the classic univocal way. In the first volume of Tillich's systematic theology, he maintains that there is only one literal statement in theology. He says:

Theologians must make explicit what is implicit in religious thought and expression; and, in order to do this, they must

begin with the most abstract and completely unsymbolic statement which is possible, namely, that God is being-itself or the
absolute.

However, after this has been said nothing else can be said
about God as God which is not symbolic.[19]

It is important that there is at least one such statement; otherwise,
the remaining symbolic language would not have meaning.
Tillich apparently came to this view as a result of a challenge by
another professor who was expressing the classical Scotist position.[20] A univocal foundation is necessary for language to have
meaning.

Tillich certainly allows much greater scope for symbolic language than Henry does, but structurally their approach is the
same. However, apparently due to the questionability of the
actual "literalness" of "being-itself," he moved to a further altera-
tion. "Being" by itself is an elusive term, as even Aristotle long
ago recognized. It is not at all clear what the literal meaning of
being-itself is. Consequently, in the second volume of Tillich's
theology, he suggested that the literal foundation of symbolic
religious language is, "Everything we say about God is symbolic."[21] This response is actually not very helpful. It may be that
Tillich's statement is literally true and that he rightly recognizes
the symbolic nature of being-itself; what is not clear is how
it provides the needed "substitution" that would provide
foundational "content" for religious language.

Another example of a liberal theologian who follows this line
of thought is Schubert Ogden. Ogden earlier followed the analogical way, but in his most recent writing firmly rejects it in
favor of the univocal way. He confessed that he was won over by
what is clearly the classical Scotist position, that unless there is a
univocal foundation, we cannot ascribe meaning to the use of
symbolic or metaphorical language. One of the examples he gives
is as follows: "The same ultimate reality that is symbolically
asserted to be the boundless love of God is literally the universal
individual whose action on all others and reaction to all of their
actions in turn are alike unsurpassable."[22] It takes little reflection

to see that Ogden is vulnerable to the same problems as Tillich. Is "universal individual" truly literal? We may have some idea of the literal meaning of each term taken by itself in its common contexts (although "universal" may present the same problems as "Being"), but when we put them together, it is not at all clear what they mean. Some would say rather that it is a contradiction in terms to speak of an individual being universal. Or others might even say that "God is boundless love," while being metaphorical, is much clearer and more understandable than "God is a universal individual." Or another way of putting the question is to ask, "Is the first phrase any more metaphorical than the second?"

In conclusion, it is apparent that the univocal way is still alive and well, but that it has its endemic problems. It may be that if the only choice is between equivocal or univocal language, many may choose the latter; but the cost is high. It is difficult to see how we can move from literal language, with its context in everyday life, to the transcendence of God without sacrificing something precious to common religious sensibilities. That is why it is often those most committed to spirituality who opt for the equivocal way. The question urgently presents itself, is there not a third way?

## The analogical way

Precisely because of such difficulties, Thomas Aquinas opted for a third way, attempting to do justice to the intentions of both of the other "ways" and yet to avoid their drawbacks. As such, his appeal to analogy became the standard model for understanding religious language and merits especially close attention. As mentioned above, he began with the *via negativa*, thus ruling out the univocal way from the outset.[23] God is not a being like other beings. God cannot be "classified" into some genus and species.[24] Every term used of God must consequently in an important sense be denied, "for what He is not is clearer to us than what He is."[25] Aquinas does not stop there, however, because he shares the later Scotist conviction that we do have cognitive revelation, that is,

23

we know something of God and can express this knowledge in language. As Aquinas says, "If, then, nothing was said of God and creatures except in a purely equivocal way, no reasoning proceeding from creatures to God could take place. But, the contrary is evident from all those who have spoken about God."[26] How do we, however, understand this "mean between pure equivocation and simple univocation?"[27]

Aquinas's answer is that we know and speak of God "analogically."[28] Aquinas's views on analogy can be interpreted in a variety of ways and may represent no systematic theory.[29] Historically, however, two of his explanations of analogy have been extremely influential, namely, analogy of "attribution" (or "proportion") and analogy of "proportionality." Analogy of attribution can be understood through an example that Aquinas uses.[30] We attribute health to persons in a literal sense, that is, persons possess health "formally." On the other hand, we might say of medicine that it, too, is healthy, but it certainly is not healthy in the literal sense that people are healthy. The reason seems to be that medicine causes people to be healthy; thus, it is healthy in a derivative or "virtual" sense. When we then turn to Aquinas's famous emphasis on God as the first or uncaused cause of the world, it follows that since God is the cause of everything, the names of everything can be virtually attributed to God. God is love because God is the cause of love. As Aquinas expresses it more fully:

> Our natural knowledge takes its beginning from sense. Hence our natural knowledge can go as far as it can be led by sensible things. But our mind cannot be led by sense so far as to see the essence of God, because the sensible effects of God do not equal the power of God as their cause. Hence from the knowledge of sensible things the whole power of God cannot be known; nor therefore can His essence be seen. But because they are His effects and depend on their cause, we can be led from them so far as to know of God whether He exists, and to know of Him what must necessarily belong to Him as the first cause of all things, exceeding all things caused by Him.[31]

A quick objection may come to mind, which Aquinas, in his usual way, anticipates, that is, this seems to prove too much. If God is the cause of everything, then everything can equally be attributed to God. How then can we distinguish between more or less appropriate characterizations of God? Is God as aptly "love" as a "lion?" To press the point further, is God as much evil as good, or in more trivial fashion, is God sour-tasting as well as omnipotent? If so, as Frederick Ferré points out, "The analogy of attribution admits of no control."[32] In response, Aquinas first of all can appeal to his understanding of evil as nonbeing to dismiss negative terms.[33] Evil, to put it perhaps more simply than the issue deserves, is the lack of being, and therefore all being, as such, is good. Evil in itself is nothing. Therefore, we cannot appeal to God as the cause of what is not. Negative characterizations of God, therefore, on the basis of the analogy of attribution, are ruled out. Second, since God is infinite, terms that are capable of infinite expansion are more applicable than terms that are not. Thus, "good" is more appropriately applied to God than is "lion." Calling God a "lion," or Jesus "the bread of life," or "the door to the sheepfold" are what Aquinas calls metaphors. He expresses the difference well:

> There are some names which signify these perfections flowing from God to creatures in such a way that the imperfect way in which creatures receive the divine perfection is part of the very signification of the name itself, as stone signifies a material being, and names of this kind can be applied to God only in a metaphorical sense. Other names, however, express these perfections absolutely, without any such mode of participation being part of their signification, as the words being, good, living, and the like, and such names can be properly applied to God.[34]

For Aquinas, and in general for the Thomistic tradition, therefore, analogy is a much more potent category than metaphor. We will find later that this estimation is exactly reversed in other contemporary traditions (see chapter 6).

A second problem, however, is that this causal approach makes the terms refer primarily to creatures and not to the Creator, whereas our theological sensibilities incline us to say that these perfections belong primarily to God and not to the creature. We would not want to claim, for example, that humans are "just" in a primary sense and God is only secondarily "just." Aquinas also anticipates and sidesteps this problem by pointing out that the effect in such a case must exist more perfectly in the cause.[35] And since he has been able to show that God is infinite and unlimited, positive attributes exist in God in a "perfect" and unlimited way. The dilemma is solved when we realize that according to our mode of knowing or signification, we must move from the created world to God the Creator. On the other hand, we are able to realize that according to the way things truly are in reality, the order of being, these perfections are predicated primarily of God.

The objection that Aquinas fails to answer has to do with the ground of his approach, namely, causation. Terms can be ascribed to God analogically because God is the cause of all things. But how is "cause" used in this case? If cause is used in a literal sense, we have claimed that all language ascribed to God is analogical – based, however, on one univocal ascription, God as cause. This is precisely the univocal approach, remarkably akin to that of Tillich. On the other hand, if cause is used analogically, Aquinas is explaining analogy by an analogy, a good example of a circular argument.[36] Thus in this sense he is caught on the horns of a dilemma. Richard Swinburne flatly concludes that this traditional form of the analogy of attribution is contradictory.[37]

A further objection relates to some of Aquinas's medieval metaphysical assumptions crucial to his argument but not as widely shared today. As indicated, Aquinas assumes that any perfection must exist more perfectly in God as its cause; thus, if love is a perfection in humans, then God, as a higher-order cause, must possess love in a more perfect way. Moreover, there must be some supremely perfect cause of any finite perfection. These assumptions, as well as the background assumption of the cosmological argument, are not nearly so self-evident after the criticisms of David Hume and Immanuel Kant in the eighteenth century, as we can see by examining virtually any modern discussion of the traditional arguments for the existence of God. If we question these foundations, though, the whole apparatus begins to totter. Is Scotus correct after all? In the end, are there only two options, univocity and equivocity? Perhaps the second attempt at an explanation will fare better.

The second approach to analogy, that of proportionality, follows from the name. We may say that a cabbage has life or is alive. Probably we would consider that it has life literally in the way that any other garden plant lives. On the other hand, we may consider that there is only a proportional relationship between the life of a cabbage and the life of an animal: a cabbage has life in the way appropriate to a cabbage, and a rabbit has life in the way appropriate to a rabbit. Life functions differently in both cases, but it is also similar, that is, analogical. When applied to God, the proportionality is simply extended. We then would say that life is to a cabbage as life is to God. God has life (or love, or goodness, or power) in the way appropriate to God. As Ferré has pointed out, however, it is not so simple. In a mathematical proportionality, both sides are actually equivalent. So we can say that 2 is to 4 as 8 is to 16 because the relationships are really the *same*. In Aquinas's case, however, the two sides of the comparison are not only materially different, they occur in ontologically different realms of reality. So we should dismiss from the outset the exactitude that comes from the misleading appearance of being a mathematical proportion. In addition, even a mathematical proportion must have three known terms in order to find the fourth. If we know that 2 is to 4 as some $x$ is to 16, we can easily deduce the $x$ as 8. Aquinas's model trades on this fact. His idea is that we can give sense to a predication such as "good" by placing it in equation with three other known terms. For example, good ($x$) is to God as good is to persons. The problem is that we do not have a way of knowing who God is either. Actually, we have two unknown terms, which means that the proportionality is useless.

Eric Mascall has attempted to solve this problem by suggesting that we can fill in the missing knowledge of God through the use of the analogy of attribution.[38] If we understand God in terms of God as the first cause of all things, we know enough to sharpen that knowledge via the analogy of proportionality. The two approaches to analogy thus complement one another. The obvious loophole, however, is that the first explanation, analogy of attribution, is itself problematic as an explanation of analogy. If we concede that the analogy of attribution is in fact a univocal approach, we can perhaps proceed. But then we fall prey to all of the arguments against the univocal approach, some of the best of which stem from Aquinas himself.

It is also evident that both types of analogy make metaphysical assumptions that are more questionable today. The likeness is based on a likeness in all being, the so-called "analogy of being." Aquinas says that things are like God according to analogy, "as being is common to all. In this way the things that are from God, so far as they are beings, are like God as the first and universal principle of all being."[39] Such an analogy of being has come under heavy attack in this century by theologians themselves, most notably by Karl Barth, who called it "the invention of Antichrist."[40] Others, as we shall see, believe that a third way can be developed quite apart from such metaphysical assumptions. In any case, the questionability of these assumptions limits the persuasiveness of the analogical way.

In light of these problems, some have argued that Aquinas's reflections on analogy are not attempts to explain analogy so much as they are attempts to express analogy, that is, that it works. Mascall says of the doctrine of analogy:

> It is not to furnish us with knowledge of God, but to explain how we have come to have it . . . If the doctrine of analogy can explain how this is possible, so much the better; if it cannot, it is the doctrine of analogy that is discredited, not our knowledge of God.[41]

David Burrell similarly suggests that when we attend to the use of analogy, we discover that its purpose is to enable an altered understanding, a metaphorical leap, not to enable a step-by-incremental-step path to the understanding of God.[42] With the new insights into the nature of both univocal and metaphorical language in the twentieth century, we will be able to make a fresh return to analogy. The medieval discussion, however, leaves us with a virtually uncrossable gap.[43] It seems that we have come to a dead end in terms of the classical debate. Real issues are raised, but each approach seems to have fatal flaws. We will see that the contemporary discussion continues to deal with the same issues, sometimes reproducing the same flaws all over again as well. Our task is to search for genuinely new possibilities that enable more adequate formulations. Nevertheless, the classical options can provide for us some initial paths to follow through the contemporary thicket.

## The Universals Controversy

In the medieval period another controversy raged over the nature of language that has had enduring effect.[44] The Platonic tradition's great influence on the church until the time of Aquinas supported an understanding of words as standing for "ideas," which although abstract, nevertheless have a "real" metaphysical existence; hence this view was called "realism" (not to be confused with the later epistemological idea of realism, which means almost the opposite, that the world exists externally to ourselves and is basically the way it is presented to us through our senses). In other words, behind the form of every concrete existing thing, there is an ideal pattern or idea that is the prototype. This Platonic notion was shifted by Augustine from the conception of a separate world of ideas to the existence of these ideas in the mind of God. John Scotus Erigena (ninth century) was a significant representative, and in the debate his conception began as the most significant one.

Against this view, some propounded the conviction that words have significance only as human constructions. Only individual things exist, and so all concepts or ideas are human abstractions, or as William of Ockham (ca. 1280–1347) once contended, mere sounds only. They are pragmatic devices for organizing human experience and have no ultimate metaphysical significance. In other words, they are names only, hence the reason why this approach is called "nominalism." Rather than the ideas existing *ante res* (before the thing), they exist only *post rem* (after the thing). Such debates may seem obscure, but vital theological issues were at stake. The realists were convinced that their view was the only one that could do justice to the doctrine of the Trinity, that God was three persons in one substance or essence. If there were no reality beyond individuals, there could be no unity in the Trinity, and hence tritheism would be the result, which was the conclusion of the nominalist Roscellinus (d. 1125).

Moreover, to take another example, the doctrine of transubstantiation was at risk. In Communion the elements retain their "accidents," the qualities of bread and wine, but have as their essence the body and blood of the Lord. For a nominalist like Ockham, realism threatened God's omnipotence and freedom since such essences would place undue limitations upon God. We may note the similarity between nominalism and the Skeptical School of ancient Greece. The nominalist view was indeed suspicious of reason, but was not altogether skeptical, tending rather to exalt revelation over reason.

A mediating way, as we may imagine, was proposed by Aquinas, who was following Abelard (1079–1142); this is variously called "moderate realism" or "conceptualism." This approach is more akin to Aristotle's view that only concrete individuals exist, but that different individuals of a species have in common a form that can be grasped or abstracted by the mind. This form or idea is not simply a human construction but is a human insight into what is, that is, the idea exists *in re* (in the thing). Universals therefore represent abstractions but are truly grounded in reality.

As we can see, this discussion blurs the distinction between words and thoughts. Actually, most thinkers continued to presume the basic primacy of thoughts or concepts over words. The closer the realists could make the connection between the thought or concept and a fitting word to express that thought, however, the more confident they could be. We will return to the issue of universals in chapter 4.

As far as language in general was concerned, the kind of philosophy of language all were considering was a univocal one. Words stood at least for created, finite realities, if not also for universal ideas. The question of how they applied to God was the debate between the negative, univocal, and analogical ways that we have already considered. The next controversy we shall consider, however, takes up in another way the vexed issue of figurative language.

## Literal and Allegorical Exegesis

Another significant chapter in the historical story concerns exegesis of Scripture. Again and again, the special case of Scripture as religious language emerges. How is the Bible to be interpreted? Is it somehow different from other texts, from other religious language? Historically, two significant alternatives in the early church are represented by the so-called Alexandrian and Antiochene schools of exegesis.[45] Although their differences are sometimes overplayed, they manifested different emphases on interpretation.

Before they developed in the third and fourth centuries, though, some traditions were already part of their legacy. Jesus and Paul, not surprisingly, used rabbinic forms of exegesis. One of the most famous examples is Paul's story of Abraham, Sarah, and Hagar in Galatians 4: 24, in which he uses the Greek rhetorical term "allegory." It is more likely, however, that Paul was using "typology," a form of interpretation in which the past events of Scripture were seen as historical but also prefiguring the time in which Paul was living. Nevertheless, Paul's apparent approval of allegory proved to be tremendously influential.

In the controversy with Gnosticism in the second and third centuries, in which the Gnostics favored the use of allegory that revealed a higher, spiritual knowledge (*gnosis*), interpreters such as Irenaeus (d. ca. 202) and Tertullian (d. ca. 222–5) argued that only the bishops of the church who stood in an authoritative line from the apostles had the authority to interpret the Scriptures. Tertullian stressed that all interpretation should agree with the "rule of faith" (*regula fides*), the basic creed of the church, also rooted in the authoritative bishops and their churches. Both sides of this controversy bear witness to the difficulty of interpretation, to the fact that meaning does not lie plainly on the page, so to speak, simply to be "read off." They already recognized that what one brings to the text is almost as important as the text itself.

The Alexandrian school, located in a city that was a major center of Greek culture in Egypt, while not regarded as being heretical like the Gnostics, nevertheless favored the more allegorical, spiritualizing approach. As we might imagine from their location, their tradition was not just the Bible but also a Greek philosophical background. An important predecessor was Philo (ca. 20 BCE to CE 50), a Jewish interpreter who creatively combined the Jewish and Greek heritage. The literal sense was not ignored but was often seen as the lower, more primitive sense that must be transcended by the higher, allegorical exegesis. Origen, the most famous member of this tradition, argued for a three-fold exegesis corresponding to the anthropological notion, rooted in Paul and in Greek philosophy, that the human body consists of body, soul, and spirit. Correspondingly, Scripture has a literal, a moral, and a spiritual sense.[46] In practice, though, the contrast was usually simply between "the letter and the spirit" (2 Corinthians 3: 6).

Augustine, too, was repelled at first by what he saw as the crudity and anthropomorphism of the Bible, which hindered his being a Christian. It was not until he learned how to allegorize such elements in the Scripture that he could in good conscience affirm it as God's word.[47] Out of this tradition came the famous medieval four-fold sense of Scripture. The common example was Jerusalem. In the literal sense, Jerusalem is the earthly city. In the allegorical sense, Jerusalem is the Christian church. In the tropological (moral, ethical) sense, Jerusalem is the soul. In the anagogical (future, eschatological) sense, Jerusalem is the future heavenly city of God.[48] It was not always necessary for every passage of Scripture to contain all four senses, although this is sometimes what exegetes attempted. The Alexandrian emphasis on the figurative sense is exaggerated by the idea that the literal sense does not allow for any symbolism whatsoever.[49] This rather wooden view of the literal meaning led to an understandable denigration of it in favor of the symbolic. The method often led to what, in our eyes, seem wild flights of fancy and imagination.

What should not be missed, though, in the midst of such speculation, which in its own time would not have seemed so far fetched, is that there were hermeneutical controls. The preeminent control was the "rule of faith." Interpretation should agree with what the church has taught, pointing to the importance of a community of interpreters. The use of allegory favored approaching the text via a theological grid. Other controls existed, such as an early recognition of the "hermeneutical circle," namely, that we should interpret a passage in context, not only in the local context but also in the context of the whole Bible. A corollary is that we should interpret the difficult passages by the plain. These hermeneutical principles still provide important foundations for modern hermeneutical method. The fact that these controls existed does not mean that they were always followed. For a more sober application, we must look to the Antioch School.

This school was critical of the flights of allegory in the Alexandrian School and emphasized the primacy of the literal, historical sense. As Robert Grant says, "The school insisted on the historical reality of the biblical revelation. They were unwilling to lose it in a world of symbols and shadows. They were more Aristotelian than Platonist."[50] They, too, were interested in the spiritual but saw it as coming through the letter. While the Antioch School did not entirely carry the day, its influence can be seen in the approaches of Augustine and Aquinas. Aquinas still recommended the four-fold sense of Scripture but firmly rooted the latter three senses in the literal sense. In fact, drawing on Augustine, he argued that the meanings of the other three senses could, and should, be found as the literal sense in other passages of Scripture.[51]

The Reformers in the sixteenth century, however, brought about an even greater emphasis on the literal sense. The magisterial Reformers, Martin Luther, Ulrich Zwingli, and John Calvin, not to mention the Radical Reformation leaders, all stressed the primacy of the literal sense alone. Luther said, for example:

> No violence is to be done to the words of God, whether by man or angel; but they are to be retained in their simplest meaning wherever possible, and to be understood in their grammatical and literal sense unless the context plainly forbids, lest we give our adversaries occasion to make a mockery of all the Scriptures. Thus Origen was repudiated, in olden times, because he despised the grammatical sense and turned the trees, and all else written concerning Paradise, into allegories; for it might therefrom be concluded that God did not create trees.[52]

For the Reformers, the emphasis on the plain sense of Scripture was tied to the shift in authority for interpretation. Rather than the church, with its creeds, councils, and popes, being the primary authority, this role fell to Scripture alone. Consequently, we can understand the Reformers' emphasis on the perspicuity and straightforwardness of Scripture.[53]

Nevertheless, their approach was not based on a simplistic appeal to Scripture; they had their own hermeneutical controls, which involved tradition.[54] Luther and Calvin both stressed the role of the Holy Spirit in illuminating the meaning of the Bible. Luther particularly mandated that the entire Scripture be read in light of its testimony to Jesus Christ and justification by faith alone, thus accounting for his antipathy towards the epistle of James. Calvin was entirely comfortable in appealing to creeds and in upholding the traditional doctrine of the Trinity.

The tension between an allegorical and literal interpretation should not be confused with the philosophical debate between the univocal and analogical approaches to religious language in general. Allegory is figurative language, to be sure, but it is interpreted by being translated into more straightforward language. One could be a supreme allegorist, but still favor a univocal approach where the meaning of allegory is provided by a substitution of univocal language. Conversely, emphasis on the literal sense of Scripture, such as we find in Aquinas, does not militate against an analogical approach to religious language in general. The literal sense in this context refers to the historical meaning; it stresses the historical reality of the referent. On the other hand, the means of referring could be analogy or metaphor. The criterion is to consider what the author was intending. As we saw in Luther, the rule usually was to prefer a literal rather than a figurative interpretation unless the context made it clear that a figurative expression was being employed, as in some of Jesus's sayings and in the bizarre imagery of the book of Revelation. In these cases, the "literal" or plain sense is the figurative sense.

In addition, much of the language of Scripture refers to this world, not directly to God, so the question of how we refer to God does not arise. However, when Scripture speaks of God, Aquinas would argue that the language must finally be analogy. For example, when 1 John says, "God is love" (1 John 4: 8), the literal or plain sense – in the context of the exegetical discussion – must be understood in terms of God being analogously love – in the context of the philosophical discussion. The problem is that the word "literal" is used in different ways in the philosophical context (whether religious language is univocal, analogical, or equivocal) and in the exegetical context. Although the philosophical issues will be most prominent in our study, the exegetical issues are also important in twentieth-century discussions. We will return to the issue of tradition in chapter 5, to the issue of allegory in chapter 6, and to the issue of the special status of Scripture in chapter 7.

With the advent of modernity and its "flight from authority," significant changes in exegesis occurred.[55] Without going into detail, the primary insight is that, with the advent of historical consciousness, the Bible is to be interpreted like any other kind of literature, as a historical document in terms of the context of its time. Thus, the ideas of the Bible can be seen as borrowings and modifications of ideas in its Near Eastern setting. This meant also that exegetes would be critical of the historical claims, leading often to skepticism about the course of events in Scripture. Historical methodology particularly was applied to the Gospels using such principles as "analogy," that is, that events happened in the past in basically the same way they happen in the present. This led many to become very critical of claims of miracles. Another principle applied to the sayings of Jesus is that no saying could be regarded as genuinely Jesus's if it were similar to other ideas of the time. This left very little, if anything, that could be attributed to Jesus. Further, preoccupation with the historical dimension of the text has often led to neglect of the literary dimensions and even directed attention away from the text itself to "the world behind the text." The success of the historical-critical method in opening up the text in an unprecedented way has led to its widespread, even if critical, acceptance. However, the dangers of these principles are fairly obvious. The principle of analogy, for example, could lead to a kind of cultural imperialism, with everything being interpreted in terms of current understanding. New developments in hermeneutics (noted in various contexts in chapters 5 to 8) call for serious revision of many of these principles, without necessarily implying their wholesale rejection.

As we begin to examine currents of thought on the philosophy of religious language in the twentieth century, we will find that the discussions, while often significantly new, nevertheless relate to the historical discussions. The issues of the nature of religious language, whether equivocal, univocal, or analogical, whether realist, nominalist, or something else, and questions of exegesis, particularly questions about the historical-critical method, will crop up again and again.

# 3

# The Falsification Challenge

In 1955 a symposium took place that dominated the philosophy of religion for the next quarter century. Published in the journal *University*, it became known as the *University* debate. It represented the legacy of one of the major philosophical movements in the early part of the century, logical positivism, which placed a marked emphasis on the univocal approach to language in general. The upshot for religious language in particular, however, was that it was considered not simply false, but meaningless, or more strikingly, nonsense. Ironically, the *University* debate centered not around univocal prose but around parables that each of the three main speakers used to convey their different positions. Before turning to these parables and to this crucial debate, we will need to consider the background.

## The Early Wittgenstein

One of the most remarkable figures in the twentieth century is Ludwig Wittgenstein. He became a key figure in two of the most significant philosophical movements in the first part of the twentieth century, logical positivism, which we will examine here, and functional analysis, which we will consider in the next chapter. Wittgenstein was still an aeronautics student from Vienna when he inquired of the famous British philosopher Bertrand Russell whether he, Wittgenstein, had the ability to be a philosopher or was a "complete idiot" and should become an aeronautic engineer. Russell reported that he had Wittgenstein write a paper on a philosophical topic and that after reading only one sentence of it, he responded, "No, you must not become an aeronaut."[1]

Russell himself was perhaps the major British philosopher of the time, an established scholar who, with Alfred North Whitehead, had laid the foundation for symbolic logic in *Principia Mathematica*. More importantly, with G.E. Moore he had shifted the impetus of British philosophy from idealism back to the strong British tradition of empiricism. The added emphasis on logic led to this school often being called "logical empiricism."

With the aid of powerful new logical tools, Russell and others were able to take up the legacy of David Hume and establish it on firmer foundations. A primary aspect of their approach was what has been called "Hume's fork." Hume conceived of only two types of meaningful assertion: propositions about "matters of fact" and about "relations of ideas." The first had to do with the way propositions convey truths about the empirical world. These assertions are contingent because they could be true or they could be false. In other words, there is no a priori reason, apart from learning by experience, why a person should know whether such a proposition could be substantiated. For example, "The earth has one moon" is a proposition that, although true, could conceivably have been false. These propositions are also called "synthetic" because we must attempt through experience to connect the meanings of the terms with their corresponding referents in order to determine whether they are true or not. The second type of proposition expresses logical relationships. This type of proposition does not say anything about the world but only about the way we use language or symbols. It is therefore necessarily true or necessarily false. We can know a priori, by the meanings of the terms, whether a proposition is true or not, without "checking" through experience. For example, "A is not 'not A'" or "All bachelors are unmarried" are examples of such logical truths. They are considered "analytic" because their truth or falsity is determined simply by analysis of their meaning.

Russell's early work in particular conceived of the world as composed of discrete particulars that are related to each other in logical relationships, hence the name "logical atomism." He believed that the more closely we can fit our language to a one-to-one relationship with sensations of atomistic particulars, as basic as "redness" or "wetness," the more adequate it will be. In other words, the more we can attain to words or symbols that stand univocally for such experiences, the better. Russell looked, additionally, to logical analysis to dispel philosophical confusion. For example, his famous theory of descriptions showed how definite descriptions that imply the existence of their referent, for example, "The present King of France is bald," can be analyzed in such a way as to avoid assuming the existence of something that is nonexistent. In fact, the implication of his position pointed towards the replacement of everyday language with a more accurate logical calculus. G.E. Moore, while more attentive to everyday language and less oriented to logic, also stressed analysis of language into its simple or atomistic components. Both of these philosophers had a great impact on Wittgenstein, and vice versa. In an obituary notice on Wittgenstein, Russell said "Getting to know Wittgenstein was one of the most exciting intellectual adventures of my life."[2]

Out of the exposure to Russell's interests, combined with the legacy of his Viennese upbringing, Wittgenstein composed as a soldier in World War I a short, enigmatic book entitled *Tractatus Logico-Philosophicus*.[3] Containing only seven major numbered propositions, it became virtually the Bible of the logical positivist movement, centered first in Vienna, hence the name the Vienna circle, and later in England and America. We find in this book Hume's distinction between two types of language, that describing states of affairs and that describing logical relationships. Wittgenstein's basic idea was that synthetic language presents a logical picture of the world. Like the way a musical piece is represented variously by sheet music, the grooves on a record, and by sound waves, facts and their relations are represented logically by language.[4] Wittgenstein is supposed to have hit upon this idea when considering the way in which a car accident had been portrayed by dolls in a courtroom setting.[5] He thus maintained that we deal not directly with things but with "facts" stated in propositions. "The world," he said, "is the totality of facts."[6] Like Russell, he argued that words only have meaning in a sentence. "Only propositions have sense; only in the nexus of a proposition does a name have meaning."[7] There must be, he thought, logical, verbal simples that correspond to factual simples, but they only have meaning as picturing an elementary state of affairs in a proposition. He suggested then that the meaning of a cognitive proposition lay in knowing what it pictured. As he put it, "To understand a proposition means to know what is the case if it is true."[8] One way to dispel philosophical confusion is to ferret out this logical structure, as Russell did in his theory of descriptions, and to reduce molecular propositions to these elementary propositions.[9] His view was that "language disguises thought", so that philosophy must be a critique of language.[10]

Wittgenstein made significant advances in logic also. For our purposes, though, it is important simply to note that, like Hume, he argued that logical truths are the only other legitimate category of meaning, but that they tell us nothing about the world. In his words, they are all tautologies.[11] Either they are necessarily true or necessarily false; they cannot possibly be false or they cannot possibly be true. The argument "If 'p' then 'q', 'p', therefore 'q'" tells us something that must be the case, whatever the symbols stand for. In this way, their most important function is to provide part of the structure for picturing the world. Logical operators or "connectors" like "if," "and," "but," and "or," and the logical operations based upon them, do not correspond to objects in the world but make it possible to picture arrangements of objects, that is, to represent facts.[12] "The propositions of logic describe the scaffolding of the world, or rather they represent it. They have no 'subject matter.'"[13]

Another key emphasis was his assertion, "Everything that can be thought at all can be thought clearly. Everything that can be put into words can be put clearly."[14] Language either speaks (or pictures) clearly, univocally, or it does not speak. A related aphorism was the last sentence in the book: "What we cannot speak about we must pass over in silence."[15] "*The limits of my language*," he thus stated, "mean the limits of my world."[16] The significance of this latter saying for the Vienna circle was to rule out anything but empirical propositions as cognitively meaningful; this included aesthetics, ethic, metaphysics, and religion. So far, they agreed with Wittgenstein. They drew the conclusion in some cases, however, that these areas were insignificant. Not so Wittgenstein. The Vienna circle could hardly make sense of Wittgenstein's enigmatic last pages in the *Tractatus*, where he said, "We feel that even when all *possible* scientific questions have been answered, the problems of life remain completely untouched."[17] "They are what is mystical."[18] Such things could be "shown," he thought, but not "said." This was true even of his own remarks about the function of logic and of propositions. The way logic functions and the way language is used to picture the world can only be shown. As Wittgenstein says, "What finds its reflection in language, language cannot represent. . . . Propositions *show* the logical form of reality. They display it."[19] Nor could the Vienna circle comprehend the fact that Wittgenstein sometimes read them poetry in the meetings.[20]

As has only recently become clear in studies of his life, Wittgenstein truly believed at the time that we should only use univocal language in clear statements about the empirical world or in necessary statements about logic. But he definitely believed that what was most important, ethics, aesthetics, yes, and religion – the mystical – made such empirical language pale into insignificance. In terms of the traditional categories, Wittgenstein regarded language in general as univocal and religious language as equivocal. This Kierkegaardian and Tolstoyian strain in Wittgenstein's thought, rooted in his Viennese education, was a deep source of continuing misunderstanding between him and Russell, indeed, the whole British context.[21] In fact, although Wittgenstein allowed Russell to publish the *Tractatus*, he felt that Russell had not understood it.

In any case, Wittgenstein was so convinced that he had solved the central problem of philosophy, the relation of philosophy to language, that he quit philosophy. His bold statement in the preface of the *Tractatus* to that effect was: "The *truth* of the thoughts that are here communicated seems to me unassailable and definitive. I therefore believe myself to have found, on all essential points, the final solution of the problems."[22] As Wittgenstein turned to gardening, to being a teacher in an elementary school, to architecture, even to considering becoming a monk, the Vienna circle took his programmatic ideas and applied them with evangelistic zeal – which became a fearsome challenge to metaphysics and religion.

## Logical Positivism

With the aid of Hume's fork and Wittgenstein's elaboration of it, the Vienna circle especially focused on the criticism of metaphysics.[23] Beginning in 1922, a group of scientists, philosophers, and mathematicians met weekly to develop an approach to philosophical problems similar to the program enunciated by Wittgenstein. Among its members were Moritz Schlick, Rudolf Carnap, Otto Neurath, Kurt Gödel, and Friedrich Waismann. In 1969, one review of the movement said:

> It was a revolutionary force in philosophy, for it stigmatized metaphysical, theological, and ethical pronouncements as devoid of cognitive meaning and advocated a radical reconstruction of philosophical thinking which should give pride of place to the methods of physical science and mathematical logic. . . . Today logical positivism no longer exists as a distinct movement, yet its effects, direct and indirect, recognized and unrecognized, continue to be felt.[24]

In 1986, Wentzel van Huyssteen, in a book on the cusp between science and theology, commented upon the stance of the logical positivists, "This stand was to lead to a logical-positivistic conception of science that many scientists adopted up to the 1960s and are adopting even today, whether consciously or subconsciously."[25]

The key was what came to be known as the verification principle, which means that the meaning of a proposition lies in the mode of its empirical verification.[26] This is a corollary of the view that cognitive language expresses an empirical state of affairs. For example, what does the proposition "A table is in the kitchen" mean? It means that if we go into the kitchen, we can see a table, feel a table, perhaps even smell a table. In a more scientific manner, we could weigh and measure the table with instruments. Especially in the early years, the logical positivists desired conclusive or absolute verification.[27] Also as a corollary, like Russell and Wittgenstein, they wished to reduce language to certain, univocal statements about matters of fact. These "protocol sentences," as they were often called, would sometimes refer to immediate sense data – psychologism or phenomenalism – or sometimes to concrete physical measurements – physicalism.[28] Moritz Schlick, the key figure holding the Vienna circle together, said:

> What was originally meant by "protocol statements", as the name indicates, are those statements which express the facts with absolute simplicity, without any moulding, alteration or addition, in whose elaboration every science consists, and which precede all knowing, every judgment regarding the world. It makes no sense to speak of uncertain facts. . . . If we succeed therefore in expressing the raw facts in "protocol statements" without any contamination, these appear to be the absolutely indubitable starting points of all knowledge.[29]

Strictly speaking, the logical positivists argued that philosophy has to do only with language, for when we verify, we are verifying a sentence or a proposition.[30] On the part of some, then, there was a dream to construct a unified science around ideal symbolic "languages" that would allow clear, unequivocal communication.[31]

When applied to less empirical disciplines such as ethics, aesthetics, metaphysics, and religion, the verification principle ruled their propositions as cognitively meaningless since they clearly could not be empirically verified. The force of the logical positivists' objection, against religion for example, is much more severe than the traditional atheistic view that religious beliefs are false. An atheist might concede that the claim that "God exists" is meaningful; the evidence, however, does not support it. For the logical positivists, religious beliefs are not yet in the ballpark of truth and falsity or of being supported by evidence. In other words, they have not achieved the merit of being meaningful, albeit false; they are simply cognitive nonsense. Along with metaphysical beliefs, they could be regarded as a certain kind of art, which might express an attitude toward life. The problem is that they do not do it well; they take the misleading form of empirical or theoretical assertions. As Carnap said of metaphysicians, "Metaphysicians are musicians without musical ability!"[32]

With the elimination of metaphysics, is there role left for philosophy? Yes, they claimed, but only as a kind of metatheory about science. Scientific language is the only meaningful type of cognitive language, but there is a place for reflection about what constitutes proper scientific language and scientific theory. Trying to avoid Wittgenstein's paradoxes, of speaking of what can only be "shown," they thought that it was possible to discuss, as a kind of metatheory, the way we use language and the way it connects up with the world.[33] Thus, philosophers could establish that the verification principle was the criterion for meaningful cognitive statements and further specify how a proposition might be empirically verified. In this approach, philosophy is reduced basically to a philosophy of science. Logical positivism is consequently powerful testimony to the hegemony of science in the modern Western world, which has had significant impact upon the understanding of religious language ever since science arose as a significant cultural force in the Enlightenment.

As discussed above, the members of the Vienna circle advanced their ideas with religious zeal, proclaiming in the spirit of Wittgenstein that they had provided the key to solving the age-old riddles of philosophy. Perhaps none was more zealous than A.J. Ayer, who conveyed these ideas in a very influential way to the English world in *Language, Truth and Logic* in 1936. He, too, dismissed metaphysics and religious language as cognitively meaningless. He, too, based this judgment on the reduction of cognitive language only to tautologies or analytic statements on the one hand and empirical statements that could pass the verification principle on the other. He thus had the same confidence as Wittgenstein, who had provided "a *definitive solution* of the problems which have been the chief sources of controversy between philosophers in the past."[34] In particular, Ayer emphasized an emotive approach to ethics. Since people use ethical language, which, however, cannot be cognitive, what is its meaning? He suggested that ethical statements express the feelings of the speaker. For example, when I say, "Stealing money is bad," this is just another way of saying "Stealing money!!" with a particularly strong show of feeling.[35] Since no factual statement is being made, you can disagree with my moral feelings but you cannot contradict me.

Despite Ayer's advocacy of these views, however, he was already showing an awareness of complications. Like a meteor that shines brightly for a while, then quickly fades, the Vienna circle *per se* faded quickly for a variety of reasons. One was the social situation. Europe became convulsed in war, leading to the scattering of the circle, as well as of much else. Its leader, Schlick, was murdered by a student in 1936. A consequence of this scattering, however, was the spread of its influence, particularly in America. Scholars like Carnap helped move American philosophy beyond pragmatism and idealism to an intense emphasis upon logical symbolism. Nevertheless, the fervor of the school abated. Perhaps the most significant factor, to their credit, was their own internal critique of the cherished verification principle. In an embarrassing way, the linchpin of logical positivism, the definitive philosophy that was an end to metaphysics and religion, appeared itself to be metaphysical and capable of being believed only on faith.

When Hume's fork was applied to the verification principle, it was seen to be clearly unempirical. How can one use empirical proof to prove that every cognitively meaningful proposition can only be empirically proven? That would be circular. Is this statement analytic then, a reflection of the way humans use language? Certainly it is not the way all people have used language in the past; it is in fact a rather recent usage. Ayer was thus driven to say that it was only a convention or a recommendation. If so, what is to keep us from rejecting it? This dilemma was never satisfactorily resolved.[36] Additionally, because of the realization that no scientific hypothesis can be conclusively verified, Ayer had moved away from an emphasis on correspondence or picturing towards saying that the value of science was predictability or pragmatic usefulness.[37] He and Carnap also moved from requiring complete verification to a weaker claim that a proposition must be verifiable only in principle to be meaningful.[38]

A further challenge was raised by Karl Popper, a philosopher of science with friendly relations to the Vienna circle. He argued that science actually does not so much strive to verify as to falsify a hypothesis.[39] In other words, the way one arrives at a hypothesis is not so important; the important thing is to know how it might be falsified and how resistant it is to falsification. This is the difference between the logic of discovery and the logic of justification. As Popper says, "According to my proposal, what characterizes the empirical method is its manner of exposing to falsification, in every conceivable way, the system to be tested. Its aim is not to save the lives of untenable systems but, on the contrary, to select the one which is by comparison the fittest, by exposing them all to the fiercest struggle for survival."[40] Logically speaking, a hypothesis can never be conclusively verified. In this strict sense, verification actually commits a logical fallacy, namely, that of affirming the consequent. Take the conditional proposition "If I jump off the rim of the Grand Canyon, I will fall." If I in fact have fallen, this does not necessarily mean that I jumped from the Grand Canyon rim; it could be from some other rim, or from an airplane. However, if I jump off the rim of the Grand Canyon and do not fall, then the proposition has been definitively falsified, at least as a universal assertion. Thus, a logical asymmetry exists between verification and falsification in favor of falsification.[41]

Popper was more reluctant than the logical positivists to universalize, to apply his falsification principle beyond science to all other regions. He contended that it was a demarcation criterion for science but not necessarily for other areas, a much more modest proposal than that of Wittgenstein or the Vienna circle. A weakness of his view is that despite the logical asymmetry between verification and falsification, it is also very difficult conclusively to falsify a hypothesis – alternative explanations can usually be found for the failure of an experiment. Popper recognized this, but he believed that his emphasis on empirical testing nevertheless mitigated spurious attempts to evade the force of evidence.[42] He did not make strong claims to truth anyway, suggesting that conclusive truth could never be found and that confidence in science rested, in the final analysis, on a decision that transcended rational argument.[43] In general, it seemed that Popper's cautious ideas were closer to the actual practice of science than to the rather utopian views of the positivists.

For various reasons, then, the fervor of logical positivism abated, and it is often said that no one would call himself or herself a logical positivist today. Nevertheless, as indicated earlier, it is not difficult to see a tacit or working employment of these principles in the approach of much of the scientific community. Moreover, the transmutation of the verification principle into the falsification principle proved to be as threatening to religious propositions as ever, as we shall see.

## The Falsification Challenge

Antony Flew in the *University* debate posed the challenge to belief in the form of a parable derived from an earlier essay by John Wisdom.

> Once upon a time two explorers came upon a clearing in the jungle. In the clearing were growing many flowers and many weeds. One explorer says, "Some gardener must tend this plot." The other disagrees, "There is no gardener." So they set up a barbed-wire fence. They electrify it. They patrol with bloodhounds. (For they remember how H.G. Wells's *The Invisible Man* could be both smelt and touched though he could not be seen.)

47

But no shrieks ever suggest that some intruder has received a shock. No movements of the wire ever betray an invisible climber. The bloodhounds never give cry. Yet still the Believer is not convinced. "But there is a gardener, invisible, intangible, insensible to electric shocks, a gardener who has no scent and makes no sound, a gardener who comes secretly to look after the garden which he loves." At last the Sceptic despairs, "But what remains of your original assertion? Just how does what you call an invisible, intangible, eternally elusive gardener differ from an imaginary gardener or even from no gardener at all?"

In this parable we can see how what starts as an assertion, that something exists or that there is some analogy between certain complexes of phenomena, may be reduced step by step to an altogether different status. . . . But though the process of qualification may be, and of course usually is, checked in time, it is not always judiciously so halted. Someone may dissipate his assertion completely without noticing that he has done so. A fine brash hypothesis may thus be killed by inches, the death by a thousand qualifications.

And in this, it seems to me, lies the peculiar danger, the endemic evil, of theological utterance.[44]

After raising the question of the problem of evil and how believers typically make qualification after qualification to explain how a perfectly good and powerful God might yet allow suffering, he ended with the question, "What would have to occur or to have occurred to constitute for you a disproof of the love of, or of the existence of, God?"[45]

We should not underestimate the power of this challenge, despite the rejoinders that can be brought to it. It identifies a serious problem for belief, the problem of evil, and a real tendency of apologetes to cause belief "to die the death of a thousand qualifications." It also correctly focuses on the major difficulty of religious language in a scientific context, that it refers to a reality that is not empirically accessible. And specifically, it underscores an important point: that if an assertion is compatible with any state of affairs whatsoever, it is empty since it literally makes no difference whether we believe it or not. These interlocking problems present a challenge that haunts almost anyone who has genuinely grappled with questions of divine providence or with God's activity in the world.

A closer look, however, reveals that Flew's approach has problems of its own. It is clear that it presupposes the falsification criterion, but applies it far beyond Popper's own restrictions. Flew makes it as universal as the earlier verification principle of the logical positivists in a way clearly inconsistent with Popper's own restrictions of it to scientific language. In Popper's terms, we could clearly concede that God's reality is not the sort of reality that falls under scientific enquiry, but it is not unique on that score and such a concession presents no problems in principle – unless we believe that empirical falsification, or verification, is the criterion for all cognitive language. But that assumption had been thoroughly explored, and found wanting, by the logical positivists themselves. The very foundation of Flew's challenge, therefore, that which gives it its cutting edge, is itself not empirically verifiable or falsifiable.

It is clear, therefore, that if we grant Flew this assumption that the only allowable proof is empirical, we are going to be hard put to defend traditional usage of religious language. What Flew has done is actually to restate the traditional teleological argument for the existence of God. In other words, does the character of the world give evidence for the existence of some kind of designer (gardener)? Without going into that issue, suffice it to say that this is an open question. It is generally not regarded as a valid proof but may be seen as a valid argument. Flew's approach restricts this whole issue in a novel way by counting only empirical evidence for the designer as valid, suggesting something that can hardly be found anywhere in the history of Christian thought, that God is empirically discernible. In fact, there are clear warnings against such an expectation in Christianity, Islam, and Judaism to the effect that such a "finding" would be actually a sign that one had *not* found God but would be close to idolatry. Flew, therefore, demands from the believer as positive evidence what the believer would regard as negative evidence. If there were some overriding reason to accept this empirical criterion, then we might conclude up front that theism was therefore incoherent; but even the logical positivists, who most wanted to defend it, could not supply such a reason.

What is also revealing are the changes that Flew made to the original context and content of Wisdom's parable.[46] Wisdom offered the parable as telling for the possibility of the cognitivity of religious belief. Without maintaining that religious language is straightforwardly cognitive, Wisdom wanted to suggest that sometimes arguments for the existence of something are not disagreements about the obvious "facts," but about the pattern of the facts. The point is, Wisdom urged, these are valid disagreements about real issues.

What remains of the challenge? Two responses were given at the time, also in the form of parables. The first was by Richard Hare.

> I must begin by confessing that, on the ground marked out by Flew, he seems to me to be completely victorious. I therefore shift my ground by relating another parable. A certain lunatic is convinced that all dons want to murder him. His friends introduce him to all the mildest and most respectable dons that they can find, and after each of them retired, they say, "You see, he doesn't really want to murder you; he spoke to you in a most cordial manner; surely you are convinced now?" But the lunatic replies, "Yes, but that was only his diabolical cunning; he's really plotting against me the whole time, like the rest of them; I know it I tell you." However many kindly dons are produced, the reaction is still the same.
>
> Now we say that such a person is deluded. But what is he deluded about? About the truth or falsity of an assertion? Let us apply Flew's test to him. There is no behaviour of dons that can be enacted which he will accept as counting against his theory; and therefore his theory, on this test, asserts nothing. But it does not follow that there is no difference between what he thinks about dons and what most of us think about them – otherwise we should not call him a lunatic and ourselves sane, and dons would have no reason to feel uneasy about his presence in Oxford.
>
> Let us call that in which we differ from this lunatic, our respective *bliks*. He has an insane *blik* about dons; we have a sane one. It is important to realize that we have a sane one, not no *blik*

at all; for there must be two sides to any argument — if he has a wrong *blik*, then those who are right about dons must have a right one. Flew has shown that a *blik* does not consist in an assertion or system of them; but nevertheless it is very important to have the right *blik*.[47]

Hare gives an example of such a *blik* as confidence in the steering mechanism of our cars. If we distrust it, no amount of successful driving will dispel our distrust. Someone who distrusts the steering mechanism would likely not drive a car. Hare consequently adds at the end:

> There is an important difference between Flew's parable and my own which we have not yet noticed. The explorers do not *mind* about their garden; they discuss it with interest, but not with concern. But my lunatic, poor fellow, minds about dons; and I mind about the steering of my car; it often has people in it that I care for.[48]

Hare clearly accepts the terms of Flew's challenge. He bluntly allows that religious language may be noncognitive, in that it does not describe the world, but his disagreement is that language may still be meaningful. It may represent a *blik* upon the world that cannot be falsified, to be sure, but nevertheless is existentially significant. This response represents what we may call a noncognitive response to Flew's challenge and is favored by other significant philosophers, a point we will take up further in the next chapter.

In light of our previous discussion, we may immediately question whether this is what believers have meant by their use of religious language. Is it a prescription for a different, perhaps more valid use of language, or does it purport to be a description of what believers really are doing in the speaking? This issue, too, though a crucial one, will be taken up later. These questions aside, some problems arise with this approach as it stands.

First, Hare is ambivalent about a point central to the strength of his position. In order to respond to Flew, he maintains that no evidence or reasons can be offered for a *blik*. Presumably, a person simply holds one or does not. The reasons may perhaps lie in some form of psychological or sociological conditioning. There is, however, no danger of lapsing into the death of a thousand qualifications. On the other hand, when the obvious question arises of what is needed to distinguish one *blik* from another one, or more urgently, an insane *blik* from a sane one, Hare indicates that we are able to make such a distinction. One *blik* is simply better than another, or sane when another is insane. But how can we tell, short of evidence? In the end, Hare seems to want the best of both worlds, but may perhaps be vulnerable to the liabilities of both worlds. If *bliks* are truly noncognitive, they seem vulnerable to charges of irrationality, even insanity. If one *blik* is better than another, but is not amenable to empirical verification or falsification, then the *bliks* are liable to endless qualification with no convincing proof.

What Hare has done positively, however, is to underline the point that empirical language is not the only meaningful language. He rightly points out that Flew's parable does not carry the existential significance and urgency of religious beliefs. The question of whether there is an invisible gardener or not, while interesting, is not vital to one's "being or non-being," which Paul Tillich says is the mark of a religious question. Beliefs can be life altering as well as being tractable to empirical proof or disproof.

An approach that may be considered a cognitive alternative is that of Basil Mitchell. His parable and explanation runs as follows:

> Flew's article is searching and perceptive, but there is, I think, something odd about his conduct of the theologian's case. The theologian surely would not deny that the fact of pain counts against the assertion that God loves men. This very incompatibility generates the most intractable of theological problems – the problem of evil. So the theologian *does* recognize the fact of pain as counting against Christian doctrine. But it is true that he will not allow it – or anything – to count decisively against it; for he is committed by his faith to trust in God. His attitude is not that of the detached observer, but of the believer.
>
> Perhaps this can be brought out by yet another parable. In time

of war in an occupied country, a member of the resistance meets one night a stranger who deeply impresses him. They spend that night together in conversation. The Stranger tells the partisan that he himself is on the side of the resistance – indeed that he is in command of it, and urges the partisan to have faith in him no matter what happens. The partisan is utterly convinced at that meeting of the Stranger's sincerity and constancy and undertakes to trust him.

They never meet in conditions of intimacy again. But sometimes the Stranger is seen helping members of the resistance, and the partisan is grateful and says to his friends, "He is on our side."

Sometimes he is seen in the uniform of the police handing over patriots to the occupying power. On these occasions his friends murmur against him: but the partisan still says, "He is on our side". He still believes that, in spite of appearances, the Stranger did not deceive him. Sometimes he asks the Stranger for help and receives it. He is then thankful. Sometimes he asks and does not receive it. Then he says, "The Stranger knows best". Sometimes his friends, in exasperation, say "Well, what *would* he have to do for you to admit that you were wrong and that he is not on our side"? But the partisan refuses to answer. He will not consent to put the Stranger to the test. And sometimes his friends complain, "Well, if *that's* what you mean by his being on our side, the sooner he goes over to the other side the better."

The partisan of the parable does not allow anything to count decisively against the proposition "The Stranger is on our side". This is because he has committed himself to trust the Stranger. But he of course recognizes that the Stranger's ambiguous behaviour *does* count against what he believes about him. It is precisely this situation which constitutes the trial of his faith.

When the partisan asks for help and doesn't get it, what can he do? He can (a) conclude that the stranger is not on our side or; (b) maintain that he is on our side, but that he has reasons for withholding help.

The first he will refuse to do. How long can he uphold the second position without its becoming just silly?

I don't think one can say in advance.[49]

In contrast to Hare, Mitchell accepts Flew's challenge. He does not concede the noncognitivity of religious language but attempts to show the limited nature of Flew's criterion of empirical falsifiability. He argues that evidence does count for and against belief, but the evaluation is not a simple matter. It may be qualified, but not to the death.

A key is that the evaluation of the fidelity of the stranger is based upon personal encounter and personal relationship. With all of the problems that encounter with God entails, it is a part of traditional claims to knowledge of God. The context is not an objective matter of physical presence that may be discerned by an electric fence but is more like the complex judgment of a person's character. Such a judgment is not purely subjective or whimsical, as anyone with a budding romance or friendship can attest, but it is not something that can always be publicly defended to everyone's satisfaction. As Mitchell argues in another context, such judgments are made far more often in life than we might think − perhaps more commonly than such open and shut cases as scientific verification − in courtrooms, in politics, in literature, and in the human sciences in general. They occur in cumulative cases, where the evidence is less like the links of a chain than the legs of a chair, representing a wholistic, more *gestalt*-like appraisal of the evidence as a whole.[50] Moreover, the issue is one that is existentially pressing, one that is crucial to one's life, and one which a person cannot easily evade. William James once similarly gave as the criterion of a religious belief that it is a "forced option." A choice not to believe is as much of a choice as a choice to believe. In these ways, Mitchell presents a more realistic picture of the actual religious context.

On the other hand, Mitchell leaves us with his own ambiguity. He asserts that evidence counts against, but the believer never lets it decisively count against faith. Doubts are a trial for one's faith, but the true believer will always pass the test. This suggests that the believer recognizes problems but will somehow find an answer to every problem, which is suspiciously close to faith being compatible with any state of affairs whatsoever, or dying the death of a thousand qualifications. In the end, evidence really cannot be allowed to count against faith. This approach, it appears, would hardly satisfy Flew.

In the course of the argument, however, Mitchell suggests a quite different position, which is more of an alternative to Flew's. He says that evidence counts against, but that we cannot predict beforehand whether it will be decisive or not. This suggests that religious belief does make a difference and that it could conceivably be falsified – and therefore is cognitively meaningful. The actual assessment is a matter of personal judgment, a cumulative case, and a complex affair. This is actually the point that John Wisdom was attempting to make with the original parable of the invisible gardener. The fact that the outcome cannot be predicted in advance, moreover, corresponds to existential matters. They often cannot be theoretically settled but must be decided in the context of an existential situation, which adds its own elements. Perhaps this is akin to the question of whether one might act courageously if one's life were threatened. One likely will not know for sure until the actual situation occurs, with all of its tacit elements. Elaborating the nature of such a cumulative case approach is crucial to the defense of the cognitivity of religious language; but at this point, valid questions are raised about the adequacy of Flew's presentation of the religious situation.

One aspect of Mitchell's parable was later emphasized as a fourth response to Flew's challenge, also in the form of a parable. Mitchell's parable suggests that the believer may have his or her belief verified or falsified in the future. While the situation is ambiguous in the present, it may be clarified later. In the religious context, this suggests what has been termed "eschatological verification," verification at the end of one's life. John Hick emphasized this point in his parable of the celestial city in 1960 as a direct response to the *University* debate.

> Two men are travelling together along a road. One of them believes that it leads to a Celestial City, the other that it leads nowhere; but since this is the only road there is, both must travel it. Neither has been this way before, and therefore neither is able to say what they will find around each next corner. During their journey they meet both with moments of refreshment and delight, and with moments of hardship and danger. All the time one of them thinks of his journey as a pilgrimage to the Celestial City

and interprets the pleasant parts as encouragements and the obstacles as trials of his purpose and lessons in endurance, prepared by the king of that city and designed to make of him a worthy citizen of the place when at last he arrives there. The other, however, believes none of this and sees their journey as an unavoidable and aimless ramble. Since he has no choice in the matter, he enjoys the good and endures the bad. But for him there is no Celestial City to be reached, no all-encompassing purpose ordaining their journey; only the road itself and the luck of the road in good weather and in bad.

During the course of the journey the issue between them is not an experimental one. They do not entertain different expectations about the coming details of the road, but only about its ultimate destination. And yet when they do turn the last corner it will be apparent that one of them has been right all the time and the other wrong. Thus although the issue between them has not been experimental, it has nevertheless from the start been a real issue. They have not merely felt differently about the road; for one was feeling appropriately and the other inappropriately in relation to the actual state of affairs. Their opposed interpretations of the road constituted genuinely rival assertions, though assertions whose assertion-status has the peculiar characteristic of being guaranteed retrospectively by a future crux.[51]

Hick is concerned to meet Flew on his own grounds, so to speak, and to show that there is at least one relatively clear-cut case when religious language can be empirically verified and thus be cognitively meaningful. Interestingly, he points out that here is a case where language may not be falsifiable but only verifiable, indicating a limitation of the falsification principle. If the unbeliever is correct, both will simply perish at the end of the journey, and no one will be in a position to falsify the believer's assertion. But if the believer is correct, both will be in a position clearly to verify it.

Several troublesome questions arise concerning this parable. First, it implies that only two alternatives exist. After being quite involved in discussions of the relation of world religions, Hick later of course recognized this. Here, however, he is assuming that the parable represents a way in which Christian beliefs may be verified in contrast with naturalistic beliefs. It is presumably possible that other views of the afterlife might be verified in contrast with the Christian view.

Another question is that of empirical verification. Hick solves this by pointing to encounter with an empirical, resurrected Jesus Christ. The problem is that such a state is so far beyond our comprehension and knowledge that the extension of our word "empirical," whose meaning in this life is understood, to the afterlife, which is so little understood, is questionable. Its usage may be stretched so far that it is at best used analogically or metaphorically. Hick himself later recognizes that the afterlife, too, may be ambiguous in determining the truth or falsity of various religious views. Perhaps each will see his or own view verified. Still, we might imagine that some kind of clear verification is possible, even if only in some way analogous to our empirical verification.

The question is, how does that future possibility help one now? Hick, like Mitchell, points to the ambiguity in the religious situation, granting to Flew that it is not an open and shut empirical matter, without conceding that such ambiguity vitiates its cognitivity. Mitchell, however, suggests the plausibility of making a decision in the present on cognitive grounds. Hick's parable provides no such grounds. It suggests something more like a *blik* that is either present like a brute fact or wagered upon, which may turn out to be true in the future. This latter view resembles Pascal's well-known wager, in which Pascal (1623–62) suggested that we should bet on belief, for if we are correct, there is an infinite good to be gained. If we are wrong, then only a finite good is lost.[52] It also falls prey to common objections to such a calculated approach to faith. It first of all does not do justice to the nature of religious belief, which is not a prudential wager but a convinced trust. Hick claims that he is only concerned to show that there is a theoretical sense in which religious claims may be considered to be empirically verifiable and nothing more. On that score, despite the questions raised about the meaning of "empirical" in this context, he scores a kind of technical or "Pyrrhic" victory over Flew. This victory has the liability, however, of not being deemed satisfactory by Flew or by other believers. In other words, it cannot be put to work.

The *University* debate, as mentioned, was a dominant force in the philosophy of religion for a significant part of the twentieth century. As has been seen, it focused on the cognitivity of religious language, asking whether it has any sense at all. The responses pointed to a plethora of ways in which that question may be answered, as well as raising questions about the very grounds of the question. The discussion gradually turned away from the bare question of verification or falsification, sense or nonsense, to a less restricted and more tolerant view of the variety of ways in which language can mean, and as a consequence, to the ways in which religious language can mean. In other words, the question is not so much whether religious language has meaning – it obviously has a use and therefore presumably a meaning. The more important question is, what kind of meaning? Astonishingly, this more open-ended and tolerant approach was based on the work of the same Ludwig Wittgenstein who provided the foundation for the more restrictive approach just treated.

# 4

## Language Games

After finishing the *Tractatus Logico-Philosophicus* and leaving philosophy behind, Ludwig Wittgenstein was persuaded to return to philosophy and to Cambridge in the late twenties, whereupon he became critical of his own earlier views. He developed a viewpoint that stood in stark contrast but which was as revolutionary as the earlier work. He shifted to a more pluralistic, tolerant approach that through his students and his one published book, *Philosophical Investigations*, exerted enormous influence on the philosophy of religious language. This shift marked a turn from being primarily concerned with *whether* religious language refers to the *way* it refers. We will therefore first examine the views of the so-called "later" Wittgenstein and his emphasis on "language games" and then consider various applications of his thought to religious language.

### The Later Wittgenstein

In the opening pages of his *Philosophical Investigations*, Wittgenstein indirectly criticized the type of view he himself had earlier espoused via criticism of Augustine's understanding of language. Wittgenstein summarized Augustine's approach in the following way. "The individual words in language name objects – sentences are combinations of such names. – In this picture of language we find the roots of the following idea: Every word has a meaning. This meaning is correlated with the word. It is the object for which the word stands."[1] This should sound familiar, for it is reminiscent of the view of language in Wittgenstein's *Tractatus*, and it represents the traditional paradigm of language delineated in chapter 1. For example, one might show someone a brick, point to it, say, "Brick," and in this way teach a language. Wittgenstein had begun to see numerous problems to this traditional view, which emphasized single words and ostension (pointing out) apart from a wider context. Wittgenstein's view was that such "naming" only has meaning in a certain context, such as bricklaying. As he said, "A great deal of stage-setting in the language is presupposed if the mere act of naming is to make sense."[2] With bricklaying, the word "brick" would be learned as one was taught to bring bricks or to lay them, not as a mere label. In order to discern the meaning of words, therefore, it is best to see how they are actually used, rather than trying arbitrarily and theoretically to come up with a definition. One of Wittgenstein's sayings therefore was, "Back to the rough ground."[3]

Many philosophical problems, he believed, were due to the failure to follow this maxim. For instance, a philosopher tries to find some common essence behind the various uses of "to be," and thus metaphysics, the study of the nature of "being," is born. In fact, this is a wrenching of words out of their living use and creates unnecessary and insoluble problems. We put cramps in words, he suggested, which can only be solved by returning words to the stream of life, or as he also put it picturesquely, by showing "the fly the way out of the fly-bottle."[4] "Philosophical problems arise," he maintained, "when language *goes on holiday*."[5] The better part for philosophy, then, is not to prescribe but to describe language use. Wittgenstein emphasized, "Philosophy may in no way interfere with the actual use of language. . . . It leaves everything as it is."[6]

When we return to ordinary language, we find that words, rather than having one kind of appropriate use, such as a scientific one, have many. Wittgenstein suggests:

> Think of the tools in a tool-box: there is a hammer, pliers, a saw, a screw-driver, a rule, a glue-pot, glue, nails and screws . . .

Of course, what confuses us is the uniform appearance of words when we hear them spoken or meet them in script and print. For their *application* is not presented to us so clearly. Especially when we are doing philosophy![7]

Another way of putting it is to say that there are many kinds of "language games."[8] Words have meaning only in the context of these different games. There is no more only one kind of usage of words than there is only one kind of game. Language is as diverse as life. More significantly, if words have a use in life, they have a meaning. We cannot therefore so easily brush aside vast areas of language as nonsensical, as did the Vienna circle and the earlier Wittgenstein himself. The upshot of this approach was to turn away from "ideal" uses of language to actual language. In fact, one of the movements influenced by the later Wittgenstein in Oxford was called "ordinary language analysis," which we will take up later.

The idea of "language games" has been enormously influential. Unfortunately Wittgenstein did not expand the idea in any systematic way. In fact, most of his writing, his earlier as well as his later, was in the form of aphorisms rather than systematic treatises, and much of it was unpublished in the nature of lecture notes taken by students or of collections of his own notes. Nevertheless, he offered a degree of further reflection on this important idea. He suggested that words have meaning in the context of life, as he called it, in "forms of life."[9] Thus, words cannot carry their meaning in themselves in a transparent way, as the positivists dreamed of achieving; rather, their meaning is supported by an entire background of actions and practices. This suggests to some extent that we must participate in or at least have some empathy for a particular form of life in order to understand the meaning of language particular to it. We cannot stand outside such an activity and legislate about it. Nor should we import rules from some other game, for example, the need to dribble with the hands in basketball to dribbling in soccer. We shall explore some of the obvious implications for religion below.

A controversy has ensued over the precise meaning of "form

of life" just as over "language games" itself. Some take form of life to mean an entire culture; another view is that it refers to particular activities within a culture, such as politics, education, various kinds of occupations, and so on. In other contexts, we might call these institutions or practices. Language games therefore may be considered to be the more specific activities within these larger activities. Wittgenstein himself gives examples of language games:

> Giving orders, and obeying them –
> Describing the appearance of an object, or giving its measurements –
> Constructing an object from a description (a drawing) –
> Reporting an event –
> Speculating about an event –
> Forming and testing a hypothesis –
> Presenting the results of an experiment in tables and diagrams –
> Making up a story; and reading it –
> Play-acting –
> Singing catches –
> Guessing riddles –
> Making a joke; telling it –
> Solving a problem in practical arithmetic –
> Translating from one language into another –
> Asking, thanking, cursing, greeting, praying.[10]

As the last example suggests, activities such as praying, worshipping, and theologizing could all be considered to be differing language games within a larger form of life.

Using "form of life" as a more comprehensive term allows us to tie it in with the provocative work based on notes from his last year of life, *On Certainty*. Closer attention to Wittgenstein's reflections in this work can illuminate his distinctive approach to linguistic and epistemological problems. In this material, Wittgenstein considers justification of our beliefs to be imbedded in the entire framework of activities and beliefs constituting our comprehensive form of life and not drawn from some independent perspective. Within a particular language game, of course, specific judgments can be made. For example, this is a brick; this is not. This brick is laid correctly; this one is not. On the other hand, when we seek for the rationale of bricklaying (and other things), such specifics often go wanting. Why lay bricks? Why build houses rather than live in tents? Why pursue science? Why struggle to live? As Wittgenstein emphasizes in *On Certainty*, the fundamental assumptions behind our answers to these questions are what we judge *with*, not what we judge.[11] If I ask myself skeptical questions such as, "How do I know that I have not been on the moon?" or "Do I know that my two hands in front of me really exist?" Wittgenstein characteristically answers, by "looking and seeing." He points to the form of life and the language games in which we have been raised to see where these questions might actually operate, and if they are pseudo-questions, he recommends how we might dissolve them.

First, he suggests, such questions have little meaning in our language game. What would it mean for me (who by all accounts has never been on the moon and still have two hands) to doubt such a question? It is not a "move" in the game. "The game of doubting itself," he says, "presupposes certainty."[12] Second, any account of my assurance on these matters would be no more certain than my original conviction. Wittgenstein asks, "What would it be like to doubt now whether I have two hands? Why can't I imagine it at all? What would I believe if I didn't believe that? So far I have no system at all within which this doubt might exist."[13] Third, then, these questions challenge my entire structure or system of beliefs, which I cannot transcend in order to justify in some neutral way. "To be sure," he says, "there is justification; but justification comes to an end."[14] At some point, we "stand fast."[15] In the *Philosophical Investigations*, he says, "If I have exhausted the justifications I have reached bedrock, and my spade is turned. Then I am inclined to say: 'This is simply what I do';" and again, "What has to be accepted, the given, is – so one could say – *forms of life*."[16] Fourth, these bedrock beliefs that, practically speaking, cannot be doubted are not simply foundational, in that they support other beliefs, but they also in turn are held in place by all of our beliefs. He says, "One might almost say that these foundation-walls are carried by the whole house."[17] In this vein, Willard Quine later suggested the metaphor of a "web of belief," in which some beliefs are more central than others but all are integrally related and supported by each other.[18] Wittgenstein himself developed yet another metaphor:

> It might be imagined that some propositions, of the form of empirical propositions, were hardened and functioned as channels for such empirical propositions as were not hardened but fluid; and that this relation altered with time, in that fluid propositions hardened, and hard ones became fluid.
>
> . . . But I distinguish between the movement of the waters on the river-bed and the shift of the bed itself; though there is not a sharp division of the one from the other.[19]

Fifth, the complex nature of our belief structure indicates that justification is equally complex. When Wittgenstein suggests that justification comes to an end, such stopping is not necessarily fickle or arbitrary. It is grounded in an entire form of life, a way of acting and living that is rooted in one's entire history of learning and in a culture's history. Wittgenstein points out, "But I did not get my picture of the world by satisfying myself of its correctness; nor do I have it because I am satisfied of its correctness. No: it is the inherited background against which I distinguish between true and false."[20] We may consequently be hard put to come up with explicit chains of reasoning that convincingly demonstrate such a belief, yet we may be so convinced of the underlying form of life that it might seem insane to overthrow it. Speculative doubt finally must finally return to practice. As Wittgenstein says: "Giving grounds, however, justifying the evidence, comes to an end; – but the end is not certain propositions striking us immediately as true, i.e. it is not a kind of *seeing* on our part; it is our *acting*, which lies at the bottom of our language-game."[21]

Some wonder whether Wittgenstein says enough at this point

to avoid the specter of relativism. Others believe his observations provide a way to avoid both the extremes of objectivism and relativism. In other words, are we left with sufficient basis adequately to evaluate what we claim to be true or false, or are we left with no answer at all except to do what we already do? Philosophers continue to wrestle with the consequences of Wittgenstein's work in this area, and we shall see how appropriation for religious language reflects this tension.

Despite this attempt to flesh out the notions of language game and form of life, we must again remember that Wittgenstein used these terms loosely and not extensively, and that they are therefore used with different meanings by various thinkers. In fact, Wittgenstein used the metaphor of a game to warn against attempts to define the meanings of words too precisely. Contrary to such attempts inspired in part by his own earlier work, he suggested that we can hardly find a common or precise definition of the term "game." Think of the various kinds of games: baseball, football, card games, games with teams, games between only two people, solitary games, and noncompetitive games.[22] There is not a common essence; rather, there are overlapping characteristics between the games at one end of a spectrum to another. An analogy, Wittgenstein suggested, is the way the strands of a rope combine to form a sturdy rope, but the strands at one end do not reach to the other. He also compared the similarity to "family resemblance," that is, to the way in which members of a family resemble one another but not necessarily in any one particular trait.[23] Consequently, Wittgenstein urges us not to press for more precision than the use of a word allows. Jerry Gill calls this "the principle of sufficient precision": only seek the kind of precision that is appropriate.[24] Wittgenstein gave the example of standing in a city square and telling someone, "Stand roughly there."[25] Is it necessary to be exactly precise, for example, to say, "Go stand over there, 5.35 feet away?" Could one ever be exactly precise (perhaps one could carry it to the thousandths or millionths, 5.356, and so on)? Is it even necessary? Obviously not. One should expect "rough edges" at the boundaries of definitions, to "leave ragged what is ragged."[26] The attempt to go farther, the passion for precision characteristic of Western thought, is an example of the "bewitchment of language," of taking language out of its context and creating unnecessary metaphysical quandaries.[27]

A further important emphasis of the later Wittgenstein, which may be surprising given his openness to the fluidity and pluralism of language, is that language is public. Traditionally, the view was that the meaning of words lies in an inner thought or idea. Words then express this idea. In order, therefore, to understand the meaning of a word, we must have the corresponding inner thought or experience. Wittgenstein countered that we learn the meanings of words through their use in forms of life, which is a more external affair. As he put it, there is no "private language."[28] Since we have no access to each other's inner states, we can never know whether we have the right inner thought or meanings. Yet language, despite its imprecision, functions reliably most of the time. This is because it is associated with outer actions and practices that are more easily learned, and also corrected. Wittgenstein even suggested that inner states may not be necessary. If a teacher tries to teach a student how to add, the important thing is not the inner state but whether the student can "go on" or demonstrate that he or show indeed can solve problems in a public way.[29] Perhaps there is no particular inner state associated with such "knowledge." Perhaps different people have different inner states associated with similar activities and similar words. It does not matter as long as they reveal that they "know" the meaning in their behavior.

Wittgenstein has therefore sometimes been charged with behaviorism, but this charge is inappropriate if it means that he denies the existence of inner states or that they can be important. He would allow that they may exist and may be correlated with certain words, but his point is that meaning does not lie only or even primarily in such experiences. If someone is learning mathematics, the important thing is that he or she can perform it, that he or she knows how to proceed. Another way in which he expressed this point was to argue that language is a matter of following public rules. The reason that words can be reliably used is that there are reliable rules that can be intersubjectively checked.[30] He did not argue for a rigid or slavish subjection of language to rules, but that intersubjective regularity provides the basis for meaningful communication.[31]

In short, the early Wittgenstein carried the traditional philosophy of language to an extreme, with fateful consequences for religious language. The later Wittgenstein, while not rejecting all that he said before, offered a virtual paradigm change in the understanding of language, with momentous consequences for religious language. Philosophers of religion influenced by the later Wittgenstein fall broadly into the cognitive and noncognitive approaches to religious language, which are similar to the two responses to Flew's challenge treated in the previous chapter.

## Religious Language as Noncognitive

Wittgenstein did not publicly express himself to a great extent on religion. What was first published tends to point in a noncognitive direction.[32] We will first look at Wittgenstein's sketchy but provocative remarks on religion and then at a contentious debate centered around the charge that Wittgenstein's thought is fideistic, that is, it leads to holding unfounded beliefs.

### Wittgenstein on religion

When Wittgenstein did turn to religion, he revealed his acute powers of analysis. He gave the example of someone who lives his life in light of the idea of the Christian picture of the Last Judgment. Then he imagines such a person trying to prove the validity of this idea. The offering of evidence as if it were a commonplace prediction of a future event in this life seems out of place. He compares this to a discussion in mathematics where a student writes on the board $2 + 21 = 13$. "For a mistake,"

Wittgenstein says, "that's too big."[33] The surprising gap between what we would expect and what is given reveals that a different language game is going on. Wittgenstein provides another example:

> Suppose someone is ill and he says: "This is a punishment", and I say: "If I'm ill, I don't think of punishment at all." If you say: "Do you believe the opposite?" – you can call it believing the opposite, but it is entirely different from what we would normally call believing the opposite.[34]

The believer's attempt to justify his faith has an apparent similarity to scientific language – but it is only an illusion. Wittgenstein concludes, "The point is that if there were evidence, this would in fact destroy the whole business."[35]

So what is left of justification in religion? Wittgenstein suggests that religion has to do with living one's life by a picture, and one either does or does not have such a picture. With reference to the idea of illness as punishment, Wittgenstein reflects:

> I think differently, in a different way. I say different things to myself. I have different pictures.
>
> It is this way: if someone said: "Wittgenstein, you don't take illness as punishment, so what do you believe"? – I'd say: "I don't have any thoughts of punishment."[36]

Wittgenstein's use of picture here is best understood in terms of his conceptions of language game and form of life. The picture is not so much a mental image as a kind of framework that orders one's life.[37] Another way Wittgenstein expressed this was to speak of the "grammar" of forms of life. In a parenthesis he once referred to "theology as grammar" (which has exerted influence far beyond any explication Wittgenstein ever provided, as we shall see in chapter 7).[38] The image of a picture is closer perhaps to the actual life of religion where, as in language, the grammar derives only from reflection upon that life. Thus he speaks of theology as grammar and not of religion as grammar.

## Wittgensteinian fideism

In light of the falsification debate of the previous chapter, Wittgenstein's later thought reveals the confusion involved in Flew's parable of trying to compare faith in God with scientific proof. They are different language games, different forms of life. His line of thought points most clearly to Hare's approach. Faith seems to be something like a *blik*, and the process of coming to faith or losing faith is left shrouded in mystery. In short, this approach suggests a kind of fideistic approach to Christian faith, where arguments, defenses, and grounds have no place.

For many years, therefore, Wittgenstein and some of his interpreters have commonly been charged with "Wittgensteinian fideism." In an influential article published in 1967, Kai Nielson detailed its features. His view of it can be summarized in the following way. First, "The different modes of discourse which are distinctive forms of life have a logic of their own." Second, "Forms of life taken as a whole are not amenable to criticism; each mode of discourse is in order as it is, for each has its own criteria and each sets its own norms of intelligibility, reality and rationality." Third, "there is no Archimedean point in terms of which a philosopher (or for that matter anyone else) can relevantly criticize whole modes of discourse or, what comes to the same thing, ways of life, for each mode of discourse has its own specific criteria of rationality/irrationality, intelligibility/unintelligibility, and reality/unreality."[39]

D.Z. Phillips has been identified as the foremost of such fideists. Although he questions whether any Wittgensteinian has ever held such views, it is easy to see how Wittgenstein's remarks could be interpreted in such a way. Moreover, even Phillips acknowledges that the perception that many Wittgensteinians advocate such a perspective has been enormously influential in the philosophy of religion.[40] The problem it raises for philosophers of religion is that it not only seems to disallow philosophy, taking philosophy to be an attempt to impose an external, Archimedean point upon religion, but it also disallows anyone but a believer to criticize a particular religion. As such, it is at the opposite end of the spectrum from the extreme of objectivity which presumes that a believer could not be objective enough to evaluate his or her own religion, so that only an unbeliever can criticize it. Manifestly, Wittgenstein's philosophy of language has significant implications not only for religion but also for philosophy. How is it to be interpreted?

In Phillips's reply to the charge of fideism, he offers a nuanced response that evades the obvious problems of a simpler position like that exemplified by Hare's parable, but continues to move in a noncognitive direction. His basic idea is that we cannot evaluate faith by standards external to faith. In other words, there is no universal standpoint from which to evaluate language games. The attempt to do so inevitably reduces religion to something else, such as science. Like Wittgenstein, Phillips sees philosophy as playing only a clarifying role. "Philosophy is neither for or against religious beliefs. After it has sought to clarify the grammar of such beliefs its work is over."[41] An example is the belief in resurrection. Again, akin to Wittgenstein, Phillips considers it a distortion to understand this belief as some kind of prediction of future events. As such, eternal life is notoriously difficult to conceive in any coherent way, and furthermore it appears to make belief in God subservient to the prudential desire to continue life; rather than God being the end of belief, God is the means to a self-serving personal end. Phillips draws the searing conclusion, "To seek an external justification for why a man should be concerned about his immortal soul is to destroy the character of that concern."[42] For a mistake, it is too big.

Similarly, with regard to prayer, Phillips questions whether it is a request for a change in a future course of events. He offers the example of a mother asking the Virgin Mary to protect her child. Expecting benefits from the prayer, Phillips charges, is akin to superstition. Rather, the mother is orienting herself and her child to the virtues of the Virgin Mary, which itself constitutes the blessing. "In the one case," he says, "the protection determines whether or not the act of bringing the child to the Virgin and the alleged holiness of the Virgin have been efficacious or not. In the other case, it is the holiness of the Virgin which determines the nature of the protection."[43]

Phillips's tendency towards a noncognitive interpretation of religious practices in his early works, in which he espoused these views of eternal life and of prayer, was so striking that he came across to some interpreters as denying the existence of God altogether.[44] In response to such criticisms, he has more carefully distinguished his view from a simple fideism.[45] First, he rejects the notion of compartmentalized language games. There is much traffic between games, and some games, like religious ones, speak to experiences of suffering and anxiety in everyday life. This means, second, that language games can be dependent upon one another and can criticize one another. He points out that if a religious response to suffering is to deny the reality of suffering, the religious belief will seriously be called into question. Or again, if a religious view attempts to compete with a scientific hypothesis on scientific grounds, it should be rejected. Third, this means that a rejection of criticism based on a universal standpoint does not mean the dismissal of criticism altogether.

In the end, Phillips's view is on the one hand a powerful caution against placing religion in a Procrustean bed in the way that Flew's parable does. On the other hand, his view is still close to Hare's *blik* theory and, while more refined, in a troubling way is itself reductionistic. Phillips purports, as does Wittgenstein, only to describe, not to prescribe. He intends, therefore, to reflect what believers actually do, how they play their religious language game. But in his tendency to reduce beliefs to attitudes about this life, ruling out belief in an actual afterlife, he seems, for good or ill, not to be describing but prescribing. His view also overlooks the fact that huge numbers of Christian believers, for example, have believed in an actual afterlife but do not identify it at all with simple continuation of this life, resuscitation of this body, or in any simple way see it as contravening scientific laws. The result is that both Phillips and Wittgenstein, while allowing for many language games, seem to privilege the scientific game when it comes to questions of cognitivity. Apart from the existence of God, Phillips's working principle seems to be to question the cognitivity of any belief that cannot be justified by scientific methodology. We can allow that religious belief means to live by a picture, a *blik*, or an attitude, but Phillips seems to go farther to rule out belief in a reality not revealable by science. In this interpretation, Wittgenstein's later thought is in significant continuity with his earlier. Scientific language is still the language with which to depict reality. What is beyond the world may now be sayable – it is not simply the mystical – but it is still clearly noncognitive.

A clearer example of this approach is that of Richard Braithwaite, who draws on Wittgenstein's "meaning as use" principle.[46] For Braithwaite, religious beliefs do not, properly understood, claim the existence of some kind of transcendental reality such as God or Heaven. Scientific language determines what is cognitive by means of the principle of verification we considered in chapter 3. Religious language, nevertheless, has a use. Like Hare, Braithwaite saw that it shapes our attitudes and the way we live. Religion gives us stories – stories which need not be true – that support the intention to live a certain moral way of life.[47] With obvious similarities to Wittgenstein, then, his view is that the difference in religions lies in the difference in their stories and in the moral convictions associated with them.

In Richard Braithwaite, we have someone who drew on Wittgenstein's emphasis of meaning as use in order to justify an entirely noncognitive approach. Unlike Phillips, he is not attempting simply to describe but is more self-consciously proposing an appropriate way to be religious. And he draws out the consequences for belief with startling candor. There are others, however, who took Wittgenstein's work in another direction.

## Religious Language as Cognitive

Several thinkers influenced by the later Wittgenstein's turn to ordinary language also shared the increased finesse of someone like Phillips in dealing with the important noncognitive dimensions of religious language; however, they were also willing to explore the different and unique ways in which religious language refers to a divine reality in ways that differ from scientific reference.

## John Wisdom

One of the most significant of these thinkers was John Wisdom, a creative Cambridge philosopher who was the original source of Flew's parable of the invisible gardener. Wisdom's version of this appeared in what Flew called Wisdom's "haunting and revelatory article 'Gods.'"[48] In the article to which Flew referred, Wisdom followed the Wittgensteinian emphasis that *"the existence of God is not an experimental issue in the way it was."*[49] In other words, the believer does not look for religion to be verified in the same way as science. For the logical positivist, that would be the end of the discussion as far as cognitivity is concerned; but Wisdom is willing to consider that the believer as well as the artist can "show us reality" – but in a different way.[50]

In Wisdom's account of an invisible gardener, he refers not to Flew's "clearing in the jungle" (see chapter 3) but to two people who "return to their long-neglected garden and find among the weeds a few of the old plants surprisingly vigorous."[51] There is no talk of electric fences or bloodhounds but of patient examination of the garden and of what happens to gardens left unattended. The end result is that they do not differ as to the facts or as to their expectations of the garden; the issue has ceased to be experimental in the scientific sense, but they continue to feel differently about the garden. Wisdom, unlike Flew, does not leave the issue there, however, but wonders whether the disagreement involves more than feeling. He suggests these kinds of things may still be "a matter about which reasons for and against may be offered, although no scientific reasons . . . are to the point."[52] But what would be to the point?

Wisdom argued that in this case it is not so much a difference of "facts" but of the configuration or pattern of the facts. He says:

> In such cases we notice that the process of argument is not a *chain*
> of demonstrative reasoning. It is a presenting and representing of
> those features of the case which *severally co-operate* in favour of the
> conclusion, in favour of saying what the reasoner wishes said, in
> favour of calling the situation by the name by which he wishes to
> call it. The reasons are like the legs of a chair, not the links of a
> chain.[53]

Wisdom suggests a process of connecting and disconnecting aspects of the situation – and doing the same with other, similar
and dissimilar, situations – in order to precipitate in someone else
the same insight. His idea here is like the later Wittgenstein's
notion of "seeing-as" but places it in connection with the way
people understand certain situations as disclosive of God.

Wisdom also compares this approach to the way someone
might try to talk a friend out of "being in love." It may seem at
first a hopeless task that is merely a matter of feeling, but reasons
of the sort we have discussed may be offered nevertheless.
Though difficult, one may be able to get through.

> It is possible, of course, that he [the friend] has already noticed the
> analogies, the connections, we point out and that he has accepted
> them – that is, he has not denied them nor passed them off. He
> has recognized them and they have altered his attitude, altered his
> love, but he still loves. We then feel that perhaps it is we who are
> blind and cannot see what he can see.[54]

Although Wisdom did not write a great deal about religious
language, he suggested different ways of approaching the issue.
By such comparisons Wisdom offered a much more appreciative view of the possibilities and distinctiveness of religious
language.

## Ian T. Ramsey

One of the first and most prominent philosophers of religion to
direct this kind of linguistic analysis in a more cognitive direction
was Ian Ramsey, former Bishop of Durham in the fifties and

sixties.[55] Ramsey tied together the traditional British empiricist tradition that emphasizes the way thought should be rooted in experience and the contemporary British turn to the uses of language. He desired a "broader empiricism" that could include religious experience and that is manifested in language in "logically odd" ways. He noted first of all that the religious form of life trades heavily on what he called "disclosure experiences" or "depth experiences" where what is at stake is the empirical and "more." As he saw it, the logical positivists limited experience too much. He gave the example of a judge waiting to consider the verdict on a defendant, who suddenly discovers that the accused is his long-lost wife.[56] No longer is the situation one of judge and accused. What was before a rather objective situation suddenly gains in depth. "The penny drops" and "eye meets eye," as Ramsey says – and the situation is transformed. The empirical data, he stresses, are indispensable, but do not explain the total disclosure. A personal depth appears that was not there before, an existential dimension dependent upon but transcending the bare facts.

A prime example of such depth, he says, is the nature of "I-language,"[57] which he claims works differently than common object-language. The "I" includes all of the empirical characteristics of a person – and something more. Hearing all of the empirical characteristics that someone might attribute to a person somehow does not capture all that the person is. Ramsey suggests that the term "God" has something of the logic of I. It includes the created world but is "more" than it. It represents a "cosmic disclosure" in which "the whole universe confronts us."[58] It is this "more," real yet not easily describable, that indicates an empirical dimension of depth. This appeal to experience and language use leads Ramsey to call his approach "logical empiricism." His broader empiricism thus includes the strictly empirical plus the discernment of these depth dimensions, which he finds indicated in language. In connection with Flew's parable of the invisible gardener, we might expect Ramsey to appeal to a broader range of experience than could be picked up by hounds or an electric fence; in other word, religious experience cannot be collapsed into what can be verified by scientific instruments.

He adds that an important element of such experiences is often the dimension of commitment. If someone is drowning and a person determines to risk his or her life, as only a poor swimmer, in order to attempt to save the life of another, an element beyond the merely factual and empirical alters the situation. We may make an absolute commitment on the basis of the facts but that goes – legitimately – beyond the facts.[59] The existential concern that alters the situation is what Hare, Mitchell, and Hick conveyed in their parables but which is lacking in Flew's.

When Ramsey turned to religious language proper, he noted that it is "logically odd," indicating the difference between the experiences to which it refers and the commonly empirical.[60] In a perceptive analysis of terms such as "immutability" (unchangeability) and "perfection," he notes that much of the traditional language for God begins with a common term and then gives it a qualifier marking its "oddness." For example, he says of "impassible" (not passible or subject to suffering), "So 'impassible' invites us to treat all "passible" stories as inadequate; to agree with all the positive points they make and to invite them to go yet further – for what purpose? Until at some point or other once again the light dawns, the ice breaks, the penny drops; until an 'odd discernment' is evoked."[61] Like the negative theology treated in chapter 2, "their main merit is evocative,"[62] but they are rooted in common experience even as they point to and initiate uncommon experiences. The difference from a strict *via negativa* is that Ramsey holds that the language not only evokes but indicates – in admittedly indirect ways – something of the content of the disclosure.

In an attempt to show that this usage of language is more common than we might think, Ramsey compared it with the role of models in science and other areas. He distinguished between picture models, analog models, and disclosure models.[63] Pictorial models are simple replicas, such as the scale model of an airplane. Analogical models, however, represent a metaphorical relationship in which the model is like and unlike that which is represented, for example, the billiard ball model of gas molecules. A disclosive model therefore could be said to be an analog model with existential depth.

The application to religious language is that "heavenly father" or "kingdom of heaven" represent models that are given their metaphorical and disclosive impetus by a "qualifier" from an "odd" or very different realm. When we begin with "father" and add "heavenly," we are alerted to the fact that language is being used in an unusual way and that a kind of reality is referred to that is likewise unusual. Ramsey explores the way the Bible, for example, is filled with such uses of language.[64] The evaluation of such language, Ramsey goes on to say, does not work like simple verification but in terms of "empirical fit."[65] It is rather more like the fitting of a shoe than the verification of a scientific hypothesis.

Ramsey's work advanced the discussion, but many have not found it clear enough. A question put to Ramsey's view is the elusive nature of this dimension of transcendence and how we validate it.[66] How can it be distinguished from spurious or hallucinatory experiences? Ramsey was a pioneer whose relatively early death indeed left some dangling threads, but in part the objections continue to reflect the demand for clear and decisive verification procedures in order for language to be cognitively meaningful. The continuing impact of the later Wittgenstein's work has been to call into question the applicability of these assumptions. As we have seen, Wittgenstein has pointed to the way validation of truth claims is rooted in communal agreement and does not always require precision. In fact, religious communities tend to have intricate tests for cognitive claims, even though there is great disagreement between religious traditions. For example, in certain traditions, people are quick to detect whether a proposal is "biblical" or not, "just" or not, "authentic" or not.[67] Ramsey neglected this communal dimension, which later thinkers such as Phillips have stressed. He is correct, however, to see that a religious dimension, if it exists, would not in any case be susceptible to simple verification. In comparison to Flew's approach, Wisdom and Ramsey represent a refreshing sensitivity to the nuances of religious language. Nevertheless, is it possible more exactly to clarify the way religious language works?

## *Ian Crombie*

Other philosophers added important insights into this question in the fifties and sixties. In the symposium at which Flew's falsification challenge occurred, Ian Crombie suggested that religious language, when it refers to God or the transcendent, does not specify its object exactly, but that in a more restrained way it indicates the "reference range" of God-talk.[68] There is a "characteristic elusiveness" about God-talk, but "it derives . . . not from the natural shiftiness of person who make theological statements, but from the uses for which such statements are devised."[69] God is a mysterious reality who demands language that is "logically anomalous."[70] We therefore cannot detail the characteristics of God, but we are not left totally in the dark either. Religious language does not necessarily die the death of a thousand qualifications.

Crombie concedes that we do not have a conception of God *per se*, but our language about God points us "outside the range of possible conception *in a determinate direction*."[71] By means of paradox and intentional "category mistakes,"[72] believers are able to delimit somewhat what they mean. As Crombie also concedes, "What we mean is something rather loose and vague."[73]

Such elusiveness is unsatisfying to a positivist mentality, but Wisdom, Ramsey, and Crombie suggest that restriction of meaning to clear and distinct ideas does justice neither to the range of our experience nor to the complexity of the object of faith.[74] Crombie may himself grant more than the work of the later Wittgenstein would indicate about the necessity of precision in concepts and may thus turn too quickly to the language of paradox. This is especially true when many positivistically inclined philosophers tend to take "paradox" as another word for contradiction. In the hands of someone like Crombie, however, paradox points beyond a contradiction on one level to a possible resolution at a higher level. Close attention to the nature of religious language helps us see that "contradiction" is too simple a category for what is occurring.

Many others contributed to this kind of analysis of religious language by paying attention to its actual use. In general, rich insights have been conveyed, but a similar kind of elusiveness that we saw in all of these thinkers persists when it comes to cognitivity. The question is whether this vagueness leads to nonsense, as the positivists suggest, or has sufficient hermeneutical control genuinely to illuminate divine reality. This work was some of the earliest to indicate how complex religious language is and how we can fruitfully understand it. We should not attempt a final evaluation, however, until we examine developments in hermeneutics (chapter 5), metaphor (chapter 6), and narrative (chapter 7) that at many points build upon and complement their contributions. As we shall see, the close attention paid to the way religious language works in these other approaches to religious language is consistent with Wittgenstein's maxim to "look and see." It is safe to say, however, that the impact of Wittgenstein's thought for religious language continues and has not yet been fully worked through.

As mentioned above, the later Wittgenstein inspired a great emphasis on the analysis of ordinary language which occurred in Oxford and became known as "ordinary language philosophy." This has had important applications to issues in the philosophy of religious language. Because this approach is so distinctive and has a trajectory of its own, we will consider it separately; but it, too, is a part of the broader turn to the actual use of language that we have been considering in this chapter.


## Speech-act Theory

The most important thinker, after Wittgenstein, with regard to speech-act theory is John L. Austin. Austin himself did not particularly apply his work to religious language, but he influenced others who have. James McClendon and some of his colleagues and students in particular have made influential applications of speech-act theory to religious language. We will therefore give an account of Austin's analysis and of McClendon's and James Smith's application of it to religious convictions. Appropriation of speech-act theory for biography and biblical narratives by McClendon and another student, Michael Goldberg, will await the treatment of narrative in chapter 7.

*Austin*

In an important essay, "How to do things with words," Austin criticized the "descriptive fallacy," which is the tendency to think that the main use of language lies in describing, in straightforward cognitive statements.[75] He pointed out that in much ordinary language, words are employed for uses that are rarely limited to simple declaration of fact. He began by pointing out that some language clearly does not so much state something as do something. For example, a mayor may say, "This road is open." What appears to be a simple declarative sentence is not that at all. He or she is not stating what is a fact; rather, the statement *makes* what is said a fact. The road is opened in the act of the mayor's saying the words. Austin called these statements "performatives," and his general theory came to be known as "speech-act" theory.

In further analyzing such statements, Austin detailed how performatives could "go wrong" or be "unhappy," which is a broader issue than their truth or falsity. If someone who was not the mayor declared the road open, or if roads could not legally be opened in that way, then the declaration, "This road is open," would go wrong or "misfire." Austin asked whimsically, "Can I baptize a dog?"[76] Or more to the point, is someone baptized in certain traditions if the priest or pastor does not say, "I baptize you in the name of the Father, the Son, and the Holy Spirit?" Is the act of sprinkling or immersing enough by itself without the appropriate words? Against the traditional philosophical preoccupation with factual, descriptive statements and whether they are true or false, Austin made a Wittgensteinian turn to consider the variety of uses of language. When he did, he found a motherlode of other types of language to analyze along with a multitude of modes of analysis.

Two related questions that he engaged throughout the essay were whether descriptive statements, or "constatives" as he called them, are themselves speech acts that "go wrong" in other ways besides being true or false, and whether sometimes factual elements are important to the felicity of performatives. The question for him was whether or not there is finally a real distinction between performatives and constatives. In attempting to answer this question, Austin tried another angle. In any sentence, there is what he called a "locutionary" dimension, which means that the statement must be a legitimate use of words in a language and make recognizable sense.[77] In other words, it must have some meaning. Gibberish, for example, represents a lack of communication. Second, sentences are uttered with a certain "force," that is, in saying things, we do something. We do not merely say something, we ask or answer questions, give information or assurances or warning, announce verdicts, make appointments, provide descriptions, and so on.[78] Austin calls this element the "illocutionary" act since it can usually be identified with what we do *in* saying something.

Finally, we sometimes accomplish things by making statements. We might warn someone (an illocutionary act) and he or she might not accept the warning, but we could not persuade someone without that person being persuaded. On the other hand, we might persuade a person to flee by means of a warning. In any case, we can distinguish between what is done *in* saying something and what is done *by* saying something. Since the effect of this third element refers to what we do *by* saying something, Austin dubbed it the "perlocutionary" act. Any statement involves locutionary and illocutionary effects that are more or less conventional and thus predictable, whereas the perlocutionary effect is unpredictable and unconventional.[79]

To return to the constative–performative distinction, Austin finally concluded that both are forms of illocutionary acts, that is, stating a fact is indeed a speech act and insofar is like a performative.[80] Moreover, constatives can be unhappy in more ways than being false. To take a debated example in philosophy, "The present King of France is bald" is a statement where it is apter to say that it is "null and void" than that it is false. This is exactly the same, Austin says, "as when I say that I sell you something but it is not mine or (having been burnt) is not any longer in existence."[81] We can still distinguish between the speech act of "stating" where a primary concern is its truth value and a speech act of "appointing," say, where factual issues recede into the background (but do not disappear), but no hard and fast distinction can be made.

Implications abound for religious language, which Austin only touched upon. As he pointed out, sometimes it is very difficult to distinguish between statements of fact and other kinds of speech acts. A believer may say, "The Lord our God is one Lord." Is she making a factual claim, confessing her faith, or praying? Can these acts be clearly separated? And how is such a speech act to be assessed?

## McClendon and Smith

In answer to the last question, James McClendon and James Smith have provided a three-fold framework for analyzing speech acts, which they particularly applied to religious "convictions."[82] "Primary" conditions refer first to the speaker expressing meaningful words in the language, similar to Austin's locutionary act. The example they use is that of someone who is dining with others making the request, "Please pass the bread." The first aspect is simply to use the words in a syntactically proper manner.[83] Such a request would "misfire" if one said, "Bread pass the please." The second aspect of primary conditions is the speech act proper, similar to Austin's illocutionary act. Does the speech act represent a convention in the language sufficient to be recognizable? "Truly, truly, I say unto you, Bread!" would be confusing at the dinner table, at best.

Meeting these "primary conditions," however, is not enough. Factual or "representative" conditions are presupposed. The situation should be that of people sitting at a dining table, and bread should be present. It would not do for one who is about to come up to bat in a baseball game to say, "Pass the bread, please." Or if the requester was already holding bread in his hands, the others would certainly look askance.

Third are "affective" conditions. This refers both to the speaker's intentionality and to the hearer's appropriate responses. The request should be made in an appropriate tone of voice, for example, not pronounced angrily. Otherwise, it is not a simple polite request but is carrying out another agenda. If a person made a promise but did not intend to keep it, it would still be a promise but an insincere one, and in that way go wrong. Additionally, in order for the request to succeed, there should be an appropriate response.[84] If the others got up and left or threw the bread at the requestor, the result would also certainly be unhappy! As can be seen both from the work of McClendon and Smith, and Austin, this kind of analysis reveals how complex apparently simple language can be and in how many ways language can go wrong. It also shows how simplistic was the traditional concentration on the descriptive type of language at the locutionary level alone.

McClendon and Smith especially noted that religious language rarely consists of simple descriptive statements; but this does not mean, as the noncognitivists were wont to conclude, that it has no "representative" elements. McClendon and Smith particularly noted that the ordinary language of believers consists of "convictional" language. This would consist of expressions such as "I believe in God the Father Almighty," "In all things God works together for good with those who love God," "The Lord our God is One," and "Allah Ahkbar." These, too, are not simply stating facts, but are expressing beliefs. These furthermore are different from theories about the nature of the world or other people but express fundamental "convictions" about reality as a whole. "Convictions, then," McClendon and Smith said, "are persistent beliefs such that, if X (a person or community) has a conviction, it will not easily be relinquished and cannot be relinquished without making X a significantly different person (or community) than before."[85] Our convictions give shape to our lives; we live by them. A conviction lies at the foundation of other beliefs. As much as it is a statement, it is an intention to act in the future in accordance with such a belief. An expression of faith, for example, could mean the intention not to despair, not to "throw in the towel," to resist, to fight back.

In terms of McClendon and Smith's analysis of speech acts, what are the conditions for a "happy" conviction? A primary condition is that it is a confession, not a question or a request or a hypothesis. The affirmation "The Lord is my shepherd" makes sense within a tradition, one that treasures the 23rd psalm. Moreover, specific communities of faith would give it its particular hues and shades, for example, as expressed in a Jewish synagogue or in a Christian church. If a believer was heard to utter in such a community, "The Lord is my idol," the other worshippers would likely assume that she was new and was confused or that they had heard wrong. More seriously, the affective conditions may be violated. Such a belief should not be held lightly or with neutral objectivity. It likely would not be changed easily or quickly. Visible emotion may be present or not, but a person would not (appropriately) express such a belief with a happy-go-lucky attitude. As McClendon and Smith note about someone who did not act like a believer, "He may, with consistency, either defend his behavior as misunderstood by the objector or plead weakness of will. If however he replies, 'So what? Never mind how I live; I'm just telling what I believe,' then linguistically something is wrong."[86]

The representative conditions are several. First of all, the context would likely be that of a worship service or of a crisis (a test or trial of faith), not, say, an academic classroom whose subject is Hebrew poetry. Second, such a statement as "The Lord is my shepherd" presupposes that there is a Lord and that the Lord acts benevolently towards the Lord's people. Even though the statement is more of an expression of an attitude and an intention than a declaration of fact, it misfires if there is no "Lord" just as surely as a request to pass the bread where there is no bread. Questions indeed remain such as how the Lord "acts" (how is it compatible with science?) and what "benevolence" means (how is God's goodness reconcilable with the problem of evil?).[87] Speech-act theory suggests, though, that these questions be seen in the context of the speech act from which they arise. To go farther in this vein, such convictions are usually imbedded within larger narratives and may be metaphorical in nature. Hence an evaluation of their cognitive significance cannot avoid the particular dynamics of metaphor (chapter 6) and of narrative (chapter 7).

This kind of perspective prevents people from assuming that when they understand that religious language is rarely simple description, they do not go on to assume that it is wholly nondescriptive. It is a nuanced way of noting the cognitive dimension without emphasizing it in such a way that it distorts the "use" of the language. This analysis does not by itself solve the problem of the verification of religious language, but it sharpens the question and avoids some misleading answers. In comparison with such an analysis, the *University* debate, even the more sophisticated response of Mitchell, appears naive and even wrongheaded. An appropriate answer can hardly be given to an inappropriate question.

For example, consider again the question raised in chapter 1: can language about God be literal? From the discussion of Wittgenstein, there is little reason to deny this possibility. If we do not begin with an unrealistic and overly demanding criterion of what counts as literal, there are probably many cases within a religious community where certain terms, while originally clearly metaphorical, have died and become for all practical purposes (which for Wittgenstein is what counts) literal. God's holiness, God's *agape* (love), prayer (talking with God), all can be seen as literal as much as they are metaphorical. The last example, prayer, reminds us that much religious language is rather straightforward. Concepts such as preaching, worship, taking communion, going to church, all are literal. In fact, some literal expressions, like "walking the aisle," can begin as literal and come to function metaphorically. Words such as salvation or peace may have "rough edges" without being thereby discredited, since all words are vulnerable to this charge. Religious language may therefore be "sufficiently precise" to function conventionally within a given community of faith. In this functional sense words can easily be regarded as literal rather than metaphorical. In this way, the traditional univocal way might be given a modern reformulation.

The impact of the later Wittgenstein, therefore, in contrast to the positivist movement sparked by his earlier work, is in the direction of the pluralism and variety of language. This leads to a more positive assessment of the profuse richness of ordinary language, which should not take a back seat to scientific language. And while not downplaying the importance of scientific language, the door is opened for a broader consideration of cognitive language. This last, however, is more controversial. We have seen that some followers of the later Wittgenstein, perhaps Wittgenstein himself, continued to give pride of place when it comes to cognitive language to scientific language. But we have also seen that the door Wittgenstein opened is not so easily closed. As the analysis of the nature of religious language continued to develop and ramify, so further insights emerged in relation to the vexed question of verification. Particularly when we turn to the discussion of narrative theology, we will find Wittgenstein as a continuing influence. Before we come to that area, however, we turn to continental discussions with their differing approaches and language; but we find them still wrestling with similar questions. They, too, take a linguistic turn and, like the later Wittgenstein, emphasize the social and pragmatic contexts of language. More than he, however, they bring in the issue of tradition, cross-cultural communication, and the issue of truth.

# 5

# *Hermeneutical Philosophy*

On the continent another approach to the issue of language and religion was developing that bore interesting similarities to the thought of the later Wittgenstein. The traditional discipline of hermeneutics, the theory of textual interpretation, became the foundation for an alternative approach to language and epistemology. While hermeneutical philosophy was based on the thought of Martin Heidegger and Hans-Georg Gadamer in the first half of the century, it has become a significant force with respect to religion in the latter part of this century.

## From Regional to General Hermeneutics

Hermeneutics as the theory of the interpretation of texts – usually ancient – has centrally been focused on the interpretation of Scripture. The conflict between the Antiochene and Alexandrian Schools, treated in the second chapter, was a hermeneutical debate. In the Renaissance, a discipline of interpreting the classical texts of Greece and Rome also developed. Additionally, a tradition of interpreting legal texts provided yet another "regional" hermeneutic.[1] In these areas, principles developed that were not necessarily transferable to the other areas. There was as yet no tradition of a general theory of hermeneutics.

The catalyst for such a general hermeneutics was the contribution of Friedrich Schleiermacher, better known as the father of modern theology. Only in recent years has his contribution as the father of modern hermeneutics also been appreciated.[2] Schleiermacher moved sharply in the direction of a general theory of hermeneutics that would be applicable to the interpretation of any text whatsœver. In connection with Scripture, this meant that the Bible should be interpreted as any other book, at least in terms of the methodology. The content, of course, can be allowed to be distinctive. Such a move was central for the modern historical-critical interpretation of the Bible, which, however, is still in dispute.[3] Such an approach, for example, is not only rejected by some Christian groups, but is sharply incompatible with the Muslim interpretation of the Koran, which even prohibits the translation of the Koran into another language. As we shall see, this principle, while largely accepted, is too simplistic and has been more recently modified.

In terms of his particular hermeneutical theory, Schleiermacher as a representative of the Romantic movement, with its emphasis on creativity and genius, emphasized the psychological dimension of reexperiencing the creative act of the original author. The most celebrated aspect of his approach, therefore, has been his idea of reproducing "the whole internal process of an author's way of combining thoughts".[4] How do we discern what a text means? This process cannot be reduced to any totally rule-governed method, but in the last analysis it depends on an imaginative act of the reader intuiting (or "divining") what the author experienced.

On the other hand, how do we move from the text to such an experience? At this point, Schleiermacher offers a more objective basis. We should be guided by what he calls grammatical interpretation, which requires consideration of the straightforward understanding of words. Hermeneutics begins when a question about such straightforward understanding arises. Misunderstanding, of course, is an endemic problem of understanding historical texts because of the historical gap. Hermeneutics therefore, as Schleiermacher conceived it, is a disciplined way to resolve misunderstandings. Beyond basic word meanings and grammatical principles, Schleiermacher also emphasized the importance of what is known as the "hermeneutical circle." We cannot understand the meaning of the whole text apart from understanding the meaning of the individual sentences, and even words, in the text. On the other hand, we cannot properly understand the individual parts apart from some grasp of the whole. So there is a back-and-forth movement between the whole and the part that enables a better understanding.[5] Additionally, Schleiermacher emphasized the interweaving between the two dimensions of psychological and grammatical interpretation, each clarifying the other.[6]

One of those most influenced by Schleiermacher's hermeneutical theory was Wilhelm Dilthey (1833–1911), who extended Schleiermacher's general hermeneutic so that it became the methodology for the humanities (the *Geisteswissenschaften*) as opposed to the burgeoning natural sciences (the *Naturwissenschaften*).[7] Dilthey recognized that the way natural science was then conceived as a methodology delivering exact and objective results, as positivistic, was unsatisfactory when it came to historiography, literature, art, and so on. The natural sciences, according to Dilthey, involve "explanation" (*Erklärung*) in terms of external causation. The human sciences, conversely, involve empathetic "understanding" (*Verstehen*). As Schleiermacher had emphasized, the human sciences require the element of intuition. Interpretation is more of an art, therefore, than a science – in the natural scientific sense, that is. For Dilthey was convinced that the humanities were scientific and objective in their own right. To apply the mechanical methods of the natural sciences to human productions is to miss what is of value in them. The inner dimension of the human can only be understood by the interpretative activity of another human.

In order to secure an objective dimension in spite of the inexactitude of the human sciences, Dilthey understood human productions or artifacts as concretions of objectified spirit. This notion, which was rooted in the Hegelian tradition, understood the movement of history as the concretion and development not just of individual human spirits but of Spirit in general. Because of the unity of the one Spirit – we might speak of the unity of the one human race – it is possible for contemporaries to empathize with the experiences of those who produced the objective artifacts. More than Schleiermacher, Dilthey sought to emphasize how objective and intersubjective this process could be, based as it is on objective outer works and on a common inner structure of humans. At this point, Dilthey understood himself also to be carrying on the legacy of Immanuel Kant in terms of providing an analysis of the common structure that undergirds the human sciences, as Kant had done for the natural sciences.

While increasingly appreciative of the hermeneutical legacy of Schleiermacher and Dilthey, our contemporaries are generally critical of the Romantic hermeneutic of divinizing the intent of the original author. First, the meaning of a text is a public matter that may transcend the explicit intentions of the author. Authors may fail, for example, to express what they intend. Second, how can we know if we have divined the actual inner state of the author? Third, what do we do with works with more complicated parentage, such as the Pentateuch or the Gospels? Two of the main thinkers who appropriated this Schleiermacherian legacy but who also modified and extended it significantly because of such difficulties were Martin Heidegger and his student Hans-Georg Gadamer.

## Ontological Hermeneutics

Heidegger was tremendously provocative but did not extensively develop his insights about hermeneutics, later rejecting the hermeneutical development of his student Gadamer. Nevertheless, he was the person chiefly responsible for the shift from a general hermeneutics to an ontological hermeneutics.

In his primary early work, *Being and Time* (1927), Heidegger modified the phenomenological method he had learned from his mentor, Edmund Husserl, from a method for precise description of essences to an interpretive method of describing human existence, first of all, and in the end, Being itself.[8] Husserl was not interested at the time, if ever, in describing changeable human existence. That was too subjective. Heidegger, however, found that such an existential description was foundational to any other enterprise, particularly that of ontology. How can we understand Being apart from the horizon against which Being appears, human existence (*Dasein*, sometimes translated by its literal German meaning, "Being-there")?

As Heidegger laid out his famous analytic of *Dasein*, the structure of human existence, he stressed the central importance of "understanding" (*Verstehen*) as the essential forward-looking or projective character of human beings.[9] This appropriation of Dilthey's category of understanding now construed as an ineradicable feature (*existentiale*) of *Dasein* implies that human existence is essentially hermeneutical; in other word, human beings exist through interpretive activity. Nothing that human beings do or know occurs apart from a hermeneutical structure. Specifically, *Dasein* finds itself "being-there," always inheriting a past, that is, "thrown" into existence, and having to move toward the future. Human beings approach anything with preunderstandings that projectively shape what is experienced.[10] And what is experienced or known is always experienced or known *as* something. Thus, all experience occurs in a temporal horizon in which the present is related to the past and to a projected future.

In language strikingly reminiscent of the later Wittgenstein's discussion of the way language is functionally rooted, and his emphasis on "seeing-as," Heidegger said, "In dealing with what is environmentally ready-to-hand by interpreting it circumspectively, we 'see' it *as* a table, a door, a carriage, or a bridge."[11] In language redolent of Wittgenstein's broader category "form of life," Heidegger maintained, "In the mere encountering of something, it is understood in terms of a totality of involvements."[12] And over against the tendency of those like Bertrand Russell and the early Wittgenstein who tended to dissolve experience into its component parts, Heidegger noted, "What we 'first' hear is never noises or complexes of sounds, but the creaking waggon, the motor-cycle. We hear the column on the march, the north wind, the woodpecker tapping, the fire crackling. It requires a very artificial and complicated frame of mind to 'hear' a 'pure noise.' "[13]

What Heidegger did, therefore, was to take the model of interpreting a text – which involves the hermeneutical circle, an inherent dimension of personal judgment, and inexact methods – as the basic model for all human understanding and experiencing. He saw human beings, therefore, as essentially or ontologically hermeneutical. This was a revolutionary move. Heretofore, as we saw with Dilthey, if the hermeneutical sciences were seen as sciences at all, they were seen to involve a different methodology and were usually seen as trying to measure up to the standards of the natural sciences, if at all possible. What Heidegger implied is that even the natural sciences themselves, along with everything else, have a hermeneutical foundation.

Gadamer saw the significance of Heidegger's intimations[14] and spelled them out in more detail. He stated clearly that his concern was ontological, namely, with the question of the basic nature of all human understanding.[15] His conclusion, with Heidegger, was that understanding was hermeneutical. He developed this insight in his *magnum opus, Truth and Method,* in three ways. First, he argued that there is an experience of truth in a work of art that is not purely subjective or a matter of taste.[16] In the process, he compared the experience of hermeneutical truth to the experience of play in which the subject matter of a text or painting, for example, controls the game, not an individual player.[17] Rather, the game includes but transcends the players. It is perhaps truer to say that the players are "played" than that they play the game. The implication is that we cannot control "truth" by some "method." Rather, only in the playing of the game do we discover what it holds. Thus, the suggestion has been made that Gadamer's book should have been entitled, *Truth OR Method.*[18] In terms of literary criticism, an implication is that authors cannot wholly determine the meaning of their work. As we saw with Schleiermacher, "authorial intent" can be helpful but is not necessarily so; it can also be misleading. Gadamer, like Wittgenstein, believed that meaning was more public – and also more dynamic – than that.[19] This is seen in the way he moved from the analogy of "play" to "a play." A play's meaning includes the way the spectators experience the play as part of the meaning of the play.[20] As Gadamer said, "Not just occasionally but always, the meaning of a text goes beyond its author. That is why understanding is not merely a reproductive but always a productive activity as well."[21]

Second, with respect to historiography, Gadamer criticized what he called the Enlightenment's "prejudice against prejudice itself."[22] Taking Heidegger's insight that one is never purely objective but is shaped by preunderstandings, Gadamer argued that preunderstandings are not always obstacles. They are necessary in order to have any understanding. Preunderstandings can certainly become prejudices in the negative sense, but without preunderstandings we have no foothold with which to understand. History can open our eyes as well as close them. In other words, history and tradition prepare us to know and to understand. We cannot stand outside of history and manipulate it as we will, but we are in history and are "played" by it as much as we "control" it. To think we can escape this immersion in history and in our situation is an illusion.

This entanglement in history is what Gadamer called "a historically shaped consciousness" (an attempt to translate Gadamer's difficult expression, *wirkungsgeschichtliches Bewußtsein*).[23] We belong to history and have been formed from the "sediments" of history. This belongingness (*Zugehörigkeit*) is what enables us to overcome the distance and alienation (*Entfremdung*) that we experience over against an ancient horizon. A bridge is already formed, therefore, between the ancient and the modern horizon. This is partly why the two cannot be cleanly separated. Any time we understand something from the ancient past, according to Gadamer, it is a matter of our present horizon dynamically "fusing" with that of the ancient horizon.[24] It is *not* a matter of being fully conscious of the present horizon, then being fully conscious of the past horizon through some strict "scientific" methodology, and then taking from it what one will.[25] This is modern philosophy's illusion of transparent consciousness and knowledge, that Gadamer and Heidegger are subverting. Rather, such hermeneutical experience transcends and grounds any methodology. For Gadamer argued, as Heidegger did, that this experience, seen preeminently in historiography, is the basis of all understanding whatsoever.

The requirement of understanding the meaning of a text in the past through integration with our own horizon means that understanding is a constructive activity. To simply repeat a text is not to understand it. "It is enough," Gadamer says, "to say that we understand in a *different* way, *if we understand at all*."[26] Gadamer drew on the Platonic tradition of dialogue in this connection, suggesting that understanding is a matter of dynamic conversation.[27] In terms similar to the game analogy, he said:

> Our first point is that the language in which something comes to speak is not a possession at the disposal of one or the other of the interlocutors . . . in a successful conversation they both come under the influence of the truth of the object and are thus bound to one another in a new community. To reach an understanding in a dialogue is not merely a matter of putting oneself forward and successfully asserting one's own point of view, but being transformed into a communion in which we do not remain what we were.[28]

Gadamer also argued that application of a text's meaning is inseparable from its understanding.[29] Traditionally, hermeneutics involved the three tasks of understanding a text, explaining or interpreting it, and then applying it.[30] In traditional biblical interpretation, this was seen as first determining what a text meant, then what it means.[31] Gadamer argues that some notion of what a text means when it is applied in the present is at least implicitly involved in interpreting what the text meant in the past. Otherwise, a text's meaning remains as a free-floating construct that never transcends its original horizon. In an unusual move, he takes legal hermeneutics as paradigmatic for all interpretation since the connection of the meaning of a law with its application is clear.[32] He acknowledges that we can and must distinguish between a text's original meaning and how it may be applied in the present, but such sharp division is already a secondary and derivative process. Application has played a prior role as part of the current horizon that enables us to grasp and understand the past horizon. Rather than sharply distinguishing understanding, explanation, and application, therefore, Gadamer sees them as initially "comprising one unified process."[33] Gadamer himself points out with regard to the Christian Gospel, that it "does not exist in order to be understood as a merely historical document, but to be taken in such a way that it exercises its saving effect."[34] In fact, he implies that the Gospel cannot be understood even as a "merely historical document" apart from some notion of the latter.

The third part of *Truth and Method*, then, was to see that when it comes to ontology, all understanding is hermeneutically shaped, thus the move to ontology and the reason for the appellation "philosophical" hermeneutics. Moreover, as a hermeneutical activity, understanding is also inherently linguistic. Against the traditional view, "it is not that the understanding is subsequently put into words; rather, the way understanding occurs – whether in the case of a text or a dialogue with another person who raises an issue with us – is the coming-into-language of the thing itself."[35] This linguistic phenomenon "points to a universal ontological structure, namely to the basic nature of everything toward which understanding can be directed."[36] Thus his well-known aphorism: "*Being that can be understood is language.*"[37] This is the linguistic turn with a vengeance.

Gadamer was often misunderstood as speaking only of the human sciences, but in the preface to the second edition of *Truth and Method* he made it clear that his description of understanding was foundational also to the natural sciences. Moreover, he clarified that he was not against methodology *per se*, but he opposed the overextension of methodology to invalidate the primacy of hermeneutical judgment. Rather, all methods presuppose hermeneutical judgment. Gadamer's ontological approach thus undercut the split between the natural and human sciences, again proposing the universality of hermeneutics.[38]

95

## Critical Hermeneutics

Because Gadamer remained on the level of ontology, he left important questions unanswered. How exactly does methodology fit with such a philosophical hermeneutic? Add to that a question that arose in a significant encounter with Jürgen Habermas of the Frankfurt School of critical theory: given this immersion in history and in preunderstanding, how do we bring criticism to bear on such preunderstandings so that they do not simply become prejudices? How can we deal with the vexed question of ideology, of unconscious views that protect vested interests and oppress the powerless?[39]

Habermas contended that Gadamer was too wedded to the constrictions of tradition so that he was left to the mercy of ideological prejudices. Even though Habermas appropriated Gadamer's hermeneutical emphasis for normal public interaction, he offered an alternative to meet our "emancipatory interests."[40] His answer was two-fold. First, he argued that we need a theory that accounts for ideology and a way to move beyond it, modeled on Freudian psychoanalytic therapy for surmounting illusions and neuroses on the individual level. Second, he believed that in the idea of an ideal speech situation, we could discern regulative, ethical norms that should guide interaction, for example, the basic equality of all speakers in a discussion, the right of all speakers to express their points of view without fear of recrimination, and the requirement of validating our views with "the force of the better argument."[41] Even though such an ideal speech situation may never exist and is therefore counterfactual, it still provides a means of evaluating imperfect speech situations and discerning "systematically distorted communication" in the present.[42] What is valid, therefore, is that upon which such a speech community would agree.

Habermas's discourse ethic is significant in its own right, but it is still developing and moves in a different direction than Gadamer's approach. The basic difference is the appeal to what he at one time called a "quasi-transcendental" basis (in the tradition of Marxist critical theory) from which to adjudicate rival truth claims. Attempting to complete the "unfinished project of the Enlightenment," he argues, unlike Gadamer, that we must transcend hermeneutics in order to find a truth that should be compelling to any rational person.[43] In that sense, his work moves in a different direction than either the Wittgensteinian or Gadamerian philosophies.[44]

Critics of Habermas have pointed out that the psychoanalytic situation cannot easily be transferred to the public sphere.[45] Instead of having a "therapist," who is the agreed-upon expert, each group is vying for the role of expert – with no one capable of standing above the fray and adjudicating. Second, there is no agreed-upon theory for what constitutes ideology and what does not, nor is there agreement on how to determine by some theory what is ideological or not. Moreover, Habermas's appeal to a democratic consensus is attractive to those nurtured in certain Western political traditions but makes little sense, for example, in the contexts of traditional Shiite Muslims in Iran or of African tribal religion and politics.[46] The appeal to an ideal speech situation, as Gadamer pointed out, remains abstract. It may be so removed from the actual realities of the present that it offers little practical help in adjudicating between different alternatives. Gadamer said, "What man needs is not just the persistent posing of ultimate questions, but the sense of what is feasible, what is possible, what is correct, here and now."[47] Despite these problems with his own constructive proposal, Habermas posed sharply the question of whether a hermeneutical approach, for its part, can be sufficiently critical.

Gadamer responded by pointing out that the challenge which ancient texts offer us, for example, is a critical one. We do not absorb other horizons into our modern one, but we fuse with them. That means that we are challenged, criticized, and changed by them. This means also that we do not necessarily let the present horizon be absorbed by the past horizon. There is always critical interaction. Gadamer did emphasize the way we already belong to traditions. As he says, "Thus the meaning of 'belonging' – i.e., the element of tradition in our historical-

hermeneutical activity – is fulfilled in the commonality of fundamental, enabling prejudices."[48] He also, however, emphasized the
distantiation involved between horizons. "Hermeneutic work is
based on a polarity of familiarity and strangeness. . . . Here too
there is a tension. It is in the play between the traditionary text's
strangeness and familiarity to us, between being a historically
intended, distanciated object and belonging to a tradition. *The
true locus of hermeneutics is this in-between.*"[49]

Even before the debate with Habermas, Gadamer had insisted
that interpretation is more than confirmation of our preliminary
prejudices. He had said first of all that a classic text often "pulls
us up short by challenging our fore-meanings itself."[50] Second,
a person normally comes to a text with the expectation that it
will teach something. Gadamer suggests, then, that part of a
hermeneutically trained consciousness is sensitivity to a text's
otherness, or "alterity." "The important thing," he emphasizes,
"is to be aware of one's own bias, so that the text can present
itself in all its otherness and thus assert its own truth against one's
own fore-meanings."[51] Dialogue with texts in fact is a way of
gaining awareness of one's unexamined assumptions.[52]

Third, this checking process involves not only one's anticipa-
tory ideas but also questioning the ideas of the text itself. Some
have taken Gadamer to be a conservative simply bowing to
authority – whether it be that of texts or of persons. Gadamer,
however, is attempting to subvert the Enlightenment dichotomy
between authority and reason.[53] The authority of a text or of a
person, he argues, is based on "an act of reason itself which,
aware of its own limitations, trusts to the better insight of
others. . . . Indeed, authority has to do not with obedience but
rather with knowledge."[54] In other words, a crucial dimension of
the hermeneutical process is challenging and checking the claims
of the text. This does not mean that one accepts only what can
be fully confirmed by reason (a reason which is always historically
situated rather than universal) but what has a reasonable claim to
insight and knowledge superior to one's own. This assumes that
one has either confirmed the text's claim to be true or that it
"can, in principle, be discovered to be true."[55] Gadamer pointed

out that such a willingness to make a reasoned acknowledgment of authority is crucial for education, but it also has obvious implications for religion. It allows for a way to affirm the authority of Scripture, for example, without basing it upon blind faith or measuring it completely by the current deliverances of reason.

Fourth, what Gadamer especially insisted upon, in contrast to Habermas's view that we must have some transhistorical theory to undergird critique, is that any critical theory is itself based upon hermeneutical judgment. The judgment of the validity of theory is finally hermeneutical in nature, involving one's own tradition, with all the inclinations and biases that it entails.[56] According to Gadamer, there is no escape from history.

This issue of the viability of criticism in hermeneutics is particularly pressing in the area of feminist hermeneutics. On the one hand, there is agreement on the need for criticism of the way patriarchy has affected even canonical texts.[57] On the other hand, one of the criticisms of patriarchy is its appeal to universal standards of reason that have tended to exclude women. Moreover, feminists tend to make the Gadamerian kind of emphasis that our perspectives are shaped by our tradition and situation. Although by and large favorable to Habermas, Seyla Benhabib criticizes him precisely at the point where he verges toward a "disembedded and disembodied" self.[58] Instead, she appeals for a situated universality, which seems closer to Gadamer's views. In general, feminists have gravitated towards some kind of ideology critique that is short of Habermas's transcendental approach and also towards a hermeneutical, interpretive approach to knowledge. At the same time, they have looked for a great deal of specificity when it comes to critique.[59]

The problem with Gadamer is that he continued to leave the way in which his approach could be allied with critical methodologies unclear. In other words, he called for the testing of claims to truth and authority but did little to specify how this might be done. At this point, Habermas and feminists have reason for concern; but perhaps the person who best continues Gadamer's hermeneutical emphasis, yet with attention to critical methods, is Paul Ricœur. Ricœur's work stemmed from the same tradition as

99

Gadamer's, from phenomenology and hermeneutics. Ricœur, however, in confrontation with the explosion of the structuralist movement in France with its insistence upon method (see chapter 8), moved beyond ontological hermeneutics to take what he called the "long route" from ontology to methodology.

## Ricœur and Critical Hermeneutics

Ricœur allied himself with Gadamer at the point of the universality of hermeneutics, namely, that all understanding whatsoever has a hermeneutical shape.[60] In a critique of the philosophical tradition, focused most sharply in Hegel, that stressed the goal of absolute knowledge and a transparent knowledge of self, Ricœur argued that knowledge is always mediated through interpretation and that knowledge of the self is no clearer than any other knowledge. In fact, our own selves are texts that call for ever new interpretation. "In contrast to the tradition of the *cogito* and to the pretension of the subject to know itself by immediate intuition, it must be said that we understand ourselves only by the long detour of the signs of humanity deposited in cultural works."[61] It is not the case, either, that some privileged knowledge, as in Kant, can be exact; rather, all knowledge demands interpretation. Nor is there some kind of solid foundation or beginning point; rather, we find ourselves already on the way, with something given to interpret. As Ricœur says of his hermeneutical philosophy:

> In contrast to philosophies concerned with starting points, a meditation on symbols starts from the fullness of language and of meaning already there; it begins from within language which has already taken place and in which everything in a certain sense has already been said; it wants to be thought, not presuppositionless, but in and with all its presuppositions. Its first problem is not how to get started but, from the midst of speech, to recollect itself.[62]

Ricœur was concerned, however, not to leave matters there, like Heidegger who turned to a kind of mystical poetizing that was largely uncritical. Ricœur, like Gadamer, wanted to transcend the Diltheyan legacy of a split between the human sciences and the natural sciences, between understanding and explanation. As we saw, however, Gadamer did not go far enough. He showed that explanation is itself rooted in understanding but not how understanding might be enriched by explanation. Ricœur became dissatisfied with Gadamer's dichotomies between truth and method, between understanding and explanation, and between belonging and alienation. He therefore developed the conception of a "hermeneutical arc" that included an initial moment of understanding followed by a moment of explanation and then a new moment of now "post-critical" understanding.[63]

Ricœur articulated the first moment of understanding initially in the context of a study of the symbolism of evil among the ancient Hebrews and Greeks, that is, "at the fundamental intersection that founds our culture."[64] His view was that philosophical, critical reflection must begin with such symbols – not from scratch, so to speak. In an expression borrowed from Kant, he said, "The symbol gives rise to thought."[65] In other words, the primary language of life (and religion) is that of symbol, metaphor, narrative, confession, worship, etc., which offer philosophical reflection something to think about. In his phenomenological studies of the will, he concluded that direct philosophical analysis cannot grasp lived human life apart from these more poetic expressions.[66] In particular, he argued that linguistic access to the experience of evil – of sin, stain, and guilt, for example – only occurs initially through symbolic expressions.[67] Therefore, in concert with Gadamer, he would agree that classic texts seize us first before we interpret them; or rather, we interpret them because they have first spoken to us. To stay with Gadamer's terminology, we find ourselves in the game before we stop to reflect. This initial moment of understanding is extremely significant, for it represents an initial sense of importance and, further, an "initial guess" at the meaning.[68] But it is not enough.

In contrast to Gadamer, Ricœur emphasizes the importance of criticism, which he brings in as the second hermeneutical moment. Through methods such as structuralism (see chapter 8), we

101

can probe more deeply into a text, or ourselves, and emerge with deepened understanding.[69] Beginning with the paradigm of the text, he argues that a dimension of distantiation is already involved in writing itself.[70] A text takes on a life of its own, distinct from the intentions of the author – versus Romantic hermeneutics. The inscription into a text means that as a structured work it stands over against not only the author but also the reader, thereby challenging the reader. We cannot make a text mean whatever we want – this against those who overemphasize the current horizon. The language of a text is not a private language, as Wittgenstein argued, and moreover its structure is not something that can be changed. This public and objective dimension offers protection from the extremes of subjectivity and underscores the scientific nature of hermeneutics.

Ricœur calls for analysis of each level of the text, the semiotic level of the word, the semantic level of the sentence, and the narrative level of the work. Moreover, he allows for a variety of approaches to the text, such as an archeological psychoanalysis into the unconscious roots of a text that point backward and a teleological dimension of the text that points forward. Comparisons have been made between this emphasis and the medieval emphasis on levels of interpretation (see chapter 2). At this point he welcomes all the critical methods in biblical study such as form criticism, redaction criticism, and structuralist criticism. Ricœur further advocates "hermeneutic of suspicion" that questions the distorting effect of ideology and unconscious motivations.[71] The resulting conflict of interpretations cannot be completely adjudicated, but in the jostle of approaches, we can penetrate deeper into the text. Again, there may be no one definitive interpretation, but a text cannot just mean anything. There can be better or worse interpretations. Ricœur's view is that the superfluity of meaning is not something to be regretted but to be embraced; his principle, which he terms "the principle of plenitude," is that a text means "all that it can mean."[72]

The danger of traditional uses of critical methodology is that they stop at this second level. This is Ricœur's criticism of the traditional historical-critical approach to the Bible. It analyzes

Scripture at different levels but never moves beyond to a post-critical understanding, or what Ricœur sometimes calls a "second naïveté" or a "second immediacy."[73] As he says:

> If we can no longer live the great symbolisms of the sacred in accordance with the original belief in them, we can, we modern men, aim at a second naïveté in and through criticism. In short, it is by *interpreting* that we can *hear* again. Thus it is in hermeneutics that the symbol's gift of meaning and the endeavor to understand by deciphering are knotted together.[74]

It is precisely in the modern age of univocal and technical language (as for example in logical positivism), he suggests, that we have a chance to "recharge" our language, for we are also an age preoccupied with symbols, an age of critical exegesis, of symbolic logic, of intricate psychoanalytic analysis.

> The same epoch holds in reserve both the possibility of emptying language by radically formalizing it and the possibility of filling it anew by reminding itself of the fullest meanings, the most pregnant ones, the ones which are most bound by the presence of the sacred to man.
> It is not regret for the sunken Atlantides that animates us, but hope for a re-creation of language. Beyond the desert of criticism, we wish to be called again.[75]

Far from considering this search for meaning as a method producing guaranteed results, Ricœur regards it as a wager, akin to the Anselmian "faith in search of understanding."

> I wager that I shall have a better understanding of man and of the bond between the being of man and the being of all beings if I follow the *indication* of symbolic thought. That wager than becomes the task of *verifying* my wager and saturating it, so to speak, with intelligibility. In return, the task transforms my wager: in betting *on* the significance of the symbolic world, I bet at the same time *that* my wager will be restored to me in power of reflection, in the element of coherent discourse.

Then there opens before me the field of philosophical hermeneutics properly so called.[76]

In this way, Ricœur stays within the province of philosophical hermeneutics laid out by Gadamer but goes beyond it with the integration of truth *and* method.

Ricœur criticizes traditional approaches, including modern historical-critical biblical studies, for focusing on the prehistory of the text, or what Ricœur calls the world behind the text, rather than on the text itself and on the world it projects, "the world in front of the text." This "refiguration" of the "configuration" of the text is a creative act involving the appropriation of all of the different critical approaches at the second level.[77] In other words, it is the level of Gadamer's fusion of horizons. The appropriation also must include application. Ricœur thus agrees with Gadamer that interpretation, or the hermeneutical arc, cannot stop short of application. This is what could also be called the existential level, where we interpret ourselves in light of the world in front of the text. Ricœur stresses, "What must be interpreted in a text is a *proposed world* which I could inhabit."[78] Ricœur's language appears to some to be too subjective and privatistic, but he uses this language in light of Heidegger's conception of "being-in-the-world," which is meant to transcend such subjectivity.[79] In other words, a text offers a certain *gestalt* on reality, which goes far beyond privatistic feelings or attitudes, yet without excluding them.

Another way that Ricœur emphasizes this third moment, in essays pertaining specifically to religious faith, is to say that appropriation is akin to the reception of testimony. Testimony implies public trial or testing. In the end, however, testimony can only be appropriated by oneself coming to testify, a personal act that cannot be entirely validated by external proof.[80] In his most recent work, he appropriates testimony or "attestation" as the basis of his hermeneutical philosophy. In speaking of reason, or the "cogito" as he puts it, he says, "As credence without any guarantee, but also as trust greater than any suspicion, the hermeneutics of the self can claim to hold itself at an equal distance from the cogito exalted by Descartes and from the cogito that Nietzsche proclaimed forfeit."[81]

So far, the discussion has proceeded with reference to interpretation of texts, with obvious implications for the interpretation of Scripture. Ricœur, however, emphasizes that his basic approach is also valid for other social sciences, for an "action" can itself be seen as a kind of text.[82] We have already seen how Ricœur views the self as a kind of text that cries out for interpretation. Actions and historical events themselves can be seen as a fixed structure that allows for interpretation and appropriation beyond the original intention of the actors involved.[83]

Ricœur's patchwork development of his approach in a variety of essays and works is not without its problems. Sometimes he leaves the impression that the hermeneutical arc is a one-way process, but it is clear from the rest of his writings that he intends something more like a hermeneutical spiral, in which a postcritical understanding may itself serve as an interpretation that needs to be further criticized and then reappropriated.[84] Moreover, it is easy to separate artificially these moments into totally discrete "acts." In reality, they flow together and are more logical distinctions than actual distinctions. Another problem is that Ricœur sometimes leaves the impression that the second moment is the objective and scientific aspect that is not subject to the ontological hermeneutical framework of interpretation, which is contrary to the basic direction of his thought.[85] If we remember this fundamental point of Gadamer's, then we can accept Ricœur's hermeneutical arc at a second level, with hermeneutical judgment being involved at every point of the arc.

This view serves to clarify the debate between Gadamer and Jürgen Habermas. According to Habermas's critical theory, with its Marxist legacy, we need an objective critique to master the distorting effects of ideology. Gadamer's reliance on tradition, according to Habermas, does not provide an independent perspective from which to discern and criticize ideology. As mentioned above, Gadamer allows for criticism *through* the challenge provided by other horizons and sharply maintains the universality of hermeneutics, that is, the impossibility of such an independent epistemological platform. Ricœur agrees with Habermas that Gadamer does not explicate the critical dimension sufficiently, but nevertheless fundamentally agrees with Gadamer. As we have seen, Ricœur, too, calls for ideology critique, appropriating the analyses of Marx, Freud, and Nietzsche, but sees this as "a hermeneutics of suspicion." In his view, the elaboration of some critical framework such as psychoanalysis is itself a hermeneutical act, as is its application. He suggests, "The task of the hermeneutics of tradition is to remind the critique of ideology that man can project his emancipation and anticipate an unlimited and unconstrained communication only on the basis of the creative reinterpretation of cultural heritage."[86] And he further says of Habermas's approach, "This tradition is not perhaps the same as Gadamer's; it is perhaps that of the *Aufklärung*, whereas Gadamer's would be Romanticism. But it is a tradition nonetheless, the tradition of emancipation rather than that of recollection. Critique is also a tradition."[87] As we have seen, Ricœur enthusiastically endorses the use of such critical theories, in a way that Gadamer does not, but agrees with Gadamer that such theories are themselves illusions insofar as they purport to be independent of hermeneutical judgments based on historical traditions.

Perhaps more than anyone else except Ricœur himself, the American theologian David Tracy has applied these insights to religious language. We will take up his thought in the next chapter since it is tied in with the treatment of analogy, but in this context, his conception of a "classic" text is significant. Rather than the modern hermeneutical emphasis on regarding all texts, including sacred texts, in common, Tracy acknowledges that classic texts exert a previous claim upon us. We do not come to them neutrally, but with prejudices, as it were. We expect them to speak to us; we regard them as having a certain earned authority arising from tradition. The classic, he says, exerts a "claim to attention, a vexing, a provocation."[88] This is all the more true of religious classics. "To risk an interpretation of the religious classics of the culture is, in its manner, to risk entering the most dangerous conversation of all."[89] Because the issues are so vital, here more than ever, "the interpreter must risk being caught up in, even being played by, the questions and answers."[90] In the Enlightenment context, as Gadamer recognizes, such an approach appears subjective and irrational. In the light of the hermeneutical philosophy that we have considered here, however, it would be irrational and unnatural to ignore the claims of classic texts. As Tracy says, "Any attempt at an autonomy so pure that it is unaffected by the tradition in which we, willingly or unwillingly, stand is the final form of the general privatization which plagues our culture."[91]

These texts, nevertheless, are open to critical analysis of all kinds, especially ideology analysis. What Tracy calls for is Gadamer's "nonauthoritarian notion of authority" and "non-traditionalist notion of tradition" to make room for a "non-classicist notion of the classic."[92] He explicitly appeals at this point to Ricœur's dialectic of understanding–explanation–understanding for the way in which critique is brought to classic texts. We may conclude by affirming or by disputing the classic's claim to such status. We cannot determine beforehand whether a classic text will stand the test, or have its interpretation substantially changed. This is itself part of the conflict of interpretations and, further, the conflict of theologies. On the other hand, the authority of classic texts cannot be gainsaid.

## Reader–response Theory

A movement that is similar to Gadamer's and Ricœur's hermeneutical philosophy that further develops their notion of the dynamic reception of meaning is "reader–response theory." This will repay our attention not only because it augments the work of Gadamer and Ricœur but also because it has been quite influential in biblical studies.

It is not surprising that we find a striking affinity between reader–response theory and hermeneutical philosophy because both have strong roots in Husserl's phenomenology; moreover, much cross-fertilization has occurred between the movements. Reader-response theory includes a wide range of thinkers and ideas, but perhaps the philosopher most widely associated with it is the German Wolfgang Iser.[93] Since he is also one of the most closely attuned to the continental philosophy significant for Gadamer and Ricœur, an explication of his approach, with its strengths and weaknesses, fits well into the themes of this chapter.[94]

Like Gadamer, Iser emphasizes that meaning occurs in between the text and the reader.[95] Without the contribution of both, there is no meaning. Iser's contribution has been to spell out in more detail the unavoidability of a dynamic response from the reader, even when the historical horizons might be similar. No text tells the whole story, or boredom would be the result. Rather, there are "gaps" or "blanks" that must be filled in by the reader, which "not only draw the reader into the action but also lead him or her to shade in the many outlines suggested by the given situations."[96] This is as commonplace as the way in which a reader constructs the way a character looks, which is why sometimes movies based on novels create a jolt when the actors do not match our preconceived notions of the way they "should" appear. The condensed prose of the account of the creation and fall of Adam and Eve in Genesis 2–3 is a well-known example of how sparse writing can yield a rich account that is almost an inexhaustible source of reflection.[97] As Iser says in commenting upon Jane Austen's writing:

> What is missing from the apparently trivial scenes, the gaps arising out of the dialogue – this is what stimulates the reader into filling the blanks with projections. He is drawn into the events and made to supply what is meant from what is not said. What is said only appears to take on significance as a reference to what is not said; it is the implication and not the statements that give shape and weight to the meaning. But as the unsaid comes to life in the reader's imagination, so the said "expands" to take on greater significance than might have been supposed: even trivial scenes can seem surprisingly profound.[98]

Any work therefore is an indeterminate schema that must be "fleshed out," so to speak, by the reader. What is spelled out and what is not are both important. In this sense, the meaning of the text does not exist apart from the creative interpretative activity of the reader, a particular kind of "fusion of horizons" as it were. Far from the work standing as a complete entity all by itself, almost as a Platonic "idea" existing in a transcendental realm separately from either author or reader, the work exists only as it is read, when the reader composes the meaning based on the structure and guidance supplied by the text. The structure of the text therefore guides but does not fully determine the reader's response. Iser's approach thus offers an intriguing exemplification of Gadamer's notion of understanding a text as "playing a game."

In the English-speaking world, reader-response theory has been a reaction against the New Criticism that prevailed at mid-century, which focused upon the completeness of the work standing by itself.[99] New critics opposed, like Gadamer and Ricœur, a Romantic hermeneutic that committed the "intentional fallacy," which saw the meaning lying in the intention of the author. They also, however, criticized the "affective fallacy," which saw the meaning lying in the effect of the work upon the reader.[100] In this, they were not far from the logical positivist's emphasis upon the proposition as a logical picture that stands by itself quite apart from a speaker or a hearer (see chapter 2). We will see a similar emphasis by some structuralists in chapter 8. Reader-response critics, however, with all their diversity, stressed the inescapability of the integrative activity of the reader.

For an example in biblical studies, Alan Culpepper, in his ground-breaking application of this kind of approach to the Gospel of John, describes in great detail the way the reader is led to project a particular understanding of Jesus as the eternal Word of God become flesh and to receive it as Gospel, or good news.[101] Along the way, the reader is led through such techniques as misunderstandings and irony to fill out the characters of friend and foe, of different kinds of disciples, and finally to identify with the viewpoint of the Gospel of John itself. Drawing on the work of Murray Krieger, Culpepper says:

It is clear that John has been used as a "window" through which the critic can catch "glimpses" of the history of the Johannine community [the world behind the text in Ricœur's terms]. The meaning of the gospel derives from the way it was related to that history. . . . In contrast to the approach to a text as a "window," Krieger offers the metaphor of the text as a "mirror." This model assumes that the meaning of the text lies on this side of it, between mirror and observer, text and reader. Meaning is produced in the experience of reading the text as a whole and making the mental moves the text calls for its reader to make, quite apart from questions concerning its sources and origin.[102]

Critics of Iser have argued that he is too sanguine about the capacity of the text to guide the interpretation.[103] We shall also see in chapter 8 how some poststructuralists, while also stressing the creative role of the reader, believe that the indeterminacy inherent in reading is uncontrollable. Iser, however, shares with both Gadamer and Ricœur the belief that there is a middle ground between the text being so complete in itself as virtually to negate the importance of the reader and being so indeterminate as to be chaotic. Iser's philosophy of language is similar to Ricœur's emphasis both on the place of methods to analyze a work and also on the fecundity of a text's surplus of meaning. Ricœur himself in his work on narratives appropriated Iser's work as consistent with his conception of configuration.

Iser points out that such indeterminacy is not just present in written discourse but also in everyday conversation.[104] Here we may remind ourselves of Wittgenstein's emphasis on the blurred boundaries of words along with their use in terms of sufficient precision. In opposition to a Platonic confidence in the clarity of face-to-face dialogue, both the written and spoken word require interpretation and allow for surplus of meaning, as many who have been "quoted" in the press would attest. What we have with the later Wittgenstein and with these hermeneutical philosophers is a philosophy of language quite different from the traditional one outlined in chapter 1. Rather than an emphasis on language having to be clear and precise, it is sufficient for language to have rough edges. In fact, the surplus of meaning in symbolic language is welcomed. Rather than determinate methodologies for establishing meaning, personal judgment within communities of tradition is inherently unavoidable. Method has a place, but it is not primary or foundational. Rather than the requirement of a foundation of univocal meanings, the conception is one of starting in the midst of a plethora of meaning and finding our way by unending interpretation. Rather than an emphasis on the author or speaker's private meaning, the emphasis is on the publicness of the work and the reader's reception of it. This shift in the basic paradigm of language is carried further with the emphases on metaphor and narrative, which we shall examine in the next two chapters.[105]

# 6

# *Metaphor, Symbol, and Analogy*

Since the 1960s, metaphor has leapt from its relegation to the sidelines of discussion about cognitive language to the forefront. As Mark Johnson wrote in 1981, "We are in the midst of a metaphormania. Only three decades ago the situation was just the opposite: poets created metaphors, everybody used them, and philosophers (linguists, psychologists, etc.) ignored them. Today we seem possessed by metaphor."[1] The growing philosophical significance of metaphor parallels its increasing religious significance. As we discussed in chapter 2, figurative language in general has long been seen as central to religious language. We saw how religious language, according to Aquinas, stretches the normal or literal meanings of words. The problem was how to explain this "logical oddness," to use the words of Ian Ramsey. Reconsideration of metaphor in the twentieth century has been central to a new answer to this question and to a fresh understanding of analogy and of symbol as well.

A major handicap historically to perceiving the significance of metaphor for philosophy and religion was the increasing marginalization of metaphor to the position of a figure of speech or ornament to language, important to rhetoric and poetics but not for philosophy. It is this situation that has radically and quickly changed, altering the philosophical landscape in the last half of the twentieth century. In order to map some of that landscape, we will first take a panoramic look at the historical fortunes of metaphor to provide the backdrop for an account of its cognitive significance. Then related developments in the context of symbolism and analogy will be explored before turning to their appropriation in exegesis and theology.

## Metaphor as Ornamental

The historical treatment of metaphor reaches back to Aristotle (384–22 BCE).[2] As Paul Ricœur points out, Aristotle provided the foundation for seeing metaphor as a deviation from "normal" speech, as a *substitution* for literal language. Aristotle also saw metaphor in terms of *single* words that substitute, for rhetorical or poetic reasons, for other literal words. The effect has been to see metaphor as a mere ornament to language, which enables us to embellish what we know – not to add to what we know. Aristotle gave some hints that metaphor might connote more than this, saying, "The greatest thing by far is to be a master of metaphor. It is the one thing that cannot be learnt from others; and it is also a sign of genius, since a good metaphor implies an intuitive perception of the similarity in dissimilarity."[3] Even here, along with the insight that metaphor cannot totally be rule governed and is based on personal judgment, Aristotle suggests that metaphor is based on an actual underlying similarity. Such an emphasis, combined with the understanding of metaphor as a substitution for a proper word, led easily to the tendency to explain metaphors by reducing their meaning to these commonalities. In other words, metaphor could be reduced to literal language. Thus, if we call Achilles a lion, we are actually saying that Achilles is courageous – and nothing more.[4]

The treatment of metaphor by Latin rhetoricians such as Cicero (106–43 BCE) and Quintilian (ca. CE 35–96) further moved the significance of metaphor away from philosophy and towards matters of style. The focus on metaphor as a trope (or figure of speech) and on the classification of its various stylistic uses continued up to the nineteenth century.[5]

Despite the prevalence of metaphor in the Bible and the widespread use of allegorical interpretation in the medieval period, the cognitive value of metaphor did not come to the fore.

As we saw in chapter 2, Aquinas minimized metaphor in favor of analogy. Allegory highlighted figurative language, but it fitted within a substitutionary framework in which the allegory could be explained by nonfigurative language. Sometimes, the use of metaphor was seen as dangerous. It could be allowed in the Bible, where it was, so to speak, authorized by God, but one had to be careful of its potential to lead astray. We can hear some of Plato's suspicion of the artists in the concern for the inflammatory and perhaps deceptive power of metaphor.

Two tendencies in the modern period made metaphor vulnerable to increased emphasis on the value of direct, univocal language. One was recourse to a mathematic model for philosophy, which prioritized exactitude and certainty. The second was the continuing tendency to see metaphor in terms of rhetoric and style. At the outset of the modern period, Thomas Hobbes (1588–1679) and John Locke (1632–1704) vehemently dismissed metaphor as harmful to the cause of truth. Hobbes said that people abuse speech "when they use words metaphorically; that is, in other sense than that they are ordained for; and thereby deceive others."[6] Even though later philosophers altered many of the views of the early empiricists and rationalists, in general they did not reject this aspect of their thought. Leading thinkers continued to question and suspect the use of metaphor. It was allowable, to be sure, as a literary or rhetorical device, but when it came to treating truth, it was not to be trusted.

The epitome of the rejection of the philosophical significance of metaphor can be seen in its dismissal by the logical positivist movement (chapter 3). Their distinction between cognitive and emotive language, between what can be said clearly and what cannot, clearly disparaged figurative language as without cognitive significance.

## Metaphor as Cognitive

In the work of I.A. Richards in 1936 and Max Black in 1954–5, a new perspective on metaphor was put forward that

114

only gained currency after the tide of positivism had begun to ebb.[7] Ironically, the British analytical tradition, which was allied with logical positivism, has supplied some of the best expositions of a cognitive view of metaphor. Black's analytical credentials certainly helped to gain credence for this view. Richards suggested that rather than being a substitute, metaphor is irreplaceable. Metaphor sometimes says what has not been said before and cannot be said in any other way. In other words, metaphor is often irreducible to literal language. Indeed, in a brash suggestion, Black claimed that metaphor does not just help us to discern reality, it creates reality. The turn to seeing metaphor at the heart of cognitive language had begun.

I shall here set out in broad strokes this new view of metaphor that has had a great deal of influence in the area of religious language. Obviously, differences exist between proponents of this view, and debates persist over the finer points of the theory. For our purposes, however, we can focus on broad lines of agreement between thinkers in order to expound a major alternative to the traditional view of metaphor.

Richards and Black pointed out, in opposition to Aristotle, that metaphor occurs not just at the level of a word but at the level of a sentence. It is actually an encounter of different frameworks of meaning within a larger context. Metaphor has been defined as saying one thing and meaning another but, more accurately, it is speaking "about one thing in terms which are seen to be suggestive of another."[8] The metaphor is not one word or another but words acting together. In Jesus's saying, "You are the salt of the earth," two networks of meaning, believers and salt, come together. In Black's interaction theory, he understands metaphor to call up the "associated commonplaces" of the different words involved, so that one "filters and transforms" the standard configuration of the other.[9] Richards spoke of the two regions as the tenor and the vehicle, Black as the frame and the focus. In the expression, "The Lord is my shepherd," the tenor and the focus is "Lord," while the vehicle and frame is "shepherd."[10] What Richards and Black are pointing

115

to is the fact that *both* terms, their related ideas, and their interaction, are crucial.

In an influential exposition in which he situates himself within the Richards and Black tradition, Ricœur agrees that the problem of traditional accounts is that they focused on the level of words, whereas in order to understand metaphor we must consider the level of the sentence.[11] What is important, then, is the interaction between words within a phrase, a sentence, or a larger context. Specifically, Ricœur argued that at one level, a "semantic impertinence" alerts us to a new "semantic pertinence." The incongruity of the literal meaning of the words, such as "All flesh is grass" (Isaiah 40: 6), is a cue to build up a new meaning out of the tension between the two frames of meaning. In Ricœur's words, a "semantic shock" moves us towards a "semantic innovation" guided by the interaction of the two terms. The new construction is then built upon "the ruins of the old." Mary Gerhart and Alan Russell suggested the image of mapping together two regions that are not usually associated to create a new configuration or *gestalt*.[12] Monroe Beardsley suggested that what commonly happens is that primary associations are suppressed, allowing less frequently considered associations to come to the fore.[13] For instance, only some aspects of grass can be applied to "flesh" or human beings. Black says of his example "Man is a wolf:"

> Any human traits that can without undue strain be talked about in "wolf-language" will be rendered prominent, and any that cannot will be pushed into the background. The wolf-metaphor suppresses some details, emphasizes others – in short, *organizes* our view of man.[14]

Creative judgment, nevertheless, is still needed to put the appropriate properties together. The relationship of disparate fields of meaning presents a creative challenge, and the effect is to reframe both sides. Wolves may seem more human-like from now on and it may be that shepherds are viewed with greater consideration after being related to God.

116

At the same time, the two regions do not collapse into one another. The two frameworks of meaning continue to be distinct. In this sense, metaphors must be both affirmed and denied. We must say that all flesh is and is not grass. Ricœur and others call this capacity to see different things at once "stereoscopic vision." Given the complexity of this process, what is striking is how successfully people use metaphors all the time – which is not to say that poor attempts at metaphor will not be made.

This process implies several things about the creativity of metaphors. First, creating and understanding metaphor is an inventive act not easily assimilable to rules. Ricœur especially emphasizes the productive and generative aspect of metaphor. Metaphor has long been recognized as a literary device that enables us to depict well-known things in striking and focused ways; in other words, metaphor adorns what we already know in dashing new clothes. Philosophically speaking, what is important about metaphor is that it can do more than embellish; it can direct us to what we have never seen before. The primary reference is negated only to open up reference at another level, "another power of speaking the world."[15] As Ricœur puts it, metaphor possesses an "ontological vehemence" that leads us to redescribe reality.[16] Understanding the Lord as a shepherd was likely at one time an insight that preceded any literal explication of its meaning, not one that simply expressed what everyone already knew.

A second implication is that rich, evocative texts cannot always be replaced by univocal expositions. In other words, a text containing powerful metaphors possesses a virtually inexhaustible fecundity. We must return to it again and again. At best, more straightforward literal description can serve to avoid misinterpretation and to explore – without exhausting – implications of the metaphor. A corollary is that the best interpretation of a metaphor, rather than being a literal exposition, may be another metaphor (note the frequent recourse throughout this discussion to metaphor in order to explain metaphor). Third, we must be sensitive to the continuing "is and is not" of metaphor lest a rich metaphor be reduced to a flat univocal meaning. The tendency is

117

for a metaphor to become flattened out through use. Taking "God as father" to mean that God is male is a prominent example.

The ensuing inexactness is precisely what has often bothered philosophers and has led them to prefer univocal language. Their major criticism is that metaphor cannot be used in a syllogism. Such usage results in the fallacy of ambiguity. However, with the work of the later Wittgenstein and others that questioned the "clarity and distinctness" of univocal language (see chapter 4), the way is open to consider metaphor as cognitive, even though inexact and imprecise. Metaphor can be creative but not chaotic. The plea to live with the uncertainty of metaphor is akin to Wittgenstein's desire to leave ragged what is ragged, even when dealing with so-called literal language.

There is great debate, nevertheless, about exactly how rule governed metaphor is. Some, like Donald Davidson, argue that it is a skillful use of literal language that is a function only of pragmatics, the use of language, that cannot be seen as rule governed.[17] It is enough that we understand. While this Wittgensteinian emphasis on the sufficiency of understanding is crucial, others like Soskice and Eva Feder Kittay have explored how we might see metaphor as rule influenced although not rule controlled (that is, as an issue of semantics as well as pragmatics). Otherwise, it is difficult to understand how metaphor is usually understood quite well. The key is that the process is neither haphazard nor exact. Against the view that metaphor is totally inexplicable, Kittay argues that language and context usually provide sufficient clues to guide a fitting, to use Aristotle's word, understanding of a metaphor. Metaphor exemplifies something like Ryle's "category mistake" (chapter 4) at one level in order to establish meaning at another. Kittay emphasizes:

> Metaphor breaks certain rules of language, rules governing the literal and conventional senses of the terms. The rule-breaking takes place not in any arbitrary way but in certain specifiable ways. Hence we can tell the difference between metaphors and mistakes, and the difference between metaphors and new, technical uses.[18]

118

What these debates have in common, however, is the simple recognition that metaphor is cognitive, that it is often irreducible, and that it is understood – quite apart from the ability to explicitly analyze it. The dream of those like the early Wittgenstein and the positivists is that language should be completely analyzable to be cognitive. The paradigm that lies behind this univocal approach, however, is increasingly under attack and questionable. Aquinas's effort led in the end to the reduction of analogical language to univocal language because thinkers seemed unable to accept the fact that analogy could be understood without being explicitly explained. The interactionist view of metaphor chimes in with the implications of Wittgenstein's work for literal language to show how meaning can reliably occur without being exhaustively specifiable.

Three further developments underscore this point. One is by Mary Hesse, Ian Barbour, and others in the philosophy of science to the effect that scientific language is shot through with metaphor.[19] Metaphor is not an optional addition to univocal language. Nor is it the key to creative advance that is then gradually replaced by univocal language. Rather, the two intertwine at every level of science. Metaphor is often used in models, that is, "extended metaphors" that structure scientific understanding, testing, and prediction. Black differentiated between replicas and scale models, which are not particularly creative, and "analog" models, which function like metaphors to illuminate in new ways. Conceiving of the brain as a "computer program" leads not only to understanding but to new inferences that can be tested. Viewing light as a wave or as a particle, while not literally true, led to advances in understanding. In this sense, such stable models are important not only for discovery but for consolidation of discoveries as well as exploration of their ramifications.

Similarly, some argue that philosophy inherently involves metaphor for its capacity both to innovate and to convey its ideas.[20] The issue is similar to the philosophy of science dispute. These thinkers argue that metaphor is not simply of heuristic value in expressing ideas, nor is it important only in discovery. Rather, philosophy trades on a continuing interplay between metaphor and literal explanation. An example would be Hans-Georg Gadamer's reliance on the metaphors of game and a fusion of horizons (chapter 5). Often background models structure the development of a philosophy; examples are an organic model for Aristotle and Alfred North Whitehead's process philosophy as opposed to a mechanistic and geometric model for much of Enlightenment philosophy. Ironically, Ricœur, who stresses metaphor so much, claims that philosophy should strive towards complete univocity.[21] However, if metaphor is as pervasive and helpful as he and others have said, there is no reason to forgo its continuing cognitive power even if we allow for the helpfulness of pursuing precision whenever possible.[22]

George Lakoff and Mark Johnson in a third development argue that our language is inherently structured by such model-like metaphors, such as "argument is like war."[23] We advance, we retreat, we win, we lose, we shoot arguments down, or we even blow them away. Soskice, working out of the analytical tradition, makes a similar point. She understands the key to metaphor as the activation of a model that allows for further extension. This is why we may have metaphor when there is little semantic shock, as when we say of a poet that her words "flow," "cascade," or "run smoothly." Almost unconsciously, we are aware that the metaphor of a river is in the background. She comments, "It is the capacity of the lively metaphor to suggest models that enable us to 'go on' which gives the clue to the richness of metaphorical description."[24] She and Johnson both suggest that behind much of our language are such background metaphors that provide a frame for even our literal language.[25] In other words, we cannot speak at all without metaphor. Such a conception of stable metaphor is important since many religious metaphors fall into this category. Understanding God as a shepherd or as a rock does not exactly arouse semantic shock any more, but nor are these meanings literal. Rather, such metaphors continue to function as a model that licenses inferences about God, such as "God is caring" or "God is reliable." Similarly, these stable or conventional metaphors sometimes serve as "root" metaphors that gather and organize other metaphors into clusters of meaning.[26] For example, seeing the religious life as a journey illuminates the fact that it requires such things as endurance and directions. It may involve getting lost or injured. Scripture can become food to sustain one on the way. Other believers become fellow pilgrims, and so on.

These developments point to different possibilities in the life of a metaphor. There are what Ricœur calls "living metaphors," which are creative, innovative, and striking.[27] There are also, however, "metaphors we live by," in the words of Lakoff and Johnson, that have not been tamed down or domesticated into literal language but continue to exert their metaphorical power in a more subdued yet nevertheless significant manner. Finally, there is literal language that can be seen for the most part as "dead" metaphors, for example, the "legs" of a chair. Practically speaking, the sign that these metaphors have died is that they are found in the dictionary, or "lexicalized." Much of our language was probably at one time metaphors that have long since become ossified. Yet dead metaphors often have the capacity to rise again with renewed metaphorical import. As we shall see below, Paul Tillich noted that symbols live and die, a process rooted more in the unconscious and consequently not under explicit control. We often cannot simply choose what metaphors or symbols continue to communicate to us, or always say why they no longer communicate. An example is the way kingly metaphors redolent of domination and hierarchy often do not speak to people today, whereas metaphors of mutuality do.

The most extreme claim about metaphor exactly reverses the tradition. The tradition says that univocal language is primary and metaphor is ornamental, superfluous when it comes to cognition. Recent philosophies of metaphor almost always challenge this hierarchy, at least indicating that metaphor is as crucial as literal language. Some, however, suggest that metaphor comes first and, like Friedrich Nietzsche and Jacques Derrida (see chapter 8), assert that all language is metaphorical. This, however, is misleading.[28] If all language is metaphorical, then the distinction no longer means anything. It is also clear that metaphor depends on literal language. It may be true that with Wittgenstein we can demythologize the model of univocal language, so that it means not exact or precise language but familiar language, language that is used without much shock value. Metaphor relies on such language to work. In the end, there is a fine line between stretched literal language and metaphor, but we have learned from Wittgenstein that we do have to be able to exactly specify the edges to make an important distinction.

## Symbol and Analogy

One of the complications in this area is that the terminological landscape is confusing. Three important traditions in this connection end up largely at the same place. One is the tradition of metaphor, described above. The second is that of symbol, and the third is analogy. The relation between metaphor and symbol is often expressed as the difference between a literary and a non-literary phenomenon. At other times, symbol and metaphor basically refer to the same thing. They are clearly based on a similar dynamic, involving a clash of meaning on a literal level and another meaning arising from the relationship of two regions of discourse. Tillich particularly stressed the way symbols express what cannot be expressed in any other way, in other words, their irreducibility. Despite the fact that in other contexts, as we have seen (chapter 2), Tillich represented the univocal tradition, his conception of religious symbolism as irreplaceable was pioneering and has had a great influence on others who prefer to speak in terms of symbols, such as Langdon Gilkey.

Tillich argues that "symbolic language alone is able to express the ultimate" because it transcends the capacity of any finite reality to express it directly.[29] He unpacks this thesis in six ways. First, symbols must be distinguished from signs. Both point beyond themselves, but symbols have more than an arbitrary or conventional relationship with that to which they point. A red light or a number has no intrinsic relationship with what it represents, but a symbol, according to Tillich's second point, participates in the reality to which it points. The example he gives is a country's flag. Third, a symbol "opens up levels of reality which otherwise are closed to us."[30] Fourth, the symbol not only opens up dimensions of reality outside of us but reveals dimensions of ourselves that would also otherwise remain hidden. Fifth, symbols are not totally intentional; they arise out of the individual or collective unconscious. Consequently, and sixth, symbols "grow when the situation is ripe for them, and they die when the situation changes."[31]

Gilkey follows Tillich closely but speaks perhaps even more broadly (and loosely) of the symbolic form or structure of a religious tradition, all the symbols of which take on a particular *gestalt* that reflects the particular ethos of that tradition.[32] He includes as symbols not only a central figure like Jesus Christ or a central event like the exodus from Egypt but "doctrinal" symbols such as creation, incarnation, and redemption. The purpose of theology is to reflect upon this symbol system, but such reflection cannot take the place of the symbols or fully express their meaning. As Gilkey says, "Granting the depth, significance, and all-encompassing character of these symbolic structures, they are not at all easy to formulate precisely – though they are crucial to the life of the community, and thus 'everyone' knows perfectly well what they point to or mean."[33]

Ricœur's early work on the symbolism of evil also focused on symbols as the central issue in interpreting religion; before philosophy, theology, or even myth, he claimed, we find symbols.[34] In particular, he was convinced that the "irrational" act of evil could only be expressed by means of the indirect language of symbolism. For example, in the early Hebrew tradition, he explored the symbols of stain as a kind of pollution, of deviation as crookedness or transgression, and of weight as the burden of the soul. He, too, distinguished at that time between sign and symbol, with symbol having a "double intentionality."[35] Only by means of the first, literal, intention is the more opaque, analogical sense given. The symbol, then, expresses primary religious meaning but also stimulates further thought, whether mythical, philosophical, or theological.[36]

Each of these approaches evinces a rather loose understanding of symbol. Soskice is more precise when she points out that metaphors are figures of speech and are not events or things, as symbols can be, although symbols can also be words.[37] A wooden cross by this strict interpretation is not a metaphor. Moreover, Tillich's emphasis on the symbol participating in the reality to which it points undoubtedly underscores a dimension of powerful religious and political symbols, but overstates the intrinsic or inherent relationship of a symbol. Is it not possible that a more distant relationship could be as powerful, as when a prophet like Amos sees in a basket of ripe summer fruit the signal of the imminence of Israel's end (Amos 8: 1–2)? In fact, it is not difficult to see in the context of symbol the same relationship between creative and conventional that we saw in metaphor; the perceived close connection of the symbol is often more a result of its frequent use and stability than of any necessary, inherent connection. On the other hand, Tillich is correct that in some cases a symbol arises because of its being inextricably caught up in a larger web of meaning, such as the cross in Christianity or a nation's flag. Ricœur's later works similarly suggest that a symbol often has a closer, more biological tie to its referent. He points to the role of symbols in dreams and as conveyor of the sacred through hierophanies (symbolic manifestations of the divine) such as stones, trees, sun, and sky. He summarizes: "This bound character of symbols makes all the difference between a symbol and a metaphor. The latter is a free invention of discourse; the former is bound to the cosmos."[38] He goes on to speak of the dialectical interplay between the two in that symbol only comes to light through metaphor, but metaphor continually draws on symbol. Ricœur's neglect of the category of conventional metaphor causes him to overstate this difference between the more stable symbol and momentary metaphor, but he undoubtedly points to an important distinction nonetheless.

Another approach, stemming from the Thomistic tradition, prefers to use the language of analogy in preference to metaphor or symbol. As we have seen, Aquinas elevated analogy above metaphor. Those in this tradition, such as David Tracy and David Burrell, make virtually the same points about analogy that others make about metaphor; for example, analogy is a creative innovation involving the interaction of two fields of meaning. What muddies the picture is that those like Sallie McFague or Janet Soskice in the metaphorical tradition, largely rooted in literary tradition, can in direct opposition to the Thomistic tradition disparage analogy in relation to metaphor. For these writers, analogy remains closer to literal language; it is basically a noncreative extension of meaning, as opposed to the genuine innovation of metaphor. Since those in one tradition often speak critically of the terminology of another tradition, it is no surprise that confusion often reigns.

On analogy as a positive term, Burrell argues that is a mistake to try, as some Thomists have done, to explain analogy, which inevitably collapses it into literal language. Rather, we must recognize that analogy is irreducible but used reliably.[39] Burrell likens analogy to the more recent understanding of metaphor detailed above, and he suggests that we cannot escape the necessity of personal judgment in understanding and evaluating analogies. Making an explicit connection of metaphor to analogy, he says:

> Yet within limits we can recognize certain "sort-crossings" as more appropriate – at least to a given context – than others. Again within limits this kind of appropriateness can be argued for and so gradually learned. But what cannot be acquired and must be presupposed is the original reflective and critical ability which issues in *recognitions* like these: that a metaphor fits the occasion.[40]

He, too, notes that since the later Wittgenstein has shown that literal language is similarly extended through acts of judgment that are not totally rule governed, we should not be concerned about a further manifestation of this activity in analogy.[41]

David Tracy also prefers to speak of analogy yet draws on contemporary understandings of metaphor in order to avoid reduction to univocal language. Rather than return to literalizing explanations of analogy, he prefers to see analogy – for theological purposes – as the perception of irreducible "similarities-in-difference" between some finite event or reality and ultimate

125

reality. Using analogy, metaphor, and symbol interchangeably, he emphasizes the negating side of analogy: "If that power is lost, analogical concepts become mere categories of easy likenesses slipping quietly from their status as similarities-in-difference to mere likenesses, falling finally into the sterility of a relaxed univocity and a facilely affirmative harmony."[42]

Soskice, on the other hand, sees analogy as simply extending univocal language rather than offering genuinely metaphorical new perspectives. She says, "Analogy as a linguistic device deals with language that has been stretched to fit new applications, yet fits the new situation without generating for the native speaker any imaginative strain."[43] As an example, she cites "riding a bicycle." Likewise, McFague contrasts analogy with metaphor. She ties both analogy and symbol to the medieval sacramental universe. In this view, because all beings participate in the source of being and thus exhibit a profound underlying connection and similarity, we can speak of an analogy of being. Metaphor, however, suggests a more radical difference. "One critical difference," she says, " between symbolic and metaphorical statements is that the latter always contain the whisper, 'it is *and it is not.*' "[44] The problem, she says, is that a sacramental sensibility has waned for modern people; thus a metaphorical approach is the most promising avenue for moderns to speak of God.

The category of stable metaphor, however, offers a way to avoid some of the impasse between those who emphasize the creativity of metaphor and the "everydayness" of analogy. The major dynamic in metaphor is seeing one thing from the perspective of another. This quality can as easily be attributed to analogy and to symbol as it is to metaphor. Soskice herself speaks of the significance of well-known metaphorical models such as "the ship of state" for structuring the way we conceive of a domain. Though she is critical of Johnson and Lakoff for overreaching and perhaps including "dead" metaphors in their category of everyday metaphor, models like those she mentions fit well into their idea of a conventional or stable metaphor that is not yet lexicalized. Soskice's example of "riding a bicycle" is probably an example of a dead metaphor, but "the ship of state" or "the Lord is my shepherd" are better characterized as well-known, familiar, but nonetheless still vital, metaphorical relations.

At this juncture in the discussion, we can probably not overcome the disparity of definition. It is arguable that metaphor, analogy, and symbol can be seen as very similar, and it is arguable that they are very different. What is important is always to be attentive to how thinkers are using their terms. In addition, allowance for a category of conventional as well as creative metaphor can avoid some false dilemmas as well as paving an important way to understand religious language, as we shall see below. In retrospect, a sea-change has occurred with regard to the understanding of metaphor, making it philosophically significant and having repercussions in many areas. Some of the most important effects have been in religion, which we will now explore more fully.

## Metaphor in Exegesis

Perhaps the most important area of appropriation in exegesis has been in the area of the parables of Jesus. A little background is in order.[45] For much of the history of the church, the parables were ripe ground for allegory. Each element stood for some aspect of the Christian life, often limited only by the interpreter's imagination. While there seemed to be sufficient scope for creativity, there was little ground for hermeneutical control. At the same time, this approach had the effect of minimizing the figurative power of the parable, for once one had the key, it was a simple matter of extracting the message, thus no longer needing the parable.

An important revolution in parable interpretation was launched by Adolf Jülicher, C.H. Dodd, and Joachim Jeremias, who argued that the parables should not be interpreted allegorically. The details, they argued, were often not that significant, except as evidence that these are simple stories taken from real life. Their advice was to look for the rather straightforward central point made by the parables, rather than the many connections made by allegory. Although this approach pointed back to a more original function of the parable and did more justice to the genre, it still tended to make the parables dispensable; once one had grasped the central point, one no longer needed the parable. This way of thinking was still in the tradition of figurative language as ornamental.[46]

Under the influence of the later Heidegger and Gadamer (see chapter 5), some theologians in the so-called "New Hermeneutic" movement, particularly Ernst Fuchs and Gerhard Ebeling, inaugurated a more dynamic understanding. They saw the parables as "language-events" that did not so much teach something as do something (similar in some ways to John Austin's emphasis on performative language that we considered in chapter 4), namely, to mediate Jesus's authentic existence or the reality of the Kingdom of God to others. In this way, the parables were indispensable. The event was unapproachable apart from the parable itself. The difficulty with this approach is that there was little exploration of the way the parables functioned, leaving them, as did Heidegger with poetic language, as a rather mysterious activity.[47]

Needed clarification came in the sixties and seventies from exegetes and literary critics such as Robert Funk, Dan Via Jr, and John Dominic Crossan, who applied the new understanding of metaphor to the parables, seen as "extended metaphors." They, too, argued that the parables were irreducible, therefore irreplaceable. The parable's meaning could not be translated into literal language and had the same dynamics as metaphor. Parables involve a clash of meaning at the literal level that opens the way for a new meaning at the figurative level. There was clear emphasis on the cognitive significance of the parables. As one of the recognized distinctives of the historical Jesus, the parables represented some of the central content of his teaching. As Norman Perrin showed, the Kingdom of God is a metaphor that is further clarified by the extended metaphors of the parables. Like the thinkers of the New Hermeneutic, these exegetes emphasized the performative and participatory aspect of the metaphoric process. Crossan in particular stressed the way parable "subverts" one's world, as opposed to myth, which "creates" world.[48] In a deft way, he showed how powerfully the parables function to disturb and unseat conventional understanding, making the very structure of the parable central to its "content." Again, the parable is irreplaceable. Crossan overemphasized the destructive power of the parable, virtually refusing to allow it any positive cognitive content. While having a distinctive "shattering" dimension, however, the parables clearly point in a discernible direction, a "reorientation by disorientation."[49] Ricœur stressed the "excessive" or "extravagant" dimension of the parables, which points to the way the Kingdom of God has not only an "in spite of" but a "how much more" dimension.[50]

In sum, contemporary understandings of metaphor provided rich soil for a fresh approach to the parables themselves as extended metaphors, which transcended previous approaches which saw them as allegories or as replaceable comparisons. As such, however, metaphor itself could not distinguish altogether parable from myth. Myth might itself draw on metaphor to "establish world" just as a parable employs metaphor to disrupt world. In fact, Via and Crossan moved quickly to narrative and structuralist approaches, which we will pursue in the next two chapters, to further identify the uniqueness of the parable. In these chapters, we will see that an approach via metaphor can itself be too atomistic; not only must we move beyond the word to the sentence but also beyond the sentence to the work in order to do justice to religious language.

## Metaphor in Theology

Although the focus on the parable as extended metaphor illustrates perhaps the clearest impact of the newer philosophical orientation, much discussion has also ensued concerning the metaphorical nature of religious language in general. Several thinkers, like Eberhard Jüngel, Sallie McFague, and Janet Soskice, stress that religious language, as language about God, is pervasively metaphorical. Language is taken from finite reality and applied to a new, transcendent region, involving a semantic clash. Of course, much language among a religious community will not necessarily be metaphorical. For example, "I am going to church this morning" is the kind of religious statement many church leaders would like to hear from their parishioners, but it is certainly not metaphorical. What we are considering here are direct statements about God such as "God is love" and "God is my rock." This claim supports Aquinas's claim of a third way for religious language, between univocal and equivocal language; but with the help of a newer conceptualization of such figurative language, it avoids the paradoxes into which Aquinas fell. Metaphor can be regarded as making a truth claim, therefore, without being reduced to being a literal truth claim. The inexactitude, or the inability to use it in a syllogism, is recognized without throwing out the truth claim itself.

Jüngel points to the special difficulty of religious metaphors by noting that in most metaphors, we have some fairly precise idea of both regions, but that in religion, we are using metaphor to shed light on the region of faith.[51] As Soskice puts it:

> It is our hope that a defence of metaphor and of its use as a conceptual vehicle will support the Christian in his seemingly paradoxical conviction that, despite his utter inability to comprehend God, he is justified in speaking of God and that metaphor is the principal means by which he does so.[52]

Soskice also points out, however, that we can exaggerate how unknown God is. We never begin in language from the beginning. We start in many cases with a great deal of understanding of the religious form of life. Even if the understanding of religious terms, such as Holy Spirit or prayer, turns out to be largely misguided, the associated set of meanings enables metaphor to work. In fact, metaphors are often used implicitly to criticize previous understandings while proffering a better. When we claim that "the Lord is my shepherd," sufficient background understanding of both terms exists to convey an understandable meaning. In fact, within the religious form of life, such an expression, while metaphorical and full of surplus meaning, may be so well understood that it contains little semantic shock; indeed, it is on its way to being literal.

Not all, however, who emphasize the metaphorical nature of religious language make the stronger realist claim that such language reveals something of God. A strong tendency exists to make metaphor refer to the believer's attitude or stance towards God or life. Soskice defends the realist claims of metaphor over against people like John Dominic Crossan, David Tracy, and Don Cupitt by comparing metaphor and models in religion to their use in science.[53] Against the suggestion that models in science are realist but dispensable and are in religion non-realist but indispensable, she argues persuasively for similar uses in both. Philosophers of science point to the indispensability of metaphors and models, as we saw above. Often these metaphors license other metaphors and are also best explained by other metaphors. For example, "the brain is a computer" implies other metaphors such as "the brain uses software and hardware and must be programmed." This reliance on other metaphors for explication is probably even more important in religion.

Traditionally, religious speakers have understood metaphors such as "God is my heavenly Father" to say something about God, not just about the believer's attitude towards life. In making this qualified realist claim, it is important to realize that, just as in science, such models are not so much exhaustively descriptive but partially depicting. In other words, they enable us to pick out in general and often vague ways some aspect of reality. Soskice emphasizes that such claims are cautious, fallible, and influenced a great deal by the social traditions in which they arise. She says, "We are saying that the theist can reasonably take his talk of God, bound as it is within a wheel of images, as being reality depicting, while at the same time acknowledging its inadequacy as description."[54] Such a "cautious realism" comes close to the cautious third way that Aquinas attempted in the thirteenth century.[55]

This metaphorical approach (or analogical or symbolic approach, depending on the thinker) allows us not only to use clear-cut metaphors but also more ambiguous terms of God such as "God is good" or "God is love." In the fourth chapter, we considered the argument that we could make a claim that these are univocal. We could equally claim that any such terms, when applied to a transcendent reality such as God, are metaphorical or analogical at best. They are rooted enough in the human context that they cannot be literally applied to God, but a metaphorical use can be affirmed in the sense that they characterize God in meaningful, albeit not in "clear and distinct" ways. Theologically, then, metaphor allows us to speak of God while doing justice both to God's transcendence and immanence, without losing the tension between the two.

Sallie McFague, more than any other theologian, has emphasized not only religious language but theology itself as metaphorical.[56] Beginning from the work of philosophers of metaphor such as Ricœur, she has argued that theology should best be understood along the lines of metaphor; metaphor itself is a metaphor for theology. Theology's language for God must be both affirmed and denied; it is and is not descriptive of God. Moreover, theology is constituted by metaphors and models in that it is organized by root metaphors, such as persons in relationships of grace before God, and in turn by subordinate metaphors and models. Analysis and concepts in a more univocal mode nevertheless have a place in terms of clarification. In the end, though, theology as a whole reflects the indirect way in which metaphor conveys its truth. Thus, theological assertions must be both affirmed and denied. They are false at one level and true at another. Hence, theology must always be tentative and open to revision. One metaphor is usually best illuminated by another metaphor. The biblical metaphors thus have no sacrosanct value as literal terms. Their meaning is what is important. They actually license the creation of new metaphors that may in our time convey the reality conveyed by them in a better way. A particular concern of McFague's is how the biblical metaphors of father, kingdom, son, and so on have such strong patriarchal connotations and implications that we should seek for other metaphors as correctives or even replacements. She suggests, for example, that the world may be seen as God's body and that the Trinity can be seen as mother, lover, and friend.[57] She has sought to follow out the implications for such metaphors and to contrast them with the implications of more traditional models.

Consistently, she says of her own suggestions that they must also be denied, are provisional, and are open to correction. What is needed is a profusion of metaphors. The fact, though, that metaphors do have cognitive meaning, and do structure life, as we recognize from the significance of seeing God as mother or the Spirit as friend, means that there is both cognitive affirmation and some cognitive control. There are substantive reasons, she asserts, why these metaphors are better, more adequate, than other metaphors. We could in principle offer substantive reasons against them. Not every attempt at metaphor need work. As Burrell pointed out in connection with analogy, the imprecision of metaphor does not rule out the role of judgment. What is important in this regard is that the metaphorical nature of *any* affirmation of God be recognized, lest it become idolatrous.

Despite the profusion and often confusion of reflection on figurative language, taking different trajectories as metaphor, as symbol, and as analogy, a genuinely new approach has opened up. It offers a viable third way between a univocal and equivocal approach, although there are still reasons to affirm either of these options. The significance of metaphor as cognitive, as irreplaceable, and as extensible into models and parables also points to another significant development that is a close cousin, narrative theology.

# 7

# Narrative Theology

Narrative theology developed in earnest in the USA in the seventies and addressed many of the same issues pivotal in philosophy of metaphor. Above all, irreducibility was a burning issue. When it comes to religion, it is immediately evident that much of the language is not only metaphorical but at a wider level is also narrative. Just as with metaphor, the tendency in the past had been to draw from the metaphor or the narrative the distilled meaning, given in univocal language. The latter meaning was then deemed the "real" meaning of the story. Over against this tendency, narrative theologians have argued that the narrative is irreplaceable. It is primary language that cannot be left behind. If systematic theology on the basis of the narrative is allowable at all – and some questioned this – then it must continually circle back and be judged by the narrative, not vice versa.

The predominant emphasis in narrative or story, however, as opposed to the metaphorical issue, lay in theological discussion. Hence this chapter will focus on theology rather than on the work of exegetes, recognizing that by the nature of the case the theological discussion was often rooted in exegetical discussions. In fact, this was one of the points that separated what seemed to outsiders to be a unified movement. In an influential essay published in 1986, Gary Comstock identified two types of narrative theology, one of which he identified with Yale University and the other with the University of Chicago.[1] Some, like the so-called Yale School, tended to focus on the Bible, while others, like what he called the Chicago School, dealt with narratives on a much broader philosophical and cultural basis. We can distinguish between *the* story, the canonical Scriptures; our story, the cultural narratives and myths that form the background framework of our lives; and my and your story, the personal autobiography and biographies that constitute a central part of our identity. Interestingly, each one of these emphases is represented by a different school, if this analogy is not pushed too far. The Yale School focuses on the biblical story. The Chicago School tends to center on the broader cultural, narrative framework. And we can identify perhaps a California School centered around the work of James McClendon, now at Fuller Theological Seminary, who focuses on biography and autobiography. The topic can be explored by examining the respective emphases of these approaches. The philosophical perspective that will be delineated in each approach is not so much developed independently by philosophers and then borrowed but is implicit in the theological discussions themselves.

## The Chicago School

The Chicago School, represented particularly by David Tracy, Langdon Gilkey, and Paul Ricœur, is a good place to begin in that they represent the broadest claims and perhaps the most commonly understood approach to narrative. For them, the biblical narratives are important, but they are always related to a wider philosophical perspective. We will concentrate on Ricœur, since he has laid the most extensive theoretical groundwork.

As we saw, Ricœur in general has emphasized on the one hand the primacy of symbolic, narrative language for religion and on the other hand the consequent secondary nature of philosophical and theological reflection. In his dialectic of understanding—explanation—understanding, he calls for critical conceptualization but sets it within a spiral motion that returns to the metaphor or narrative with a post-critical receptiveness (chapter 5). In the previous chapter, we saw his emphasis on the

135

way metaphor is irreducible to complete paraphrase, demanding a creative, semantic innovation. He sets narrative within the same dynamic. Narrative, too, cannot be reduced to a theological truth or a systematic theology. Narrative "gives rise to thought," but the philosophy or theology that it yields is continually funded and judged by the narrative.

Even while he was concentrating on metaphor, Ricœur began to integrate his views on metaphor with narrative. He suggested that metaphor provides a clue for understanding the *sense* of narrative, and narrative provides a clue to understanding the *reference* of metaphor. Understanding a metaphor means to draw an appropriate meaning from the various semantic fields connected with the words of a sentence. This suggests the way in which the meaning of a work as a whole must be constructed. Ricœur says, "The text is not only something written but is a work, that is, a singular totality. As a totality, the literary work cannot be reduced to a sequence of sentences which are individually intelligible; rather, it is an architecture of themes and purposes which can be constructed in several ways."[2] The hermeneutical circle is at play in this connection, where one moves from the parts to the whole and back again.

What becomes clear in narrative, he believes, is the way in which a possible world is disclosed "in front of the text" (see chapter 5). Rather than a Romantic hermeneutic that sought the author's intentionality "behind the text," Ricœur's hermeneutical approach (like Hans-Georg Gadamer's) looks for the fusion of horizons between that of the work and that of the reader. The "reference" of the work is thus to the meaning and application for one's life; this of course is different than the meaning or "sense" of the internal world of a text. For example, following the story of David in 1 and 2 Samuel or Jesus in Mark's Gospel is one thing; determining its application for one's life today is another. As Ricœur puts it, "Sense is the 'what' and reference the 'about what' of discourse."[3] He further explains the difference between this approach and Romantic hermeneutics:

In that tradition, the emphasis was placed on the ability of the hearer or reader to transfer himself into the spiritual life of a speaker or writer. The emphasis, from now on, is less on the other as a spiritual entity than on the world which the work unfolds. To understand is to follow the dynamic of the work, its movement from what it says to that about which it speaks. Beyond my situation as reader, beyond the situation of the author, I offer myself to the possible mode of being-in-the-world which the text opens up and discloses to me. This is what Gadamer calls the "fusion of horizons."[4]

Ricœur then indicates how this power of disclosing a world in front of the narrative text suggests the fuller implications of the creative power of metaphor to project new meaning. Metaphor, too, is engaged in such larger disclosure and, in fact, usually contributes to the disclosure of the narrative as part to the whole.

In his three-volume trilogy on narrative, *Time and Narrative*, Ricœur refines his understanding of narrative.[5] He draws the characteristic connection between a phenomenological analysis of human experience that reveals a temporal, narrative pattern, which is then related to narrative *per se* and also to historiography. Drawing particularly on Augustine's reflections on the human experience of time in the last books of the *Confessions*, on the work of Edmund Husserl on time-consciousness, and on Martin Heidegger on the temporal structure of human existence, Ricœur concurs that there is an incipient "configuring" or "emplotting" process that is the experiential foundation of the human capacity to write literature and history. Stephen Crites, whose article "The narrative quality of experience" in 1971 is seen by many as the beginning of the American movement, expressed Ricœur's point well in his title.[6] This ineradicable narrative texture of our lives is the basis for the cultural stories and myths that shape our identity. In other words, *our* story is always a narrative context for *my* story.

From Augustine, Ricœur notes the "discordant" aspect of time; from Aristotle's *Poetics* he identifies "emplotment" as the capacity for ordering or providing "concordance" to time. Ricœur says, "I see in the plots we invent the privileged means by which we re-configure our confused, unformed, and at the limit mute temporal experience."[7] As he summarizes the thesis of *Time and Narrative*, "Time becomes human to the extent that it is organized after the manner of a narrative; narrative, in turn, is meaningful to the extent that it portrays the features of temporal experience."[8]

In *Time and Narrative*, Ricœur describes a dialectic of prefiguration–configuration–refiguration that roughly parallels his earlier understanding–explanation–understanding. As mentioned above, the configuring process is one of "emplotment," which refers to the capacity to bring together creatively the features of a text into a coherent temporal flow. Figuration also refers to the "mimetic" capacity of the text in the Aristotelian sense not just to "imitate" actions but through the productive imagination to convey an admirable way of being-in-the-world. As Ricœur says, "*Mimesis* is *poiesis*, that is, construction, creation."[9] Thus Ricœur also terms his dialectic "$mimesis_1$–$mimesis_2$–$mimesis_3$."[10] $Mimesis_1$ refers to "lived time," which as Augustine saw, is partly concordant, partly discordant. It is that preunderstanding that first draws us to the configuring power of texts and in turn enables us to grasp them. $Mimesis_3$ or refiguration corresponds with our appropriation of the reference of texts, with the integrative appropriation of a world in front of the text. Ricœur's focus on configuration or $mimesis_2$, therefore, "is the concrete process by which the textual configuration mediates between the prefiguration of the practical field and its refiguration through the reception of the work."[11] In a later book based on his Gifford Lectures, *Oneself as Another*, Ricœur connects his views on narrative even more closely to an anthropology that is narratively – and therefore linguistically – constituted.[12] With narrative as the base, Ricœur is fond of speaking even more broadly of the way our "world" is textually construed, "For me, the world is the ensemble of references opened up by every kind of text, descriptive or poetic, that I have read, understood, and loved."[13] This broad-based "intertextuality" of our experience, however, is challenged by the Yale narrative approach that follows.

Personal identity, then, is not so much an abstract set of characteristics as the coherence of a story. The implication that these thinkers draw from this fact is that all of our understanding is imbedded within a narrative framework. Using the language of myth rather than narrative, Gilkey argues for the continuing reality and relevance of myth (and symbol) as the broad backdrop of our lives even in a scientific and secular age. It is an ideological illusion, he contends, to think that we no longer live by myths. Rather, what is important is to become aware of and to thematize "the myths we live by," to adapt Lakoff and Johnson's phrase.[14] As we saw in chapter 5, David Tracy particularly stresses the importance of such ideology critique, drawing on Ricœur's hermeneutical spiral in connection with narrative. It is true that we already are grasped by stories, the classics that have shaped us and continue to shape us, but it is also possible to criticize them, moving to a post-critical appropriation.[15]

These thinkers certainly undergird the first-order nature of narrative as opposed to systematic prose. Thus, they virtually reverse the priority of the tradition, which tended to make figurative language of all kinds secondary. What is distinctive, however, in the Chicago thinkers is the manner in which they set narrative within a larger theological and philosophical frame-work and in which their approach is rooted in continental hermeneutical philosophy (chapter 5). The distinctiveness of their views can be seen further in contrast to those of the Yale School.

## The Yale School

The Yale school, represented above all by Hans Frei, and loosely including, among others, George Lindbeck, Paul Holmer, Brevard Childs, David Kelsey, and even Ronald Thiemann (Frei's student) from Harvard, is quite different.[16] The biblical narratives *per se* are much more the central focus, and their philosophical roots lie more in the later Wittgenstein than in the

139

continental phenomenological, existential, and hermeneutical traditions. In fact, they try not to root their emphasis on narrative in universal anthropological structures but rather to describe the nature and importance of narrative in the Scriptures. Sharing a Wittgensteinian antipathy for metaphysical speculation and a Wittgensteinian penchant for description, leaving things as they are, they seem to be uncomfortable with the broader philosophical and anthropological explorations characteristic of those in the Chicago school. In order to get a fairly full-orbed picture of their approach, we will look at Frei, Lindbeck, and Thiemann.

## Hans Frei

In a ground-breaking work in 1974, *The Eclipse of Biblical Narrative*, Frei showed how the narrative dimension of the Bible was lost or distorted in light of the developing meaning-as-reference schema from the sixteenth through the eighteenth centuries.[17] This is none other than the traditional univocal paradigm that we have discussed. The meaning of biblical narratives, Frei argued, increasingly lay in the reality of their historical reference, that is, in the empirical states of affairs that corresponded to the words. Conservatives defended the truth value of these references. Conversely, liberals rejected the historical truth value but then often overlaid another meaning upon the text. As Frei put it, "It is no exaggeration to say that all across the theological spectrum the great reversal had taken place; interpretation was a matter of fitting the biblical story into another world with another story rather than incorporating that world into the biblical story."[18]

Frei argues that this is ironic considering the development of the realistic novel in the eighteenth and nineteenth centuries in France and England, which should have given an insight into the biblical materials; but for a variety of reasons, this possibility was unexploited.[19] In any case, for him, the narratives of the Bible should be seen as "history-like," representing the familiar world of real people. The meaning, therefore, is constituted by the stories themselves, in their plain or literal sense, and not in some philosophy or even salvation history (*Heilsgeschichte*) external to the text. Like Ricœur, Frei opposed the location of the meaning of the text in the world behind the text – whether it be a reconstructed history or the consciousness of the author. He explains, "By speaking of the narrative shape of these accounts, I suggest that what they are about and how they make sense are functions of the depiction or narrative rendering of the events constituting them – including their being rendered, at least partially, by the device of chronological sequence."[20] As he puts it in another place, "Simultaneously it [literal depiction] depicts and renders the reality (if any) of what it talks about."[21] In this way, narratives offer a world in which we may or may not choose to live. In explaining John Calvin's approach to Scripture, he stresses this point:

> Through the coincidence or even identity between a world being depicted and its reality being rendered to the reader (always under the form of the depiction), the reader or hearer in turn becomes part of that depicted reality and thus has to take a personal or life stance toward it. For Calvin, more clearly than for Luther, not the *act of recital or preaching* of a text, but the cumulative *pattern constituting the biblical narrative* . . . is the setting forth of the reality which simultaneously constitutes its effective rendering to the reader by the Spirit.[22]

This depiction of a world to be appropriated is distinct from the questions about its historical reference, which is another issue. But to begin with the latter issue is to distort the nature of the biblical claim upon us.

In fact, in another book, *The Identity of Jesus Christ*, Frei argues that the function of the biblical narratives is one of the major functions of narratives in general – to render the identity of a person (an agent).[23] The identity of Jesus Christ and through him, of God, is given to us in an irreducible way in the Bible. Moreover, the identity of Jesus Christ is such that to understood who he is to understand him as existing.[24] We cannot divorce interest or faith from understanding the story in this case. Thus theology is rooted in narratives in an indispensable way.

141

It is apparent that general anthropological speculation is behind many of the insights here, which again mitigates the difference that is often claimed between the Yale and Chicago Schools. In fact, in the emphasis on identity, the similarities between the phenomenological analysis of human identity in the Chicago School and the narrative understanding of identity approached through the Wittgensteinian tradition in the Yale School are striking. In a posthumously published work, however, Frei distinguishes two major types of theology.[25] In one approach, the correlate with theology is philosophy, usually as a foundation for theology. In the second, the sister discipline is interpretive social science. He adds, "What is at stake, externally or internally, is understanding a specific symbol system interpretively rather than reductively."[26] Throughout his writings, Frei has identified Gadamer, Ricœur, and Tracy with the former reductive approach. Ironically, Gadamer and Ricœur in particular, with their nonfoundationalist hermeneutical approach, have been more allied with the interpretive social science ethos than with a traditional foundationalist, "reductive" philosophical approach. William Placher, one of the editors of the book, has argued that Gadamer and Ricœur are closer to the Yale School than is often thought and indicates that after contact with Tracy, Frei likely moved him out of that category.[27] What is important to realize here is that the lines between these two approaches may well have been overdrawn.

Differences in emphasis, at least, remain. Frei is uncomfortable with any extensive role of philosophy or even of the social sciences. As he sees it, unlike Ricœur he is advancing only a regional hermeneutic that turns out to be helpful to the interpretation of Scripture, not an argument for a general hermeneutic that in turn warrants a narrative reading of Scripture.[28] The latter, he fears, is a foundationalist enterprise that subordinates the world of the text to a philosophical theory. Frei's strength, therefore, has been in upholding the priority and indispensability of the narrative shape of Scripture against any reductive approach. While it is debatable whether Ricœur is using philosophy in a way inherently different than Frei is using the social sciences, it is true that Ricœur explores and develops the philosophical dimension much more than Frei. It is also evident that the theologians Tracy and Gilkey lend themselves to a foundationalist interpretation more easily than Ricœur. And we shall see that Lindbeck and Thiemann are even less reluctant than Frei explicitly to appeal to philosophy. In this sense, the Chicago thinkers have a much more hospitable attitude towards ancillary disciplines than the Yale thinkers typically exemplify.

One of the results of Frei's concern about the importation of foreign elements into the text is that he sometimes goes out of his way to minimize the contribution of the reader to the meaning of the story. In the following passage, it is not difficult to imagine Gadamer as the unnamed opponent he is rejecting:

> The meaning, pattern, or theme, whether upon literal or figural reading or, most likely, upon a combination of both, emerges *solely as a function of the narrative itself.* It is not imprinted on the text by the interpreter or by a multifarious interpretive and religious "tradition," a collective noun standing for the story as a product of the storyteller's own mind together with subsequent interpretations of it down to the present and latest reader, for any of whom this interpretive mental accretion itself, and not the text, becomes the cumulative story which is taken to be the text's real subject matter [emphasis added].[29]

This is virtually a rejection of reader-response theory as well as of Gadamer, but it does justice neither to their emphases nor to other tendencies in Frei's own work. Frei does not here take into account the way in which tradition and preunderstandings do not get in the way of but actually open up the meaning of the text and the way in which the reader inevitably is a creative participant in following the lead established by the text. Nor does he recognize the critical dimension of such hermeneutics that helps to avoid unconscious ideological distortion and a replacement of the text by the prejudices of the reader. Certainly tradition can obscure the text, but it is difficult to imagine how meaning is

143

solely a product of the text itself, apart from any engagement with the sometimes vast difference in horizons between text and reader.

Moreover, some of Frei's work points in quite a different direction, to a sociological approach which suggests that the community shaped by a particular tradition can become the virtual arbiter of what a text can mean. In this account, a particular community establishes the "form of life" that determines even a text's "plain" or literal sense (*sensus literalis*). In an interpretation of Frei's work, Kathryn Tanner suggests in a manner similar to Wittgenstein's emphasis on "meaning as use" that the plain sense is not identified with what the text immanently says, but "the plain sense is instead viewed as a function of communal sense."[30] We can therefore go in two different directions with Frei: one emphasizes the sufficiency of the immanent meaning of the text, the other emphasizes the community of faith as determining the meaning of the text. In either case, ironically, the concern about Frei is often similar to that about Gadamer, that he is too conservative and uncritical in relation either to the past or to a community's interpretation of the text. As Frei's supporters also indicate, however, his writing was creative and provocative, not an attempt to be particularly systematic; tensions are a result. On the other hand, the tendencies noted here are also found in Lindbeck and Thiemann.

Some of the discrepancies between the Chicago and Yale Schools may be seen in their respective philosophical and theological sources. The major theological influence on the Yale School is Karl Barth. His emphasis on heeding scripture as opposed to external philosophical influences is an important support for the Yale approach. As Lindbeck says approvingly of Barth, "Christian theology must in the first place pay heed to the language of the Christian community from the Bible to modernity," rather than vice versa.[31] Barth's reluctance to seek a point of contact between faith and other religions or between other disciplines is markedly similar to that of the Yale thinkers. Ironically, given Barth's antipathy to philosophy and his own rootedness in the continental tradition, there is a striking match between the philosophy of the later Wittgenstein and the views of Barth, both of which the Yale thinkers explicitly affirm. The commonly cited problem of both of these approaches, however, lies in the tendencies toward insularity, which has yielded the charge of fideism against both thinkers. This is where a fruitful alliance between the approach of the Chicago School, with its roots in the Gadamerian concern for the encounter of different horizons, and the Yale School, with its emphasis on the biblical text, might be profitable.

## George Lindbeck

George Lindbeck's work *The Nature of Doctrine* was perhaps the most influential book in North American theology in the 1980s.[32] In it he identifies three different types of theology. The traditional approach he terms the "cognitivist" approach, upon which he spends little time. This type stresses the way religion provides information and makes truth claims about objective reality.[33] The approach he considers the most dominant in modern theology is what he criticizes as an "experiential-expressive" approach to religion, which identifies a root experience that is then expressed in different ways. Preeminently identified with Friedrich Schleiermacher, the key to this perspective is that the basic experience of religion is the same. In this way, religions can dialogue with one another around the assumption that their differences are verbal but not substantial. Ecumenical and interreligious dialogue is a matter of finding agreement in words about a common experience. As he points out, "There is at least the logical possibility that a Buddhist and a Christian might have basically the same faith, although expressed very differently."[34] In particular, he identifies the Chicago thinkers with this approach.

Drawing on the later Wittgenstein, Lindbeck prefers diversity, emphasizing that it is truer that language structures experience than that experience structures language. The meaning of theological terms, like all terms, is rooted in the form of life of which they are a part. His emphasis, therefore, is not on the "intertextual" relations between different traditions but on the "intratextual" context within Scripture and the Christian tradition.[35] Making an emphasis on the importance of Scripture similar to Frei's, Lindbeck says, "Intratextual theology redescribes reality within the scriptural framework rather than translating Scripture into extrascriptural categories. It is the text, so to speak, which absorbs the world, rather than the world the text."[36] In this vein, he favors, as did Frei also, a recovery of the typological reading of Scripture, where a later event is interpreted through the grid of an earlier one. This implies several important connections between two events: one is a historical connection or likeness between the two; the second is an interpretive connection; and the third is a promise-fulfillment connection. Following David Kelsey, Lindbeck suggests that the most important task of the overall canonical narrative is to "render the character" or "identity description" of God as agent.[37] Taking Frei's cue to turn to the interpretive social sciences, Lindbeck terms his approach a "cultural-linguistic" approach, as well as calling it "postliberal."

Such a perspective stresses the way the tradition and the community shape even the feelings as well as the language of religion. "A comprehensive scheme or story," he says, "used to structure all dimensions of existence is not primarily a set of propositions to be believed, but is rather the medium in which one moves, a set of skills that one employs in living one's life."[38] Unlike the experiential-expressive type, the emphasis is on the influence from the outer to the inner. He provocatively concludes, "If one follows this account, Luther did not invent his doctrine of justification by faith because he had a tower experience, but rather the tower experience was made possible by his discovering . . . the doctrine in the Bible."[39]

With his longtime interest in ecumenical dialogue, Lindbeck suggests that on this basis partners in ecumenical dialogue should not assume similarity but difference.[40] Thus, different language games may have little or nothing in common. "They can regard themselves as simply different and can proceed to explore their agreements and disagreements without necessarily engaging in the invidious comparisons that the assumption of a common experiential core make so tempting."[41] Such discussion can thus proceed more fruitfully on a cultural-linguistic basis.

Perhaps Lindbeck's most significant suggestion is his so-called "rule theory of doctrine." Again taking a cue from Wittgenstein, he suggests that theological doctrines function like rules for religious language; in other words, as Wittgenstein intimated, theology is grammar. As such, theology should not be construed so much as making ontological truth claims but rather as a way of ordering language. In Christology, for example, one is prohibited from denying either Jesus's full divinity or full humanity, but within these "rules," a great deal of freedom for theorizing exists. Following Frei, he argues that in Christianity the biblical narratives provide the first-order vocabulary, the "thick description," of faith, whereas doctrines are second-order grammar.[42]

Lindbeck's approach has been rightfully applauded for the way it avoids reductionism and serves to illuminate the rich depths of a tradition. As with Frei, however, the question of truth or reference in interreligious dialogue is left dangling.[43] Lindbeck's brief references to the problem of cognitive truth helpfully suggest that a form of life must be evaluated as a whole. Specifically, he states:

> There is . . . a sense in which truth as correspondence can retain its significance even for a religion whose truth is primarily categorial rather than propositional. A religion thought of as comparable to a cultural system, as a set of language games correlated with a form of life, may *as a whole* correspond or not correspond to what a theist calls God's being and will. As actually lived, a religion may be pictured as a *single gigantic proposition*. It is a true proposition to the extent that its objectivities are interiorized and exercised by groups and individuals in such a way as to conform them in some measure in the various dimensions of their existence to the ultimate reality and goodness that lies at the heart of things. It is a false proposition to the extent that this does not happen [emphasis added].[44]

147

Lindbeck says, however, little more than this. While suggestive, it raises a number of questions. Who evaluates a religion as a whole? The issues we dealt with in connection with Wittgensteinian fideism arise here. Are only the adherents able to judge? Lindbeck deals well with the issue of how believers within different religions may begin to understand one another by appreciating the distinctiveness of their faiths, but when we move from understanding to appraisal, there is little guidance.[45] A second question concerns what constitutes a religion. In Christianity, is it the Roman Catholic, Eastern Orthodox, or Protestant tradition? Is it more specifically the Anglican, Lutheran, Reformed, Baptist, or Pentecostal tradition? Is it the early church, medieval, modern, or even twentieth-century version of the church? Within the same time frame and the same denomination, is it the first world or third world form of church, the northern hemisphere or southern hemisphere? A third issue has to do with how the evaluation proceeds. Is it measured by the "truthfulness" of the ways its adherents live out their faith or by its "truth" in correspondence to reality? Lindbeck suggests both, but he provides little help in determining how much weight one puts on the "pragmatic" test and how much on the actual "correspondence" text.

To be fair, the "truth question" is daunting for anyone. There are no easy answers, as we have seen already in the attempt by the logical positivists to find clear and determinate criteria (chapter 2). The wider dialogue of narrative approaches, however, offers more direction. First of all, as we saw in chapters 4 and 5, the Wittgensteinian approaches are adept at internal description but tend to leave fideistic and relativistic question in terms of dialogue across forms of life. Hermeneutical philosophy, with its starting point of understanding texts across cultures, tends to have the opposite strengths. The two approaches can therefore be helpfully complementary in terms of the dynamics of dealing with the truth question. Second, the last "school" that we will treat tends to focus more on the truth question and offers helpful suggestions. In the Yale tradition, Thiemann, whom we will consider next, also makes a contribution.

Before turning to Thiemann, though, we need to question, as we did with Frei, the adequacy of Lindbeck's dismissal of the hermeneutical tradition. A complementary approach, such as the one I have suggested, is a startling proposal when the two traditions are seen as contradictory. Frei and Lindbeck are more on target in their reference to Gilkey's and Tracy's appeal to "common human experience." As "revisionist" theologians, as they have been called, they seek to correlate the theological symbol system with contemporary experience. Tracy's early work, as he himself confesses, was particularly vulnerable to the reductionist and foundationalist charges. He tended to make the theological horizon subject to the contemporary philosophical horizon.[46] The Yale thinkers rightly criticize both Tracy's and Gilkey's rather simplistic appeal to common human experience. This does not mean, however, that Gilkey and Tracy sought to ground theology in philosophy; rather, the spirit of their approach is closer to a Gadamerian fusion of horizons. Lindbeck's critique is more *à propos* the early work of Tracy and of Gilkey than of Gadamer and Ricœur. All of the Chicago thinkers we have considered certainly emphasize the importance of language for shaping experience. Tracy particularly points out:

> The problem is that Lindbeck is apparently unaware that thinkers in the very tradition he targets for criticism have addressed precisely these issues [of culture and language] as their own major questions for at least fifteen years. . . .
>
> Indeed, anyone who has read modern hermeneutics in either philosophy or theology can discover that the major claim from Gadamer (whom Lindbeck does not mention) through Ricœur (whom Lindbeck bizarrely lists as one more "experiential-expressivist") has been to rethink the dialectical (not unilateral) relationship between experience and language.[47]

This is a stinging rebuttal, but since that time (1985), as Tracy himself suggests, the sharp lines between the two camps have been eased. Lindbeck himself obviously draws on general anthropological perspectives, such as a Wittgensteinian approach to language, to support his approach. What is different is not so much the presence of philosophical grounding as the stress on philosophical grounding. The Yale thinkers tend to want to be descriptive of the confessional community, with occasional forays into apologetics, while the Chicago thinkers tend to start the dialogue with the wider contemporary horizon and look for more connections. Does this make the latter thinkers foundational and reductionistic, or is this basically a difference in emphasis between people who are primarily theologians and philosophers? An answer better awaits consideration of Thiemann, who particularly articulates these issues.

## Ronald Thiemann

Ron Thiemann, former student of Frei and former Dean of the Harvard Divinity School, carries forward the distinctive themes of the Yale School that we have seen in Frei and Lindbeck. He stresses the narrative character of Scripture, the importance of thinking from within the Christian faith, the reticence about philosophical connections and support, and the tendency to prioritize the understanding of the Christian message over its truth. Thiemann, however, goes into more detail on the latter two issues.

Explicating a theme touched on in both Frei and Lindbeck, Thiemann particularly elaborates the *ad hoc* nature that theology's recourse to apologetics should take. Besides its narrative nature, Thiemann stresses the nonfoundational nature of Christian theology. As Frei pointed out, much of modern theology has sought to ground its claims outside of the biblical narrative in some kind of universal rational structure.[48] Thiemann charges that this has often taken the guise of a doctrine of revelation that defends its epistemological propriety in public terms external to the Christian faith, making its primary emphases epistemological and apologetic. Conversely, Thiemann stresses the Wittgensteinian point about the way meaning is imbedded in traditions. He argues:

Since a nonfoundational theology is concerned with justification internal to the Christian framework, its *primary* interests are neither epistemological nor apologetic. In the process of seeking justification it will surely on occasion need to engage in conversation with positions external to the Christian faith. Though the Christian faith has its own internal integrity, it does not exist in a vacuum.[49]

It may therefore occasionally borrow from non-Christian perspectives. In this case, however, "such borrowings are employed for distinctive Christian uses and sustained by distinctive Christian practices and thus are no longer *systematically* ruled by the original context. They are annexed for Christian purposes and ruled by the new Christian context."[50] Such an appeal beyond the Christian story is at best only *ad hoc*.[51]

The primary purpose of theology as a second-order activity is to "re-describe" the first-order form of life of Christian faith. Like Lindbeck, he seeks to set out the grammar or logic of faith. As such, theology does directly imply truth claims. More emphatically than Frei or Lindbeck, Thiemann discusses the unavoidability of dealing with the truth claims implicit in Christian faith and their import beyond the Christian community. In particular, he believes the nature of the Christian Gospel as "narrated promise" implies the background belief of the "prevenience" of God (belief in God's priority and sufficiency in salvation). He focuses especially on the Gospel of Matthew as having the illocutionary force of making a coherent and intelligible promise of salvation through Jesus Christ, thus the category of "narrated promise."[52] As a whole, the story implicit in the Christian canon renders God as its agent and ground. This is not an epistemological foundationalism but a theological foundationalism that sees its origin in God, even if it starts, epistemologically speaking, from elsewhere. Since God's prevenience is disputed, he engages in what he calls "retroactive justification," which begins with matters of agreement and seeks to find what these agreements presuppose.[53] He explains:

Nonfoundationalist or holist justification is not a matter of devising a universal theoretical defense of Christian language-as-such or of discerning the causal relation between our concepts and their external referents. Holist justification consists, rather, in seeking the relation between a disputed belief and the web of interrelated beliefs within which it rests.[54]

Thiemann believes that he can establish a theological consensus around God's prevenience even if a cultural consensus is lacking.[55] Indeed, seeking the latter is difficult, and not that crucial anyway. It is enough for the reader to see that the biblical story is coherent and intelligible. Anyone who decides for its truth is therefore making a meaningful claim. He adds:

*How* the reader comes to such a decision is a complex matter not easily subject to theological analysis. The act of coming to believe is a person-specific act with both reasons and causes related to that person's individual history. Theology ought not seek to devise an explanatory theory for the subjective conditions for the possibility of faith, for such theories obscure both the diversity and the mystery of human response to the gospel. . . . If a reader comes to believe the gospel's promises, the theologian, as member of the Christian community, can simply join the chorus of witnesses in glorifying God for his miracle of grace.[56]

At this point, Thiemann still suggests that we understand from within a community's narrative and that we may or may not draw connections to the wider horizon. In a later collection of essays (1991), however, Thiemann tries to distance himself from Lindbeck in stressing the way the Christian community has not only an obligation but an inherent necessity to construct a public theology.[57] In this work, Thiemann reiterates his basic Wittgensteinian stance and believes that offering a thick description of a certain narrative tradition is the best explanation and defense of the validity of their beliefs.[58] Nevertheless, he argues that Christian language inevitably describes and makes truth claims about the one world in which we all live. "Because that language describes our common world of experience, it must be related to other forms of human discourse, but the terms of that relation must always be ruled by the logic of the Christian gospel."[59] In other words, he believes that the publicness of truth claims within the community of faith necessarily engage the public outside the Christian community.

What he has not recognized is how the wider contemporary horizon is already involved in understanding from within the community of faith. In other words, as we saw in the discussion of Wittgensteinian fideism in chapter 4, language games are not compartmentalized. This is where the emphases of the Chicago School could be complementary. Drawing on Gadamer, I suggest that the fusion of horizons is already a dynamic in the understanding of faith itself, long before we may make a conscious decision to connect faith with those other horizons. This realization takes some of the excessive mystery out of the way people may find themselves convinced of the truth of a certain faith tradition. Implicit in the understanding of a faith tradition is already a dialogue about its connection with one's horizon and its possible application in one's life. Thiemann's view also does not allow much room for criticism of the tradition. As we saw with Lindbeck and Frei, this approach is vulnerable to charges of a conservatism that permits little ideology critique. The Ricœurian hermeneutic of suspicion serves as a corrective at this point, while not going so far in the foundationalist direction as a Habermasian ideology critique.

Thiemann, like Frei and Lindbeck, indicates how a social-linguistic approach to faith has advantages over foundationalist enterprises. He explicates more clearly than the others an *ad hoc* apologetic that preserves the integrity of both theology and philosophy. He also stresses more than they do the way faith inevitably engages the public world. Nevertheless, he tends to leave the community of faith as a self-enclosed world that can be understood on its own terms before engaging wider horizons, and he also leaves the truth question unnecessarily shrouded in ambiguity and mystery. While retaining the emphasis on the centrality of narrative, the California School, as I have called it, tends to deal more directly with both of these problems.

153

## The California School

A third approach to narrative theology that concentrates more on biography as a way of illuminating theology is that spearheaded by James McClendon, formerly at the Graduate Theological Union in San Francisco, California, and now at Fuller Theological Seminary in Pasadena, California. Two of his former students Michael Goldberg and Terrence Tilley have also written important books on narrative theology. McClendon himself, as mentioned in an earlier chapter, worked out a logic of convictional language based on Austin's speech-act theory. He then expanded on this approach when he turned to *Biography as Theology*.[60] At present, he is writing a three-volume theology in which biographies are central.[61]

### James Wm McClendon Jr

McClendon continues to focus on theological convictions but adds that they are rooted in the texture of a life. We discover a person's convictions by discovering his or her story. Concepts such as grace and courage have meaning only when seen in the context of a biography such as that of a Martin Luther King Jr, a Dag Hammerskjöld or a Clarence Jordan. McClendon summarizes:

> By recognizing that Christian beliefs are not so many "propositions" to be catalogued or juggled like truth-functions in a computer, but are living convictions which give shape to actual lives and actual communities, we open ourselves to the possibility that the only relevant critical examination of Christian beliefs may be one which begins by attending to lived lives. Theology must be at least biography.[62]

In this way, like the other narrative thinkers we have examined, McClendon argues that narrative is a primary or first-order language that grounds theology. In the first volume of his sytematic theology, he treats practical theology or ethics first, which is his way of saying that systematic theology (volume 2) and philosophical theology (volume 3) are grounded in life. In the first volume, discursive theological and historical reflection are interspersed with key biographies of Sarah and Jonathan Edwards, Dietrich Bonhoeffer, and Dorothy Day. In the second volume, due to the enormous amount of material to be covered, the biographies are less prominent but are still interspersed with the more traditional theological content. In McClendon's view, then, theological convictions can be derived from life-stories. The convictions can in turn be evaluated in terms of their "primary, representative, and affective" dimensions, just like any speech act (see chapter 4).

One of the problems with McClendon's approach is that, despite his rhetoric about the centrality of biography, he seems to be interested in abstracting convictional concepts that are then evaluated apart from the narrative structure behind them. Goldberg, on the other hand, moves the evaluative procedure to narratives themselves. In so doing, he addresses one of the problematic aspects of narrative theology. Granted that the emphasis on narrative is extremely helpful in understanding meaning, how do we evaluate the truth of narratives without subordinating the narrative to the doctrine or principle or conviction derived from it? In other words, is it possible to evaluative "narratively" as well as to read narratively? In the eyes of some observers, narrative approaches are a convenient way of avoiding the problematic truth question. From the narrativists' perspective, focus on the truth question is what caused the "eclipse of the biblical narrative" in the first place. The meaning is too quickly subordinated to an alien perspective that focuses on history or science rather than the power of fiction to configure a world.

## Michael Goldberg

Goldberg appropriates the flexibility of speech-act theory in order to avoid this either/or. He continues to relate narratives to

155

convictions, but unlike McClendon, he applies speech–act theory directly to narrative.[63] We must consider the adequacy of the primary conditions or "meaning," as Goldberg also terms it, which would refer to the construction of the narrative. How do particular narratives relate to a particular genre? What kind of narratives are they? Are they fables or myths that may genuinely "*as* stories have no valid meaning in and of and by themselves?"[64] Is Genesis 1: 11, for example, an example of modern historiography or even modern science, or is it something quite different? What is the nature of a parable? Are the Gospels primarily historiography or theology or a genre distinct from either? Goldberg points out, "In this regard, one of the mistakes of fundamentalists and secularists alike is the failure to draw distinctions among the different narrative genres present in the Bible, the fundamentalists accepting them as histories and the secularists rejecting them all as myths."[65] Given the understanding of a certain genre, are the stories well constructed, or confusing? Can a competent speaker of the language manage to follow the story? The meaning and the truth of a work cannot be considered apart from these issues.

Such questions are particularly significant for Goldberg as a Jew, for he argues that Thiemann's claim that Christ is the fulfillment of God's promises to Israel is inconsistent on purely intratextual grounds. Thiemann had suggested that the canonical story is coherent enough to warrant the connection between the God of Israel and the Father of Jesus Christ. Goldberg wonders if the story is not marked by more discordance. He notes that Thiemann leaves out all together the covenant at Sinai. The fact that in the Gospel of Matthew God enacts both the role of the divine and of the human and that Jesus rather than the people of Israel fulfills the covenant is in sharp contrast to the Mosaic covenant, thus calling into question the consistency of the agent rendered. Goldberg says, "At many crucial junctures in Matthew's story line, the character of the work and person of Jesus Christ appears to be strikingly *out of character* for the One, who by dint of certain characteristic redeeming acts attributed to him in the going out from Egypt, originally became acknowledged as

Israel's God and Lord."[66] In other words, the attempt to discern a coherent narrative can cause us to downplay the discordant element in the overall canon of Scripture and to miss what is radically new and different in the Gospel's stories. This is an issue treated at the level of primary conditions before dealing with the representative conditions.

Representative or "truth" conditions are also important. It may well be the case that narratives are often history-like and not history, as Frei indicates, but there is a referential dimension nonetheless. Just as in many speech acts, the representative dimension is not primary, but it is necessary. This is of vital importance in the Gospel stories. It is obvious that they are not modern histories, but we can argue that the logic of the story in the text implies a historical referent such as an actual Jesus, an actual death, and an actual resurrection. Otherwise, the narrative is "unhappy" or "infelicitous." As George Stroup says, "The discovery by historians that Jesus did not die on the cross but died fat and happy of old age in Palestine would render the claims of Christian narrative false."[67] Such historical-critical judgments should not detract from the narrative world, as happened in the modern period analyzed by Frei, but nor should they be dismissed as irrelevant. What is important is that they arise from the narrative itself and not be an external imposition. Goldberg summarizes:

> In the case of convictions for which some historical account is claimed as ground, the representative conditions will require appropriate attention to matters involving the "historical" facticity of persons, events, and the like. By contrast, convictions based in fictions, fairy tales, and fantasies will lack that kind of representative force – and that is something *true by definition*.[68]

Historical events thus are not the only kind of pertinent representative conditions. Recall Thiemann's point that the narratives of Jesus Christ necessarily imply the prevenient activity of God. If the stories are "valid," there must truly be a prevenient God.

157

This does not mean that every element in a broadly historical document like the Gospels, say, is historical or that things happened exactly as recorded. The actuality of the crucifixion of Jesus is more crucial than having an exact chronology of Jesus's life or of the details of the feeding of the multitudes (for example, how many times did it occur, or is it a theological construction?). The parables of Jesus are history-like but do not suggest a historical referent. The fact that the Gospels could not be modern histories and that they are primarily didactic and evangelistic makes of them a distinctive genre; they nevertheless imply a historical basis without predetermining the specifics of that basis. Similar issues arise with respect to the example Goldberg uses, the Exodus event. Whether the crossing was at the Sea of Reeds or the Red Sea is an issue, but not as crucial an issue as whether those crossing were the people of Israel. Both questions involve a range of historical, archeological, and biblical judgments that rarely take "the form of a flat yes or no."[69] The most crucial question, namely, whether it was indeed God who led them out, can be evaluated only in and through the story. Here the broader Old Testament canon comes into play. One can ask the question, "Is that the kind of thing that YHWH would do?"[70] The nature of YHWH derived from the larger narrative context is thus crucial in determining the answer. Goldberg provocatively suggests, "One might say that a genuine Exodus-based theology cannot justifiably speak of God in terms of some timeless and unchanging *essence*, but rather in terms of a *character* developed over time."[71] In this way, Goldberg provides a way for the historical and theological truth questions to arise while "keeping them in their place," so to speak. It is easier to see how they are important while not obtruding on the primary purpose of the biblical narratives, which is proclamation. Moreover, he indicates the way the truth issue cannot be considered in isolation from the genre. The kind and extent of historical question we raise is determined in part by the purpose of the material, whether it is a narrative at all or some other genre like law, letter, or wisdom literature. If narrative, is it a Gospel, a wisdom story (like Job), or a theological history (such as the Deuteronomic history)?

158

Finally, affective conditions ("rationality") are also relevant. Narratives are not simply descriptions; they often proffer a new world "in which we are to fit," as Frei emphasizes. Is the execution of the narrative and the response for which it calls consistent with the world of the text? This is what is often called the "pragmatic test." If a person claims to follow the Torah or to be a disciple of Jesus Christ based on his or her reading of the Gospels, yet is a scoundrel, it calls into question the efficacy of the "speech act" involved, even if it be a narrative. Perhaps in this case the issue could better be stated as one of "truthfulness" rather than "truth" *per se*. Additionally, is it possible to have a story appealing for truthfulness that is based on a representative condition of falsehood? If Jesus never lived at all, for example, many Christians would say that the gospels "misfire."

Goldberg, no more than anyone else, can offer an easy answer to the validity or truth of a narrative or a religious conviction based on narrative. However, much more than others, he has offered some of the detailed ways around which people of different narratives and convictions can converse. As he concludes, "Our assessment will, in all likelihood, involve a more textured and nuanced response, judging a narrative theology to be perhaps fully justified in some respects, totally without justification in regard to others, while being to some extent justifiable at other levels."[72] Much more needs to be done in this area of evaluation, but Goldberg has provided a helpful beginning in alerting us to the various dimensions of narrative.

## Terrence Tilley

Tilley represents a sharper turn to narrative. Even more than Goldberg, he is interested in the appraisal of narratives on their own terms apart from the convictions or theologies to which they give rise. He, too, seeks a variegated way of discerning the various forces of stories. Although his categories are somewhat different, they are roughly similar to the speech-act appraisal suggested by Goldberg. In the end, he suggests that the category of truth must be more flexible. "First," he says, "there are many kinds of stories told in many contexts, for many purposes, for many audiences. No one story can do the work of all of them. No story can be called true for any and all purposes in any and all contexts."[73] Second, no one story is likely to be called true by everyone. The upshot, though, is not relativism but a pluralism that allows for dialogue, conviction, and continued growth.[74]

In an essay on narrative theology, he distinguishes between an approach that does not lead to relativism and one that does. He suggests that most narrativists affirm incommensurability between different forms of life, which means that "there is no tradition-neutral position from which to compare and evaluate religious doctrines and practices. . . . Rather, it shows that the justification of religious beliefs is not a task undertaken from an Archimedean platform or accomplished wholesale by foundational theology."[75] Beliefs may be compared, but the adjudication is so shaped by the different narrative backgrounds that it cannot be neutral.

While appreciating much about the intratextual approach of the Yale School, Tilley is here making a Gadamerian point and worries that the Yale approach leads to fideism. As he puts it, incommensurability by itself does not lead to fideism, but incommensurability combined with intratextuality does.[76] He raises several of the concerns mentioned above about Frei and Lindbeck. He sees the Christian tradition as more than "one framework" that can stand over all of the historical frameworks in which it has existed. Rather, the Christian story has shared in and been influenced by all of these different traditions. The Christian frameworks of Irenaeus, Augustine, Aquinas, Luther, Schleiermacher, and Barth were very different worlds, working against the notion that there is a simple common Christian story.[77] Against the idea that the biblical text can by itself establish a world, he argues that texts alone cannot establish a world without the contributions of the reader, including the wider dimensions of their form of life. This is the kind of emphasis that reader-response theory makes, which implies an unavoidable "intertextuality" that is always at work. He also reminds us of Goldberg's emphasis that the canon of Scriptural intratextuality has not always been the same canon and has been seen differently be different communities.

Tilley pushes the Yale School closer to the side of Frei that stresses the way a community shapes even the literal reading of their canonical text. He calls this a "dirty intratextuality" as opposed to a "pure intratextuality."[78] In short, a heavier hermeneutical or interpretive dimension points to a more serious "conflict of interpretations," as Ricœur puts it, that does not necessarily lead to fideism but to a more hermeneutical, dialogical approach. It does not preclude McClendon's convictions, by which we live or die, but in our world they will likely be contested. Sometimes determining the exact biblical world that is to absorb all the other worlds is itself a matter of *ad hoc* conversation.[79]

After considering these three narrative schools, some observations are in order. We have come a long way from the traditional paradigm of language. The contextual emphasis of the later Wittgenstein and the hermeneutical emphasis of Ricœur and Gadamer militate against a strict univocal model. In these last two chapters, we have seen the insistence on the irreducibility of metaphor and narrative for the cognitivity of religious language. Even systematic theology itself cannot avoid the inclusion of metaphor at its center and a surrounding narrative for its periphery. The three approaches considered here help further to spell out the implications of narrative. The Yale School deserves the attention it has received as the most prominent representative. The various thinkers involved have explored more than others the singular importance of the narrative texture of Christian identity and the *ad hoc* nature of borrowings from other disciplines. More than the others, however, they tend to leave the truth question in obscurity and to downplay the extent to which they interact with other disciplines. The Chicago thinkers, tending sometimes towards foundationalism, nevertheless accentuate the inescapable dialogue between different horizons that is involved in any interpretation of a narrative. The California School emphasizes both the importance of biography and an approach, based on speech-act theory, that promises a nuanced and nonreductionistic approach to narrative. While the exploration of the issues is still in full swing, they point to a way in which the truth question can be raised without eclipsing the biblical or any other kind of narrative. The specter of relativism and fideism that hovers over many of these approaches is not easily exorcised, however. As Tilley pointed out, balancing intratextuality with intertextuality in the Gadamerian sense can help. Intertextuality *per se*, however, does not avoid the problem, as we shall see in the next chapter. In it we will see the most serious presentation of the challenge of relativism – in poststructuralism.

# 8

# Structuralism and Poststructuralism

In the early sixties the structuralist movement burst upon the consciousness of France in a manner in some ways reminiscent of the existentialist movement of the forties, because of its cultural popularity, but sharply unlike in other ways in its antagonistic stance to the individual subject and to history. In the late sixties some who were identified with structuralism challenged many of its central tenets and inaugurated a poststructuralist movement. In the United States the structuralist movement had its great impact on biblical studies in the seventies only to be followed by a preoccupation with poststructuralism in the eighties and nineties.

## Structuralism

In France the most notable thinkers identified as structuralists in the mid-sixies were Claude Lévi-Strauss, Jacques Lacan, Roland Barthes, and Michel Foucault. It is generally agreed that the actual catalyst of the structuralist movement, however, came much earlier, in the linguistic work of Ferdinand de Saussure in the twenties, in his *Course in General Linguistics*.[1] Several emphases that he made in that book became central to the later structuralist movement in France.

### De Saussure's influence on structuralism

One such emphasis was a primary distinction between "language" (*langue*) and "speech" (*parole*). De Saussure stressed the difference between "language" as *structure*, a network of interrelationships, and as actualized in the activity of "speech." Language therefore is a system of relationships that can be analyzed with some precision, whereas speech is an accidental happening that may or may not follow the rules of language.[2]

In light of this distinction, greater emphasis was laid on language as opposed to speech. Despite the fact that de Saussure himself was interested in both (if anything stressing speech),[3] the structuralists appropriated this distinction as a way of moving away from the vagaries of speech to a concentration on the more impersonal structure of language. Thus, they saw language as a *system* that can be *scientifically* analyzed. So much weight then was placed on "language" that the personal element involved in speech could be minimized and virtually seen as peripheral. What was important was the system and not the individual, providing an ideological bludgeon against the prevailing existentialism, of which many were beginning to tire.

This difference between language and speech could also be seen temporally. Language is a matter of a cross-section at any one time. To study language, we must freeze, so to speak, the condition of language at a certain time. Thus, this "synchronic" dimension is atemporal; history is irrelevant to it. On the other hand, speech is more a matter of history, the "diachronic" dimension; it deals with how language changes over time. Traditionally, it was the diachronic dimension that had been of concern in linguistics. This was also true in many areas under the impetus of Hegel in philosophy. In biblical studies, the historical-critical method has been dominated by historical concerns, such as determining the sources historically behind the Pentateuch or the "historical" Jesus. Structuralism, however, sharply challenged this preoccupation with history in biblical studies with its synchronic focus on the texts. In a sense, we need only the text at hand and do not need the historical concerns about the "world behind the text" to address structuralist issues. We will explore below the question whether these two orientations in biblical studies might be integrated in a helpful way or whether they are inherently antagonistic.

164

A further key move with respect to language is that an element within the system cannot be defined in terms of itself but only in terms of its relationship, its *difference*, to other elements in the entire structure. That is, the meaning of a term can only be seen in its differentiation from other terms. Meaning is hence a matter of *structure* and not of ostensive definition. The word "ball," for example, as a toy is characterized by its distinction from other kinds of toys such as bats, dolls, miniature cars, and so on. As a part of a game, it is distinguished from elements of other games and also distinguished from other activities such as work, reading, walking, etc. In a sense, then, the content of a word is "nothing," nothing, that is, apart from its relationship to other terms. Its meaning is thus arbitrary apart from its connection with other signs. This enabled the structuralists to counter the atomistic tradition of the modern period and also the tendency, which Wittgenstein identified, to define meaning as simple ostension, pointing out the object. Philosophically, the movement was clearly distinctive.

So far, though, we have not seen the full discrimination that de Saussure made possible. Differentiation between meanings is only one type of differentiation, one which was sometimes played down in favor of another by later structuralists and poststructuralists. De Saussure termed the differentiation of meaning of which we are speaking that which a term "signified" (*signifié*), which is a mental distinction. On the other hand, a term can be distinguished from other terms by its verbal or by its written form. "Ball" stands out due to its differentiation from the form of other words such as "bull," "bill," "call," and so on, in sound as well as in writing. As long as we can distinguish between these alternatives, there is room for variation and accent in pronunciation. This dimension of terms de Saussure called the "signifier" (*signifiant*), the material dimension of a sign. These two dimensions, however, can only conceptually be distinguished; in reality no signified can occur apart from a signifier.

In addition signs can have two kinds of relationships. One is a "paradigmatic" relationship to other words that are similar or contrasted. In the verse, "In the beginning was the Word," (John

165

1: 1), "Word" (*Logos*) has had a long history of associations (such as reason or wisdom or, in the context, Jesus Christ). On the other hand, there are linear "syntagmatic" relations, which are the means by which subjects, verbs, predicates, etc., connect with one another. In following Roland Barthes's analysis of clothing as like a language, an "outfit" is like a sentence where we can choose a variety of blouses (paradigmatic relations) to go with a certain skirt (syntagmatic relations).[4]

## Structuralist thinkers

De Saussure is indeed the foundation; structuralist thinkers *per se* added some characteristic emphases of their own. Perhaps the most significant was the insight that virtually every cultural field could be depicted in this structural mode; everything is structured like a language, to use the phrase Jacques Lacan used of the unconscious. Lacan applied structuralism to his own field of Freudian psychoanalysis; Lévi-Strauss applied it to ethnography; Vladimir Propp applied it to fairy tales; Roland Barthes applied it to cultural fashion; A.J. Greimas applied it to narratives; Michel Foucault applied it to different historical periods in relation to treatment of the insane, the criminal, and the sick. The Western search for a unified science that we saw in the positivists is on full display here in the form of a dream of a universal science called structuralism or "semiotics:" the science of signs.[5] Over against the empiricism that was regnant in the social sciences, structuralism vigorously moved in the rationalist direction of the ordered, internal constraints of the human mind over external reality.[6] Contrast its universalizing approach *vis-à-vis* behaviorism in psychology and the emphasis on pluralistic, incommensurate cultures in anthropology.

Structuralism became a cultural event in France like existentialism a decade or two earlier.[7] There is some irony in that fact because structuralism is virtually a rejection point by point of existentialism, but the dismissal of the previous philosophical generation is surely no accident. Structuralists often self-con-

sciously rejected existentialism. Pointing out some of the oppositions may help to position structuralism philosophically.

Existentialism focuses on the individual subject; structuralism
displaces the subject in favor of anonymous structures. Existentialism looks to the intentionality of the actor; structuralism looks
to the work itself and to the patterns it exemplifies. Existentialism
emphasizes consciousness and freedom; structuralism looks to
unconscious deep structures that determine action "behind the
back of the author," so to speak. Existentialism considers one's
immersion or "thrownness" in history and one's life project – a
diachronic interest; structuralism is aggressively synchronic,
ahistorical (which accounts for its tension also with Marxism, an
aggressively historicist philosophy). Existentialism stresses the subjective and fragmentary nature of our knowledge; structuralism
represents a renewed search for objective scientific foundations.
A more complete opposition can hardly be imagined.

Lévi-Strauss, for example, examined kinship not in terms of
the effect on individuals but in terms of the patterns determined
by signs structured in terms of binary oppositions such as those in
the family and those not. As he saw it, people circulate between
groups just like words circulate in language. He said, "The error
of traditional anthropology, like that of traditional linguistics, was
to consider the terms and not the relations between the terms."[8]
The spirit of his approach is captured in this summary of his early
work, *The Elementary Structures of Kinship*:[9]

> In *Les Structures*, behind what seemed to be the superficial contin-
> gency and incoherent diversity of the laws governing marriage, I
> discerned a small number of simple principles, thanks to which a
> very complex mass of customs and practices, at first sight absurd
> (and generally held to be so), could be reduced to a meaningful
> system.[10]

Another example is his examination of culinary matters in
terms of oppositions like "the raw and the cooked, the fresh and
the decayed, the moistened and the burned."[11] Such relationships

are not so much reflections of a reality that imposes itself upon the mind but the reflection of structures that compel the human mind inveterately to classify its world. There is structure and meaning, but not necessarily correspondence. Lévi–Strauss imagined that we could find beneath all cultural practices a "deep structure" of binary oppositions that reflect the universal structure of the human mind.[12]

Lévi–Strauss attempted to develop a more complex calculus that has not been widely adopted,[13] but others such as Propp, Greimas, and Tzvetan Todorov provided a deep structure of narratives that has been appropriated in biblical studies, as we shall see below.[14] In this account, every narrative presupposes a common structure. A story may not utilize all of these elements, but they are always in the background to be drawn upon. Propp's analysis of fairy tales showed that not only are individual tales constructed according to a common syntagmatic deep structure, but combined they draw upon each other in a paradigmatic manner. In other words, one story does not tell the whole story. Greimas developed an influential "actantial analysis," whereby every narrative contains a similar pattern of six related functions (actants). Put simply, an object proceeds from a giver, and a subject desires either to have the object or to convey it to a receiver. The subject may be aided by a helper or obstructed by an opponent. The consequent grid is seen frequently in structuralist studies:[15]

$$\text{giver} \;\rightarrow\; \text{object} \;\rightarrow\; \text{receiver}$$
$$\uparrow$$
$$\text{helper} \;\rightarrow\; \text{subject} \;\rightarrow\; \text{opponent}$$

To illustrate, we can draw upon its use in studies of Jesus's parable of the Good Samaritan. In the parable, according to one interpretation, the Samaritan is both the giver and subject, who provides aid and healing (the object) to the traveler (the receiver). The Samaritan is helped by the oil, wine, donkey, etc., and is opposed by the priest and Levite. The diagram would then look like this:

Samaritan     → aid & healing → traveler
               ↑
oil, wine, etc. → Samaritan     → priest and Levite[16]

Michel Foucault went in a different direction in his early work in seeking to uncover or provide an archeology of the deep structures or *epistemes*, as he called them, that underlie different cultural epochs.[17] These are the autonomous cultural codes that make possible the specific statements (*parole*) and practices of a given period. Typical structuralist emphases are apparent. He looked at the whole structure of language in a synchronic way. He did not try to analyze genetically how the classical period or modern period developed, but what they were. In fact, he emphasized the ruptures and discontinuities rather than the continuity between periods. Again, he did not search for what individuals such as a Descartes or Kant contributed but for the structure within which they made their contributions. He was thus interested in the underlying "discursive system" that unconsciously set the parameters for what could be said, which he called an "archeology of knowledge."[18] His emphasis was also on the relations between statements, not on the statements themselves.

For example, in his early book *Madness and Civilization*, he examined how sanity could not be understand apart from insanity.[19] Madness defines reason and vice versa. In *The Birth of the Clinic*, an "archeology of medical perception," he explored how so-called developments in medical disciplines for health reflect changing configurations of death and finitude.[20] A technology of healing replaces the mystery of death. In different epochs, both sides of the equation, death and health, revolve around each other. In *The Order of Things*, he explores in the areas of language, biology, and economics the epistemes that shape them. In the preface to the book, he expresses succinctly his unusual structuralist "history:"

> Quite obviously, such an analysis does not belong to the history of ideas or of science: it is rather an inquiry whose aim is to rediscover on what basis knowledge and theory became possible;

within what space of order knowledge was constituted; on the basis of what historical *a priori*, and in the element of what positivity, ideas could appear, sciences be established, experience be reflected in philosophies, rationalities be formed, only, perhaps, to dissolve and vanish soon afterwards. I am not concerned, therefore, to describe the progress of knowledge towards an objectivity in which today's science can finally be recognized; what I am attempting to bring to light is the epistemological field, the episteme in which knowledge . . . grounds its positivity and thereby manifests a history which is not that of its growing perfection, but rather that of its conditions of possibility. . . . Such an enterprise is not so much a history, in the traditional meaning of that word, as an "archaeology."[21]

There are obviously Kantian parallels to the structuralist program.[22] Structuralism provides a set of transcendental conditions of possibility that make knowledge possible and also call into question the nature of its correspondence to the "thing in itself." Foucault speaks little of universal structures, however; he is more interested in particular configurations in European history. On the other hand, he clearly assumes that these configurations are coded according to the basic structuralist paradigm. He underscores the potential of structuralist thought as a type of "hermeneutics of suspicion" or ideology critique, despite his antipathy towards Marxism, whereby the apparent objectivity of the developing human sciences is seen to be rather arbitrary and actually conceals tendencies of confinement and control that are more dubious than "enlightened," an emphasis that is heightened in his later work.

In *The Order of Things*, which hit the bestseller list and made Foucault probably the most famous French philosopher since Jean-Paul Sartre, he also takes the structuralist critique of "modern man" to its greatest height.[23] Foucault argues that modern man "is a recent invention" within European culture since the sixteenth century, "and one perhaps nearing its end." "Modern man" is thus the creation of a certain structural code without any necessity in its particularities. He goes on to say, "If those arrangements were to disappear as they appeared, if some event of which we can at the moment do no more than sense the possibility ... were to cause them to crumble ... then one can certainly wager that man would be erased, like a face drawn in sand at the edge of the sea."[24]

## Critique

Structuralism obviously has numerous philosophical consequences. When it comes to the meaning of words and other symbols, however, what is its value? Generally structuralists believed that what structuralism discovers is intrinsically important in that it uncovers the underlying pattern of all that we do. In other words, the meaning lies in the structure.[25] Lévi-Strauss says of kinship patterns:

> Of course, the biological family is ubiquitous in human society. But what confers upon kinship its socio-cultural character is not what it retains from nature, but, rather, the essential way in which it diverges from nature. A kinship system does not consist in the objective ties of descent or consanguinity between individuals. It exists only in human consciousness; it is an arbitrary system of representations, not the spontaneous development of a real situation.[26]

Sometimes it appears that the structure is itself the *only* value; it does not say anything further or suggest a way to evaluate practices. Even here, structuralist analysis can make sense of what otherwise seems to be irrelevant and unrelated items in myths and rituals. In a further move, Lévi-Strauss analyzes the movement of binary oppositions in terms of reconciliation of tension, which gives it a more practical and existential flavor. For example, it may be that life and death are in opposition, but this opposition can be mediated by a conception of some kind of life after death (which may give rise to a further opposition, and so on). The analysis can thus provide the key for the way actual life conflicts are resolved. Yet another step, to follow Todorov, is to see the way the human mind universally structures its world as a reflection of reality itself.[27]

In general, structuralists emphasize the way humans impose

meaning upon the world, not as the tradition had held, namely, that the world imposes meanings upon humans. Perhaps it is better to say that the structure of the mind, which is structured like a language, imposes meanings upon humans, who collectively configure the world according to a common deep structure but develop a multitude of surface structures. As we saw with Foucault, the centered subject of modernity, the conscious inventor of meanings, may become radically decentered, the center at best of a node of signifying relations. As Jonathan Culler says of the various semiotic sciences, "Although they begin by making man an object of knowledge, these disciplines find, as their work advances, that the self is dissolved as its various functions are ascribed to impersonal systems which operate through it."[28]

Structuralism undoubtedly reveals much about the workings of language itself and the constraints within which specific "speech acts" occur. Like many other of the movements we have considered, it reminds us that ours is a linguistic world. Knowledge and truth are inseparable from the prism of language through which and in which it emerges. Structuralism is especially helpful when it comes to myths, where the medium in many ways is the message. Foucault's manner of elucidating the background assumptions of a period are also helpful and can serve both as explanatory and as ideology critique.

On the other hand, structuralism suffers from two liabilities. First, it is less helpful as a comprehensive interpretive grid when it comes to the message of a specific narrative, parable, or discourse. Structuralist methods may uncover some of the dynamics by which a specific message is configured, but they cannot easily convey the uniqueness of a particular message, in part because they are geared to the stable and universal structures that are used to state particular messages. Culler underscores this fact: "Just as the task of linguists is not to tell us what individual sentences mean but to explain according to what rules their elements combine and contrast to produce the meanings sentences have for speakers of a language, so the semiotician attempts to discover the nature of the codes which make literary communication possible."[29] As de Saussure saw, there is a dialectic between *langue* and *parole*. Both are important. A particular statement uses the structure of language, but the structure of language is itself not the whole message. When we consider the message of particular Scriptures or theologies, awareness of deep structures may help elucidate what is said but does not wholly determine or explicate it. Structuralism has shown that the codes of our various forms of communication cannot be ignored and has thereby corrected the unbalanced emphasis on diachronic approaches in the past. As a totalizing method that points only to itself, however, it is insufficient to do justice to religious speech and religious documents.

Second, it offers little help in dealing with the truth question. It contributes in terms of advancing understanding and in terms of poking holes in ideological pretensions. Understanding the conditions of making any truth claim is certainly important, just as understanding grammar is important in understanding a particular sentence. The grammar, however, does not in itself select between several well-formed sentences, some of which may be regarded as true and some as false. For example, "God exists," and "God does not exist," are both grammatically correct and follow the "rules," but that does not get us very far.[30] When it comes to truth, then, structuralists sometimes call into question the possibility of truth (a tendency which is heightened in the poststructuralist phase) or neglect the issue because of their focus on the conditions for stating any such truth claim. Again, as a totalizing approach, it leaves significant questions unanswered. Paul Ricœur, who is quite appreciative of structuralism, points to a more balanced account in his hermeneutic philosophy, and the appropriation of religious scholars has by and large followed this more moderate approach.

## Structuralism in Religious Studies

Structuralism became quite the rage at certain points of religious studies in the seventies and early eighties.[31] Paul Ricœur also

173

responded directly to French structuralism in much of his work in the seventies, carefully pointing out both its strengths and weaknesses, while integrating it within his own linguistic project. He provides a philosophical response. After considering his work, which ties in with our treatment of his work in other chapters, we will look at how some biblical scholars have appropriated structuralism.

## *Ricœur*

Ricœur placed his own work between the emphasis upon the author by both Romantic and existentialist hermeneutics, on the one hand, and the emphasis upon the text by the structuralists on the other. He contrasts the Romantic interest in recreating the experience of the genius to the anonymity of structuralism. Ricœur thus says, "The principal task of hermeneutics eludes the alternative of genius or structure."[32] He proposes in their place an emphasis on discourse, which draws on both *langue* and *parole*. He acknowledges that "language" in the structuralist sense "has no relation with reality, its words returning to other words in the endless circle of the dictionary."[33] This centripetal force of *langue* is opposed to the centrifugal nature of *parole*, which casts the words out into the world. He argues, however, that a dialectic occurs in which the two are not so much contradictory as complementary. As he puts it, "Just as language, by being actualised in discourse, surpasses itself as system and realises itself as event, so too discourse, by entering the process of understanding, surpasses itself as event and becomes meaning."[34] There is a "meaning which endures" in any language event that becomes part of the fixed system that structuralism studies.[35] The result is a stable field of signs that refer not to the world but to each other, yet this field supplies "the condition for communication for which it provides the codes."[36] The event of language itself includes a dimension of distantiation, where the work transcends the intentions of the author and also stands over against the horizon of any particular reader. Such distancing from the event of communication enables both the publicness and objectivity of language necessary for the dictionary meaning of a word and also for a world of the text that does not necessarily correspond to the world behind the text.[37]

In Ricœur's dialectic of understanding–explanation–understanding, developed about this time, this enduring fixity means that structuralism is the approach *par excellence* that allows for disciplined, scientific analysis at the second moment of explanation. For Ricœur, however, interpretation cannot stop at this point. With reference to Lévi-Strauss's work, he says, "We can indeed say that we have explained a myth, but not that we have interpreted it."[38] He argues that in fact such a structural "algebra of constitutive units" is impossible apart from the actualization of discourse where the oppositions that the myth mediates, such as birth and death, blindness and sight, sexuality and truth, are existential realities. He concludes, "I really believe that if such were not the function of structural analysis, it would be reduced to a sterile game, a divisive algebra, and even the myth would be bereaved of the function . . . of making men aware of certain oppositions and of tending towards their progressive mediation."[39] In other words, the explanation of the text, which operates at the level of the sense of the text, must move towards the reference of the text, the way it opens up a possible world in which the reader can live. According to Ricœur, then, structuralism is an essential ally towards this end, opening up the depth structure of which we might otherwise be unaware, but it points towards a postcritical appropriation by the reader that goes beyond structuralism *per se*.

## Thiselton

Anthony Thiselton appropriates certain emphases of structural linguistics with regard to its impact specifically on biblical studies. He points out that at the beginning of this century, semantics in general was hampered by the following false assumptions:

(1) that the *word, rather than the sentence or speech-act,* constitutes the basic unit of meaning to be investigated; (2) that questions about *etymology* somehow relate to the real or "basic" meaning of a word; (3) that language has a relation to the world which is *other than conventional,* and that its "rules" may therefore be prescriptive rather than merely descriptive; (4) that *logical and grammatical* structure are basically similar or even isomorphic; (5) that meaning always turns on the relation between a word and the object to which it *refers;* (6) that the basic kind of language-use to be investigated (other than words themselves) is the *declarative proposition* or statement; and (7) that language is an *externalization,* sometimes a merely imitative and approximate externalization, of inner concepts or ideas.[40]

Several of these assumptions have been challenged by the philosophies of language that we have considered in previous chapters, but structuralism particularly calls them into question. It certainly points beyond focus on atomistic words apart from their synchronic context. Words do not refer on a one-to-one basis apart from broader linguistic structures.

Thiselton additionally points out that traditional Greek and Hebrew lexicons take an atomistic, diachronic approach that looks to etymologies, or the history of a word. For example, the Greek word *leitourgia* earlier meant a work (*ergon*) by the people (*laos*). However, even by the time of Aristotle, as Thiselton indicates, it meant little more than a generalized "service," yet the earlier meaning is sometimes read into the New Testament use. We can be so led astray, as he says, that sometimes we lapse into "sheer anachronism, as when we are told that 'witness' (*marturion*) means 'martyrdom'; or, worse still, that *dunamis* in the New Testament 'properly' means 'dynamite!'"[41] It would be better to look at the contemporary paradigmatic network of words with which it contrasts or differs along with the larger syntagmatic and narrative structures in which words are imbedded.

The surface or grammatical structure, moreover, may not reflect the deeper structures, as we have seen. Thiselton notes, "Biblical scholars, however, have been quick to draw far-reaching conclusions about Hebrew or Greek 'thought' on the basis of vocabulary-stock."[42] In other words, if the vocabulary lacks a word, the idea ostensibly is absent. In actuality, many alternative structures exist for saying something similar.[43] Certainly differences between cultures exist that are reflected in language and in larger narrative structures, but this is a much more complex issue than simply similar vocabulary or grammatical form. Moreover, as speech-act theory also showed, the referential or descriptive function of language is not its chief function, and when it is descriptive, usually more is going on than just description. Finally, no simple atomistic connection exists between a word and a referent, the latter which exists "out there" quite apart from the intermediary of language. Nor is there a concept that exists "in here" dislocated from the mediation of the structure of language.[44]

## *Patte*

Daniel Patte also takes a moderate approach while at the same time vigorously advocating the significance of structuralist methods for New Testament studies. He argues that structuralism is not just another method added to text criticism, literary criticism, form criticism, and redaction criticism. Rather, the latter belong to a historical, diachronic approach whereas structuralism represents a linguistic, synchronic approach – all of which, however, are important. He says, speaking of the former methods:

> They presuppose that biblical texts are to be seen primarily as sources for reconstructing some kind of historical process. By contrast the structural methods assume a linguistic paradigm, that is, that expression in language is to be taken as a fundamental category and not as an access to something else, e.g., history.[45]

As in the work of Ricœur, then, the focus is on the world of the text, not the prehistory behind the text. This means that, as Thiselton pointed out, the meaning of words and patterns is

177

sought in terms of that time, not in terms of etymology. Patte further adds that structuralism does not concentrate on the historian's stock in trade, the conscious, intended meanings of agents in history, but on the unconscious structures that shape what they do. In other words, diachronic methods look to the significations imposed by the author; structuralism looks to the significations that are imposed upon the author.[46]

Drawing upon various kinds of structuralist studies, he says that the structuralist exegete looks to uncover the linguistic, narrative, and mythical structures. Underneath all of them are the universal deep structures. Together they constitute the various structuralist levels of meaning, although the universal deep structures are of most interest to the structuralist.

## Crossan and Via

As we intimated in the discussion of metaphor and the parables of Jesus (chapter 6), John Dominic Crossan fruitfully applies Lévi-Strauss's ideas to the parables.[47] In that chapter, we saw that the parables challenge or subvert the normal expectations of the world. Crossan argues that this can most easily be seen at the deeper structural level rather than at the level of manifest content. He begins by looking at the mythical structures of Western movies that portray a conflict between good and evil in terms of cowboys and Indians, which can then be challenged by a good Indian or a white person who take the Indians' side. In such a challenge, a whole pattern or "structure of contempt" may be laid waste.[48] In the parables, Jesus is constantly confronting cultural oppositions and breaking them down, perhaps opening the door to a new perspective. In the Good Samaritan parable, the binary opposition between good and evil in terms of Jews and Samaritans (and also between clergy and laity) is reversed – but not in such a way that it easily mediated by a new contrast between the now good Samaritans and evil Jews. In fact, Crossan argues that myths, in terms of structuralist analysis, offer the possibility of mediation in principle, of reality that is quite manageable; in other words they "establish world." Parables, on

178

the other hand, question such easy mediation, if they do not question mediation altogether; they "subvert world." As he pungently expresses it, "You have built a lovely home, myth assures us; but, whispers parable, you are right above an earthquake fault."[49]

Crossan's example also shows how the underlying pattern may not be fully revealed in any one parable, but, somewhat like Propp's emphasis that fairy tales can only be understood as a whole, Jesus's parables together constitute a larger message. He looks at patterns in the parables that reveal motifs of advent, reversal, and action.[50] As we saw in chapter 6, Crossan probably overestimates the "world-destroying" nature of parable, but his insights are nevertheless illuminating. Crossan's version of the deep structure, however, is probably not deep enough for most structuralists. What Lévi-Strauss wanted was perhaps simply the basic oppositional structure, abstracted from any particular content, while content is extremely important for Crossan. Crossan, however, shows both the limitations of a strict appropriation of Lévi-Strauss and the possibilities of a more limited appropriation.

Both Crossan and Dan Via Jr analyze the Good Samaritan parable in terms of Greimas's actantial analysis (see above).[51] Via elucidates the same kind of reversal of expectations that Crossan emphasizes, while utilizing the whole context rather than a simpler, reconstructed, more original saying. This illustrates the different ways these methodologies can be employed. Crossan uses metaphorical and structuralist analysis to reconstruct the sayings of the historical Jesus and to illuminate the "world-destroying" action of the parables. Via uses the same methods to understand the present form of the text and allows for some "world-creating" implications.

The common criticism, however, of structuralist methods in biblical studies is that the apparatus is so complex that the rewards for appropriating it yield little more than traditional exegesis reveals.[52] For example, Via and Crossan, using the more straightforward metaphorical analysis, came up with basically the same results that they attained using structural analysis with much less confusion.[53] It often appears, in addition, that the elusive basic structure is often forced to fit narratives, suggesting that there is no way of verifying or falsifying the thesis of a basic structure. The chameleon-like quality enables it to fit everything, meaning that it may not actually say anything. Its value is more clearly seen in the broader philosophical context exemplified by Foucault and Barthes, in linguistics as in de Saussure and Thiselton, and in the kind of applications in ethnology and folk tales evinced by the work of Lévi-Strauss and Propp.

Moreover, the claim to universality or transculturality, whether in structures of the human mind or of reality itself, is highly questionable. The illuminating results of many studies are not dependent on so universal a hypothesis. The further claims to universality in terms of the foundation of all the sciences, coupled with claims to scientific precision and the avoidance of history and the subject, are extremely problematic and largely unfulfilled. Ricœur has shown, for example, that the binary elements themselves are rooted in and derive their meaning from the existential life-world, making structuralism at best a moment in a hermeneutical arc – but certainly not self-sufficient. If structuralism has value in exegetical studies, it is in terms of a balance to one-sided emphases on the importance of the self, of history, and of atomistic facts. However, the most penetrating criticisms came from within the movement itself, leading to a poststructuralist movement, better known as deconstructionism.


## Poststructuralism

The most incisive critique of structuralism was launched by Jacques Derrida, who at one time was himself seen as a structuralist.[54] His thought is certainly rooted in certain structuralist ideas, making the description of poststructuralist *à propos*, but it is doubtful whether he ever had enough in common with the structuralists to be considered one of them, in contrast, say, to Foucault, who went through a structuralist then a poststructuralist phase. In a continuing series of interpretive essays, which are at once scintillating and bewildering in their variety and effect, Derrida has launched a sustained dissection of the foundations of Western philosophy – with language as his instrument. His work, and that of the later Foucault, has been variously called poststructuralism, postmodernism, and deconstruction. The term "postmodernism" comes from the withering critique of the rationalism of the modern period by these thinkers, pointing to a different paradigm of reason.[55] "Deconstruction" is particularly Derrida's term; its meaning, along with that of "poststructuralism," should become clear in the course of our discussion.

## Derrida

Derrida took up the structuralist theme of meaning as constituted by arbitrary difference with a vengeance, drawing applications that went in another, much more radical direction. He argued that since a term is constituted by its difference from other terms, meaning is never fully present in the one word itself; it is "deferred," constituted as much by absence as presence. Playing on the ambiguity of the French verb *différer*, which can mean "to differ" or "to defer," he came up with his own neologism, *différance* (the noun form meaning "difference" is spelled *différence*).[56] The only distinction lies in spelling, not in pronunciation, which underscores another emphasis, that writing is at least as important, if not more, than speaking. In this way, Derrida challenged the traditional emphases on what he termed a "metaphysics of presence" and a verbal bias. Western thinkers have desired to grasp meaning fully, a goal best expressed by Descartes's criteria "clarity and distinctness." Going back to Plato, as we saw in chapter 1, philosophers have tended to favor conversation over writing because of the feeling that one can thereby better assure meaning and because speech allows an immediate presence as opposed to the absence of writing. In terms of the traditional goal of univocal language, Derrida says reproachfully, "A noun is proper when it has but a single sense. . . . No philosophy, as such, has ever renounced this Aristotelian ideal. This ideal is philosophy."[57]

In some of his most skillful works, Derrida argues that this univocal goal and the metaphysics of presence is an illusion. In a series of masterful essays, Derrida shows how attempts by Plato, Rousseau, Husserl, and leading structuralists such as Lévi-Strauss and de Saussure to privilege speech over writing, presence over absence, founder in their own inconsistencies and bear the marks of writing (of course) and absence themselves.[58] Univocity is inevitably implicated not only with ambiguity and imprecision but with metaphor.[59] Derrida's "deconstructive" technique, as it has come to be called, uses a work against itself to show how it sows the seeds of its own destruction. For example, he points out how Plato used writing to argue against writing, poetic myth to outlaw myth. Plato saw writing as a "poison" (*pharmakon*), but implies that Socrates, his great protagonist, was himself such a poison or, playing on the ambiguity of the word *pharmakon*, at the same time a "remedy." In the end, Derrida shows how even Plato failed to disentangle speech from the hazards of writing. In a point he makes against Husserl, words always involve repetition, having left their unrecoverable origin, thus creating an unavoidable fissure between word and transparent presence. Derrida's conclusion is that writing actually has a certain priority in that it reveals that speech is like writing, possessing the same instability and ambiguity as writing. In one well-known comment, he claims that "there is nothing outside of the text."[60]

In a manner akin to Ricoeur's, he emphasizes the distantiation of writing, but he goes farther to indicate that a like gap occurs even in speech with a corresponding necessity for interpretation. In similar forays into the works of numerous other thinkers, Derrida attacks what he terms "logocentrism" in favor of his "grammatology" in order to show how difficult it is to be able to be clear and distinct about anything. Using Wittgenstein's language, he is saying at the least that there are always rough edges to words. Another way he puts it is to say that what we have is only a trace, the mark of meaning, but not the full revelation. Christopher Norris writes:

> Above all, deconstruction works to undo the idea – according to Derrida, the ruling illusion of Western metaphysics – that reason can somehow dispense with language and arrive at a pure, self-authenticating truth or method. Though philosophy strives to efface its textual or "written" character, the signs of that struggle are there to be read in its blind-spots of metaphor and other rhetorical strategies.[61]

As in structuralism, Derrida also downplays the subject, suggesting that the subject is not a thing in itself but an implication of texts, or a creation of texts. If there are texts, there are readers and authors, but only by implication. The critique of the substantial subject begun by Hume is transposed to a textual mode.

Using structuralism against itself, he takes the binary oppositions of the West – speech, mind, life, father, and light over against writing, body, death, mother, and darkness – and breaks them down without finding a higher synthesis.[62] He shows how they lead to dead ends, or aporias, that must be endured in "an interminable experience," rather than surmounted.[63] The result is a ceaseless play of interpretation without a fixed stopping point, a profligate dissemination.

Taking the idea of reader-response theory that what is not said, the blanks, are as important as what is said to a more radical conclusion, Derrida stressed the importance of absence and the margins of what is written. In fact, meaning is so deferred that we can make the signifier as important, or more important, than the signified. Thus, especially in Derrida's later work, what we find are endless word plays that have to do more with the signifier than the signified. Conversely, Derrida depicts logocentrism as a search for a "transcendental signified," a final stopping place, a guarantee of indubitable meaning.

As in Wittgenstein and Gadamer, the idea of play is significant. The play for Derrida is more anarchic, however. By such playing with texts, he intends to undermine the view that they have a fixed meaning, that we can privilege certain interpretations, and that there is a limit to interpretation. In fact, he sees the criticism of a text as a creation in its own right, as another "poetic" text itself. His own work, in fact, has been as much literary criticism as philosophy, as much literary production as criticism upon literary productions, thus breaking down the sharp distinctions between these activities.[64]

His Jewish heritage has been cited to underscore the element in Derrida's thought of never-ending written commentary upon texts, commentaries which themselves become fodder for further commentary.[65] Consequently, Derrida stresses an "inter-textuality," an interrelationship of all the texts in our horizon.[66] Sometimes the connections he finds, centered as much on the signifier as the signified, are to average eyes arbitrary and forced, but this underscores the structuralist emphasis on the interweaving of the entire sign universe.[67] Gadamer's emphasis on understanding as a creative production is extended further. As a famous attempt at dialogue with Gadamer showed, however, Derrida incessantly evades an attempt to pin him down, to fix his meaning, but remains always elusive.[68] In the end, he himself leaves only a trace. He leaves all readers somewhat in the position he at one point leaves Nietzsche, "a little lost in the web of his text, lost much as a spider who finds he is unequal to the web he has spun."[69] Some question whether there is any hermeneutical control at all in Derrida's view.

We must counter that concern, however, by noticing how intent Derrida is on the close reading and careful analysis of texts. His purpose, however, is not so much to reveal the meaning but to reveal the "unmeaning" in the texts. Like Wittgenstein, he does not want to offer a metaphysic of his own but to be parasitic, so to speak. He offers a kind of therapy that disabuses one of an impossible illusion of absolute mastery.

## Foucault

As Foucault turned from his more structuralist phase of performing an archeology of historical periods or epistemes, he focused more than Derrida did on a historical analysis (or "genealogy") of the particular ways in which language, knowledge, and power are intertwined.[70] Significantly influenced by Friedrich Nietzsche at this point, he emphasized that knowledge is inevitably power and ends up inscribing itself in the body, in prisons, in medical treatment, in treatment of the insane, and in handling sexuality. His word for this is "bio-power." Like Derrida, he eschewed any large-scale theory, an implicit critique of his early analysis of epistemes, in favor of delineating "micro-practices" or a "micro-physics of power."[71] Rather than something like a grand Marxist critique, for example, he suggested that it would be best if there were numerous small-scale acts of criticism. He advocated the "specific intellectual" rather than the world- and cosmos-comprehending "general" intellectual. Like the later Wittgenstein, he avoided the craving for generality and emphasized pluralism.

Foucault's later work turned more to the practices in which discourse is imbedded than to the discursive systems themselves, much as the later Wittgenstein saw a "form of life" as including language *per se* but also the practices in the stream of life in which the language is set. Also uncannily like Wittgenstein, Foucault's earlier work now seemed too general, too precise, and too focused on the autonomy of a discursive system apart from its setting in life. The effect of his later work is more of an ideology critique than ever before, although he still hardly allows for any way to talk of truth or better or worse judgments. Language and practices may be analyzed, therefore, but they leave us in an inescapable labyrinth where the play of power undermines any claim to traditionally objective knowledge.

Foucault continued to take a broadly structural approach in that the subject is not so much the actor who produces but the one who is produced by the network of relations of power. A surprising turn, however, in his history of sexuality is an avowed interest in the subject and how it produces itself – even in its self-understanding. He explored for instance the "technologies of the self" such as Stoic and Christian techniques of self-examination.[72] The one who proclaimed the death of "man" seemed concerned about becoming an authentic self.

## Critique

On one reading, the effect of Foucault's work is anarchic, like Derrida's. He implies that anything one does will be itself ideological. He never offers a way out. Derrida offers no escape from the endless play of difference in texts. Foucault offers no escape from the endless play of violent power. Both have been criticized, however, for inconsistently excluding their own work as authors from the critique they brings to others.

On still another reading, however, their work is not so anarchic. Foucault's work can be seen, like Derrida's, as deconstructive from within, not rejecting power but the abuse of power, not rejecting the sciences but their ideological pretensions. Rather than standing above the fray, he increasingly engaged in political struggles himself, in "micro-resistance." His work is aligned with those who generally have little voice: the insane, the criminal, the sick, the politically oppressed.[73] He never offers much of a positive program, any more than Derrida does, but his work serves to underscore the finitude and limitations of all of our knowledge.

The greatest value of these philosophers' work lies in its role as "ideology-critique." Both Derrida and Foucault are masters at uncovering vested interests.[74] And perhaps in their own praxis, we can glean some indication of a more positive vein. Nevertheless, the lack of a constructive alternative is seen by most as a weakness, by some as a strength – as a statement of the truth about things. The problem is that neither gives any indication that there is such a thing as truth or reflection of reality. They seem to transcend both correspondence views of truth and relativism, leaving us with no place to stand. Despite the implication of their work that we are enmeshed in the system or in the text, both often leave the impression that somehow they are outside the system. They assert the truth of their views while debunking any attempt to assert the truth. A more positive reading, however, sees them as transcending the alternatives of objectivism and relativism, offering a more chastened, perspectival approach to

186

truth, much like the later Wittgenstein and the hermeneutical philosophies of Gadamer and Ricœur.

An illuminating illustration of these different perspectives lies in their appropriation by feminist philosophers. Poststructuralism has been a matter of concern for feminist thinkers. On the one hand, the structuralist–poststructuralist framework helps elucidate the problems of patriarchy. The binary opposition of man–woman led to one side dominating the other. The wider systems of language and practices reveal this one-sidedness where women have been regarded as less than "man," as property, as not having the right to vote, as being farther from spirit and thus from God (women are paired on the negative side of the spirit–body, mind –body dichotomy), and so on. Poststructuralism in particular appears to be an ally in challenging the patriarchal ideology. On the other hand, as some feminists have countered, just as women are gaining a sense of independent selfhood, poststructuralism dissolves the self, which seems another cruel trick history is playing on women.

The final feminist assessment of the attractiveness of poststructuralism depends on whether it is given a more radical or more moderate interpretation. Those who see them as nihilistic usually reject them.[75] Those who see the poststructuralist critique as consonant with a more moderate critique of modernity like Gadamer's, for example, see it as offering perhaps the best alternative. It provides room for a necessary ideology critique of patriarchy, or as feminists often describe it, of the Cartesian autonomous, disembodied, rational self without lapsing into a totalizing Enlightenment-style discourse that suppresses otherness (see the discussion in chapter 5). As Susan Hekman says, "The gaps, silences and ambiguities of discourses provide the possibility for resistance."[76] Likewise, feminists regard selfhood as largely constituted by tradition and socio-linguistic practices.[77] Some see poststructuralism as helping to avoid making the mistake, as they see it, of some feminists of simply reversing the hierarchy, of making the qualities associated with women superior and "masculine" qualities inferior or of accepting the hierarchy and trying to bring women to the masculine side. This finally allows for creative development of a view of the self that sets male–female relationships on sounder footing.[78]

The feminist poststructuralists such as Julia Kristeva, Luce Irigaray, and Hélène Cixous move in this direction.[79] Their early work, influenced significantly by the structuralist psychoanalyst Jacques Lacan, tended to continue the traditional male–female dichotomy even while challenging it. For example, Kristeva, following Lacan, saw the "symbolic" as the "male" side of language that institutes order; the "semiotic", however, the "female" side, is the origin of creativity and revolutionary change. She spoke of an on-going dialectic between them.[80] While displacing the traditional hierarchy, she did not undo entirely the bipolar opposition. In her more recent work, however, she continues to use these categories but sees the problem of identifying one side or the other with male or female.[81] Susan Hekman speaks positively of her approach:

> The reconstitution of the subject proposed by Kristeva constitutes a radical departure from the Cartesian subject because she challenges its constituting role. She replaces the constituting Cartesian subject with a subject that is constituted by discourse, but one that is by no means passive. Opposed to the fixed entity that is Descartes' knowing subject, she presents a subject in process, one that is constituted differently by different forms of discourse.... Like Foucault, Kristeva rejects the dichotomy between the constituting Cartesian subject and the passive constituted subject. Instead she explodes these categories by describing a subject that is both constituted and revolutionary.[82]

A similar dynamic based on the conflict of interpretations of the poststructuralists is reflected in their use in religious studies.

## Poststructuralism in Religious Studies

Three possible appropriations of the poststructuralists for religion have emerged. One is a frank rejection. This approach emphasizes the anarchic, even nihilistic, reading and therefore finds little to glean that would offer something positive for faith. Another accepts virtually the same reading yet finds in its radicality resources for a religious perspective akin to the negative way considered in the first chapter. A third gives a more moderate reading and sees much hermeneutical value in it.

Anthony C. Thiselton is an example of the first approach. As we noted, he sees much value in structuralism, and he thinks the poststructuralists plausible insofar as they remain within that linguistic framework. In general, however, he sees them as disguising a world view "in semiotic dress" that is relativistic and nihilistic.[83] A more moderate interpretation would see them sounding similar themes to thinkers he favors, such as Wittgenstein, and the hermeneutical tradition we have seen in Gadamer and Ricœur. Thiselton, however, considers the poststructualists (whom he refers to as postmoderns) as going so much farther as to be unusable for Christian hermeneutics. He says:

> The post-modernist attack on the fixed and immobile accords with hermeneutical insights after Hegel and after Dilthey into the historical, contextual, and finite nature of human understanding and of language. But this insight is to be distinguished from post-modernist suggestions that all truth and falsehood and all critiques of idolatry remains so contextually conditioned as to become unstable and radically pluralistic.[84]

Such a radical approach would seem to limit its appropriation by religion, but we should remember the negative way emphasized in the first chapter. There has been a constant tendency in many religions to use a negative critique of language to protect the "otherness" of God and even the mystery of faith itself. Perhaps the best-known appropriation of Derrida in America is that of Mark C. Taylor, who has an affinity with such a rejection of univocal language in religion in seeing deconstruction as the appropriate hermeneutic of the death-of-God movement. He says, "The death of God was the disappearance of the Author who had inscribed absolute truth and univocal meaning in world history and human experience . . . Since the world text no longer

189

had an authoritative author who established its intrinsic intelligibility, interpretation by necessity became creative rather than imitative. Poiesis, in other words, replaced mimesis."[85] What is left for religion? Just as in the death-of-God movement, what is meant is that the God of tradition has died, only to be incarnate in the world. "The death of God, the disappearance of the Father, is the birth of the Son, the appearance of the Word – the appearance of language as sovereign."[86] Often writing in metaphors and playful forms, he suggests that God seems to be a kind of mystical reality now incarnate in texts, between the lines, in the margins, in difference, never present but never totally absent either . . .[87] Likewise, the self is both lost and found much in the way it is in Foucault. "Making the language that denies the self into a center rescues the self linguistically at the same point that it asserts its insignificance, its emptiness as a mere figure of speech. It can only persist as self if it is displaced into the text that denies it." Sounding the similarities between this approach and mystical traditions, Taylor concludes, "If theology is to have a future, we must learn to speak of God godlessly and of self selflessly."[88]

While also seeing the ties with negative theology, John D. Caputo has contended for a less textual and more ethically engaged reading of Derrida. He laments:

> Unfortunately, the significance of Derrida's work has been obscured by a particularly perverse misunderstanding of deconstruction, one which, to anyone who has taken the considerable trouble required to gain familiarity with his texts, seems quite ironic (if not amusing). For the notion has gained currency that deconstruction traps us inside the "chain of signifiers," in a kind of linguistic-subjective idealism, unable to do anything but play vainly with linguistic strings. That, were it true, would be an odd result for a philosophy of alterity, a very unkind fate to visit upon a philosophy whose every effort is bent upon turning toward the other.[89]

As this quotation indicates, Caputo sees in Derrida and other poststructuralists not a relativism or infinite play of texts so much as a prophetic critique of oppressive power in language and life. In an ironic twist for a philosopher like Derrida who as much as anyone else has undermined authorial intent as the key to the meaning of texts, Caputo appeals to Derrida for support of this less radical and more prophetic interest. He quotes from an interview of Derrida that deserves to be reproduced:

> There have been several misinterpretations of what I and other deconstructionists are trying to do. It is totally false to suggest that deconstruction is a suspension of reference. Deconstruction is always deeply concerned with the "other" of language. I never cease to be surprised by critics who see my work as a declaration that there is nothing beyond language, that we are imprisoned in language; it is, in fact, saying the exact opposite. The critique of logocentrism is above all else the search for the "other" and the "other of language." Every week I receive critical commentaries and studies on deconstruction which operate on the assumption that what they call "post-structuralism" amounts to saying that there is nothing beyond language, that we are submerged in words – and other stupidities of that sort . . . This misinterpretation is not just a simplification; it is symptomatic of certain political and institutional interests – interests which must also be deconstructed in their turn. I totally refuse the label of nihilism which has been ascribed to me and my American colleagues. Deconstruction is not an enclosure in nothingness, but an openness toward the other.[90]

Caputo then suggests that this concern for justice and for the singular over against the merely academic and the general reflects a different paradigm, a Jewish rather than a Greek paradigm.[91]

Caputo also adds to the emphasis on the "other" (alterity), as opposed to reducing difference to the "same," Derrida's affinity with the mystical tradition.[92] Although Derrida does not simply adopt the *via negativa*, which is interested finally in a positive knowledge, albeit beyond words, Caputo sees that Derrida's notice of the fault line in all of language is something the theologian would want to say about God-language as well.[93] We cannot simply keep silent, as the negative theologians themselves evince. When we speak of God, however, the *différance* of language means that our language may be used illicitly to oppress – but also in the sense of negative theology to point to God.

As Caputo indicates this positive sense of a "Christian deconstruction" in theology, Stephen D. Moore calls similarly for the positive value of a poststructuralist hermeneutic for biblical studies in a book provocatively entitled *Poststructuralism and the New Testament: Derrida and Foucault at the Foot of the Cross*.[94] He also notes the connection with negative theology and finds it most useful in opening up new readings of texts in ways that challenge the ideology of both reader and text. He takes a more moderate reading that allows it and feminist hermeneutics not to disregard the text but to open up liberating meanings of the biblical text.[95]

Despite the appeal of Caputo and Moore to Derrida's authorial intent, it is apparent that all three readings of Derrida (and Foucault) are possible. Their texts are sufficiently wide ranging, unsystematic, and rhetorical for us to be able to go in several directions. In the most positive sense, however, the broad interest in poststructuralism in the American Academy of Religion in the eighties is probably attributed to the resonance of Derrida's work with a theme like that of the Apostle Paul, "We see in part."[96] It is a sobering reminder that all of our language about God is limited. A second value is its effectiveness as ideology critique. Poststructuralism is a deft tool for uncovering structures of power that alienate and exploit people. In more traditional religious language, the structuralists aid in offering a prophetic critique of sinful and exploitative practices.[97] It is another thing to ask, what next? While negative theology has been a strong current in Western religion, most theologians have felt the need for religious language to refer in some analogous or univocal sense to God. Perhaps appropriately, deconstructionist philosophy is most helpful in a negative way. Whether or not a positive view of God and of religion can be worked out in concert with such a philosophy remains to be seen.

# 9

# *Conclusion: A Changing Paradigm*

After wrestling with language to express the mystery of the Trinity, Augustine apparently wondered if it might be better to say nothing at all. He finally concluded, however, that on a matter so important he must speak, but only that he might not be wholly silent. What we have seen in the twentieth century is that this kind of grappling with religious language has extended to all of language. Language has come to the forefront of philosophical discussion, and all of the options that emerged in the religious context have emerged for language *per se*. The logical positivists and the structuralists turn to the precision and exactitude of a univocal approach. Poststructuralists and others suggest a *via negativa* that stresses difference and the endless play of intertextuality, leading to a pragmatic and possibly mystical approach to the meaning of language. Other movements that have looked to hermeneutics, metaphor, and narrative incline towards more confidence in the reference of words but only in an indirect and mediated way – a type of *via analogia* if you will. The ferment in language philosophy *per se* rebounds, however, back upon religious language, leading to new approaches to exegesis, theology, and philosophy of religion.

After consideration of this plethora of approaches to religious language, what conclusions can be drawn? More specifically, given the set of alternatives offered by the traditional approaches to religious language described in chapter 2, has any new light been shed? Recall that their legacy was an impasse, each approach possessing strengths and yet being internally incoherent.

193

Moreover, what can be said at this point about the legitimacy of the dominant historical paradigm in philosophy, the univocal? If that paradigm is broken down in philosophy, what remains of truth claims?

## Reducing the Contrasts

From a Wittgensteinian perspective, the sharp contrast between a univocal approach, representing the dominant philosophical paradigm, and the analogical is greatly reduced. As Wittgenstein never tired of illustrating, even what we could call "literal" language is rarely precise. Words cover a great many instances that can be identified well enough in practice, indicating agreed-upon conventional uses, but they often have 'rough edges' and cannot be identified with a complete and exact description. In this light, as indicated in the chapter on Wittgenstein, there is a fine line between stretching a literal term to cover a new case and a metaphorical use of a literal term. Especially if we consider that in a given Christian community terms such as "salvation," "enlightenment," "prayer," "conversion," and so on can come to have a rather fixed conventional meaning, a strong case can be made for regarding these terms for all practical purposes as literal.

We may even regard some terms, as ambiguous and full of mystery as they may be, as univocally applied to God but only indirectly applied to persons. Examples would be holy, righteous, and even "loving." This would be consistent with Thomas Aquinas's argument that all such terms apply primarily to God in "the order of being," though not in "the order of knowing." In light of the later Wittgenstein, however, we may actually in the order of knowing ascribe literality to these terms as they apply to God, given the conventionality of a certain community's use. Or we could argue that both believers and God are "holy" in a literal sense, but recognize the great range and fluidity of the term. In such ways, the univocal approach might be reappropriated and reinvigorated.

Also in contrast to Aquinas's approach to analogy, recent developments suggest ways to renew the analogical way. Metaphors, symbols, and analogies may be regarded as cognitive and "in order" as they are, quite apart from an explanation or foundation in literal language. Where univocal language remains significant is that the semantic innovation is constructed, as Ricœur puts it, "out of the ruins" of literal language, even if we understand literal language from a Wittgensteinian perspective. Metaphorical language such as "Jesus is the vine" can hence be seen as irreducible and practically irreplaceable by literal terms. The role of explanation in an approach such as Ricœur's is important, but must begin with and return to the fecundity of the original metaphor. Explanation does not replace the metaphor but rather stands in the secondary relationship of literary criticism to a literary work. In other words, the metaphor may "give rise to thought" as a stimulus for theological systematization, but it remains, not only as the origin, but also as the test of such work.

Further, the philosophies of metaphor and narrative that we examined indicate that all language is shot through with metaphor and is embedded in a narrative context, whether we speak of theological or of scientific language. George Lakoff and Mark Johnson contend that even univocal language is framed within certain common metaphors. The narrativists argue that prosaic language is itself emplotted within a larger temporal frame – which in turn may be dominated by a key metaphor. The equivocal way itself, which stresses the instrumental or catalytic role of language in precipitating faith, finds sharpening in the way all religious language has a performative dimension. In other words, even univocal language has an instrumental role. In some ways, then, we may argue that recent philosophy of language breaks down entirely the categories in which the traditional philosophy of religious language has been formulated.

As a result of these modifications, the identification of language as univocal or metaphorical is much more fluid and relative to a particular community's usage. In fact, the question of the correct label is not so important as the question of whether we understand the meaning or not, or whether we can "use" it adequately or not. In medieval language, this is suggestive of the nominalist tradition, but realist intentions may well remain. Access to truth may be mediated through linguisticality, as the discussions of hermeneutical philosophy, of metaphor, and of narrative attest, but it is not ruled out. Part of the shift in these areas is to underscore the cognitivity of metaphor and narrative over against the tradition that denigrated the capacity for truth of figurative language. These movements in fact reduce the difference between the truth-bearing capacity of language. Both univocal and symbolic language are indirect and inexact pointers to truth, but both may point to truth. This likeness on the issue of truth further calls into question the tendency to identify religious language as all symbolic or as all reducible to univocal language. What appears to be the case is a fluid and complex "stream of life" in which words are both fixed enough to convey a surprising amount of stable meaning without being specifiable enough to overcome imprecision and rough edges.

Perhaps the most remarkable implication of recent developments for religious language is the affirmation that despite irreducible imprecision and metaphorical language, religious language is communicable and understandable. Even if religious language possesses more indeterminate and figurative language, it is not so unlike other language, even scientific language. The attempts to find univocal precision and to reduce figurative, analogical language to univocal is seen as the imposition of false and unnecessary requirements. Rather than attempting to determine whether we can explain a metaphor precisely in other, usually literal, terms, the important thing is to do with metaphor what we do with univocal language, namely, to determine its meaning. To put it in Wittgensteinian terms, we must "look and see" its use in a community of language users. Of course, a structural insight is to note the pattern of connection with other words and also with other metaphors. We often find that even though exact descriptions cannot be defined or that the meanings may be in conflict with those of other groups, the words have a reliable usage and consequently a meaning.

# A Changing Paradigm

Most of the movements that we have considered here are surprisingly compatible, given the diversity and variety of the contexts and traditions from which they spring. Starting with the later Wittgenstein's rejection of his own earlier positivist views, groundwork is laid for a convergence with continental hermeneutical approaches. If we take a moderate critique of structuralism by the poststructuralists, which challenges any univocal approach to meaning without necessarily excluding the human subject or stable meaning altogether, a broad but distinctive paradigm of language emerges. The philosophies of metaphor and of narrative also point in the same direction.

As we noted in chapter 1, the dominant approach to language in general has been one which makes the following emphases: words are secondary to ideas or thoughts, they function primarily to picture objects in an atomistic way (the descriptive fallacy), clarity and precision are crucial, figurative language is ornamental – not cognitive – and broader narrative and historical contexts are ignored. The univocal approach in religious language derives from this view. Likewise, the early Wittgenstein's picture theory of propositions is a classic example, although he already moved beyond words to the sentence as the primary unit of meaning. The structuralists, too, emphasize the broader context but maintain the stress on precise relations and universality.

The general paradigm of language to which the movements we have considered point is quite different. All of them question the sharp separation of thought from language, which is why language cannot be considered simply a matter for rhetoric and poetics but is a central philosophical concern. In the context of religious language, it is closer to the analogical or even the equivocal way. Most challenge what John Austin termed the descriptive fallacy, namely, that language is primarily referential. Following Austin further, language is always an action (a speech act) that has multiple dimensions. A representative or cognitive dimension is usually present, to be sure, but it may well be

197

subsidiary to other dimensions ("primary" and "affective," to use the language we developed in chapter 4). Against his own earlier, positivistic thought, Wittgenstein underscored the immense variety of language games and the kinds of misunderstandings that occur when the uses of the words are not taken into account. The result, he thought, is like an ancient city, where new roads and neighborhoods have sprung up in seemingly cluttered and disorganized fashion.[1] Neither language, nor thought, nor life, can be reduced to the absolute formal precision required by logic. Wittgenstein would never reject a function for logic in its own right, but it should not be made primary. Rather it is now seen as a kind of artificial special case for restricted, albeit important, use. In general, he saw the craving for such precision as akin to walking on ice, too slippery to be very effective.[2] Further support comes from Gadamer's "fusion of horizons," which means that understanding is always dynamic and creative, and Derrida's *différance*, which points to the inherent ambiguity of language. Significantly, Wittgenstein was not alarmed about the rough edges of language, noting that he was not prescribing something different but offering insight into what people have been doing and will continue to do. The main advantage, if there is a prescription, is to prevent unnecessary and impossible demands upon language that it cannot meet. In other words, he hoped to dispel philosophical confusion and anxiety but not basically to reform language.

The philosophies of metaphor and of narrative point in their own way to these conclusions. Metaphor is inherently elusive, but this does not prevent its common use and understanding. It need not be reduced to univocal language to be understood. In fact, as we noted in the previous section, it may be impossible to demarcate clearly metaphorical and literal language in that even prosaic language may be structured by everyday "metaphors we live by," to use the words of Lakoff and Johnson. Whether it be the hard sciences or historiography or poetry, metaphor with both its dynamic creativity and inherent ambiguity plays a crucial role. Narrative, too, loosens up the atomistic universality of terms. Rather than words standing on their own apart from any context, they are imbedded in larger frameworks of meaning. This may be as basic as the structuralist and poststructuralist emphasis that words have meaning in terms of difference and likeness to other terms in wider networks of meaning. Or it may refer to an inherent storied form hovering in the background of all of our conceptuality. Without some grasp of this deeper texture, as Wittgenstein would express it, language keeps going on holiday.[3] Alasdair MacIntyre, for example, points to the effect on modernity of the Enlightenment belief that it transcended narrative and tradition, making it a story that believed it was not a story.[4]

Narratives, however, are not easy to pin down precisely or to evaluate exactly. They call for hermeneutical competence, but this is not the same as formal, logical analysis. Nor do they allow for easy solutions to the ensuing "conflict of interpretations." On the other hand, as Ricœur and others would point out, nor do they necessarily leave us in compartmentalized forms of life without any possibility of argumentation or adjudication at all. Within forms of life, often clear and precise decision procedures for resolving questions exist, whether it be a group of physicists or a group of Methodists (who agree on their tradition). As Jean-François Lyotard puts it, "There are many different language games – a heterogeneity of elements. They only give rise to institutions in patches – local determinism."[5] Against Lyotard, even in larger discussions, sufficient ground is also usually available to continue discussion, if not settle it (that is, as long as other interests are not working to capsize the debate, which in the real world is too often the case). Gadamer's wonder at the capacity, despite all difficulties, to understand ancient texts is testimony to the possibility of crossing horizons, whether ancient or contemporary. Ignoring the narrative context is often why arguments seem to float past one another, as ships passing in the dark – because they are in fact missing the context of the other's language.

An advantage of the implications of these more recent movements is that they point the way out of the aporias in religious language left as the legacy of the tradition and also left by logical positivism. We are not then totally perplexed by living traditions of religious language that use language in their everyday lives in perfectly normal ways but somehow use religious language in inexplicable ways. The lead, as Wittgenstein would emphasize, is taken from the language use itself, rather than imposing an a priori framework in which meaning, sense, and nonsense would have to fit. All such attempts at finding universal meanings have so far come to nought. What is called for in understanding religious language, as in any language, rather are the virtues of patient observation, a certain degree of participation and empathy, and a talent for "thick description."

In the terms of the philosophy of religious language, language philosophy in general is moving from a univocal paradigm toward an analogical or even equivocal paradigm. Whereas the analogical has been dominant in the Western religious tradition, the univocal has been dominant in terms of language in general. An interesting kind of "merger" is occurring with important implications for the relationships between the two. One implication is that less suspicion about religious language, with its mystery and inexactitude, should exist since all language is pervaded by similar dynamics. These characteristics may be more pronounced in religious language, but this is a difference in degree, not in kind. A related implication is that the religious community should be less inclined to try to fit its language into a supposed Platonic ideal of language that is a Procrustean bed of uncomfortable proportions. The falsification challenge is a case in point, where the initial assumptions made it impossible to give an adequate answer. Religion, by and large, would betray its "object" if it found some materially empirical verification. It is indeed difficult to give a good answer to a bad question.

Even though in the religious community, religious language has been understood primarily along analogical lines, an enormous increase in the dynamic complexity of religious language has occurred in the twentieth century. The "fusion of horizons" of Gadamer, Ricœur's hermeneutical arc, the complexities of metaphor, and the nature of narrative, all apply directly to understanding the various kinds of religious language, whether it be

Scripture, creeds, prayers, sermons, or systematic theologies. In fact, one of the benefits is to do justice to these various genres without reducing their difference to a flattening sameness. The insights into parables as extended metaphors, Lindbeck's conception of doctrine as grammar, and Thiselton's proposed revision of lexicons based on structuralist insights are examples of specific gains from increased attention to language, many of which have occurred only in the last half of this century. And the ferment is not at all at an end. If the momentum to a different paradigm continues, we may expect its outworking to continue well into the next century.

In this book I have focused on new movements of language that have significantly impacted the philosophy of religious language and have consequently neglected defenses of a more traditional approach. In this section, I have emphasized the continuity between these movements. It is crucial to realize, however, that not everyone agrees with the direction of these movements, nor do adherents always agree with each other. Along the way, we saw how narrativists radically opposed the later Wittgenstein and Gadamer, how poststructuralists differentiated themselves sharply from Gadamer and Ricœur's hermeneutical philosophy, and how critics struggle between the different readings of the poststructuralists. We should not imagine that what we have is a tidy and manicured landscape; rather, we have something more like a wilderness with groups making forays deep into the forest, sometimes working together and sometimes working against each other. Some perceive promising new opportunities; others see only dead ends and wasted effort. This book is written in order to help the readers gain a better understanding of these efforts and to make their own judgments. Judgments, however, imply claims to truth, and that has been one of the vexed questions about these new movements.

## Religious Language and Truth

The question of truth is difficult, and it certainly remains an important question. The verification challenge is still significant in that it raises the question of whether and how religious language makes a difference. Subsequent movements, however, underscore how we cannot limit that difference to simple empirical verification. The evaluation of the truth of religious claims is similar to the question of the truth of certain beliefs of cultures quite different from ours. The intensity of that question shows that it cannot be answered easily, that it is quite complex, and that in many cases it involves the evaluation of a raft of claims all at once.

As Wittgenstein saw, many beliefs are so entangled in other claims that a person can hardly take one out by itself and examine it. Furthermore, we must be attentive to the full range of criteria for evaluating language, for example, primary, affective, as well as representative meanings, everything in other words that makes a speech act "happy."

The belief in Jesus as the Son of God, for instance, involves a range of issues such as consideration of what it means in the broader context of the Judeo-Christian tradition as well as a persons's particular confessional tradition. It implies background beliefs about a God who could have such a Son and subsequently raise him from the dead and about the possibilities of such an event occurring, in large part at least, beyond this space–time continuum, which in turn relates to how porous or open this time–space continuum is. It also involves beliefs about how historical questions are judged, for example, whether or not we rely on close analogy between what happens occasionally in the present and what can happen in the past. It must be perceived as the expression of a religious conviction and therefore cannot be divorced from the dynamics of convictional speech acts. As is evident, numerous angles and several levels are involved in the appraisal of such a momentous claim. As we saw in the chapter on narrative, the way to judge the truth of a narrative is still in dispute. If we do not reduce a narrative to a proposition or a conviction, how is it judged as a narrative?

In the end, such judgments are irreducibly personal, based on a particular perspective that cannot conclusively be redeemed.

There are "rough edges" to arguments as well as to the meanings of words. On the other hand, debate about truth claims is not necessarily a private or idiosyncratic issue. The publicness of language means that words are not ours to bend as we will and that standards for judgment are usually available, sufficient at least to continue the conversation. Occasionally, enough consensus exists even among religious believers definitively to settle issues, but this is rarer than in the natural sciences. The concern for a "hermeneutics of suspicion" and "ideology critique" does not necessarily undermine all truth claims, but it is a test of all unchallenged claims, whether public or privatistic. Inevitably, as we saw in chapter 5, all such critiques are themselves rooted in a tradition that must itself be scrutinized for sinful plays of power. These "checks and balances" are inexact, but they at their best serve to enlarge the discussion, to raise the question of truth, and to test claims to truth. This is the case not only with religion but also with judgements about many other issues in life as well, such as ethical judgments, political judgements, and medical judgments. There is thus no short cut to the attempt at conversation, at dialogue, at seeking for common ground in order to build up consensus and understanding.

The approach to language evinced here thus does not inevitably lead to a non-cognitive or functionalist view of religious language as in the equivocal tradition or in more contemporary approaches such as that of a Richard Braithwaite (chapter 4) or a Mark C. Taylor (chapter 8). As their work indicates, a non-cognitive and even mystical approach is still viable. A strictly univocal approach in connection with the traditional paradigm of language, however, is called into question in light of the basic viewpoint that experience is mediated by language and that language cannot be reduced to such precision or straightforwardness. We may feel the inadequacy of words to capture an event, but an experience untainted and unshaped by such words would appear to be an impossibility. It is a way of saying that there cannot be a human experience without a human frame of reference. Part of the problematic behind the traditional univocal approach is the view that only univocal language is properly cognitive language and then that the standards for what is to count as cognitive are raised too high. Sensitive religious persons easily find that their experience is distorted.

Once we break the spell of this standard, however, new options are opened up. Greater possibilities of regarding much religious language as univocal are present; metaphors can play a central cognitive role in and of themselves; great diversity in community usage is possible and likely. The kind of paradigm that emerges is something like the idea of language as a colored or translucent window, not a transparent one. Language is one of the frames, perhaps the central one, through which we encounter and understand our world. The fact that we cannot get outside of this frame does not in and of itself mean the window is opaque. It means that human forms of life will always shape and color what is seen. It likely means that broad agreements and precise agreement upon descriptions will be hard to come by. Yet communities will still accredit and take for granted certain meanings and usages. In other words, more forms of life are possible than we perhaps can imagine and sometimes than which we can comfortably accept.

In the end, evaluation is certainly possible and probably inevitable. The results of such evaluation cannot be predicted beforehand apart from the personal judgment of the evaluator. In many cases, however, wide consensus will likely exist between communities on certain judgements such as the prohibition of slavery or religious child sacrifice. There may be wide consensus within communities on questions such as the truth status of the Koran or the Christian Bible. Then there will be pockets of varieties of judgments about the way to be a disciple of Christ or of Confucius or of Buddha. An understanding of the philosophy of language can contribute to these discussions. It may sharpen the debate in some cases and bring people back to the rough ground in others. The philosophy of language, however, can rarely settle truth claims. If it can enhance discussion and lead to greater sensitivity to the role of language, it will already have made a significant contribution. What is surely the case, despite all demurrals against the adequacy of language to express what for many are the deepest experiences of their lives, is that the philosophy of language will continue to be needed, for people will continue to use language about religion, "that they may not be silent."

# Notes

## Chapter 1   Introduction

1   See the essays in the book by this title: Richard M. Rorty, ed., *The Linguistic Turn: Essays in Philosophical Method* (University of Chicago Press, Chicago, IL, 1992).

2   Augustine, *The Trinity*, trans. Stephen McKenna, The Fathers of the Church, vol. 45 (Catholic University of America Press, Washington, DC, 1963), 5.9.10 (the reference is not to the page number but to the book, chapter, and section, respectively).

3   See George M. Marsden, *Fundamentalism and American Culture: The Shaping of Twentieth-Century Evangelicalism, 1870–1925* (Oxford University Press, Oxford 1980), chapter 13. On Kierkegaard, see any of his pseudonymous authorship.

4   Langdon Gilkey, *Naming the Whirlwind: The Renewal of God-Language* (Bobbs-Merrill Educational Publishing, Indianapolis, IN, 1969), p. 10.

5   Maurice Merleau-Ponty, *Phenomenology of Perception*, International Library of Philosophy and Scientific Method (Humanities Press, New York, 1962), p. xix.

6   Helen Keller, *The Story of My Life, with Her Letters (1887–1901)* (Grosset & Dunlap, New York, 1905), pp. 23–4.

7   Paul Ricœur, *The Symbolism of Evil*, trans. Emerson Buchanan, Religious Perspectives, vol. 17 (Harper & Row, New York, 1967), p. 349.

8   Mark Johnson, ed., *Philosophical Perspectives on Metaphor* (University of Minnesota Press, Minneapolis, MN, 1981), p. ix.

9   John Sturrock, ed., Introduction in *Structuralism and Since: From Lévi-Strauss to Derrida* (Oxford University Press, Oxford, 1979), p. 12.

10   Jonathan Culler, *The Pursuit of Signs: Semiotics, Literature, Deconstruction* (Cornell University Press, Ithaca, NY, 1981), p. 25.

11   Standard introductory accounts of the history of philosophy in English (and the volumes that deal with the Greek origins) are Frederick

Copleston, *A History of Philosophy* (Image Books, Garden City, NY, 1985), vol. 1, and W.T. Jones, *The Classical Mind: A History of Western Philosophy*, 2nd edn (Harcourt Brace Jovanovich, New York, 1970), vol. 1.

12  See, for example, Plato's *Gorgias*, in *The Dialogues of Plato*, Great Books of the Western World (Encyclopedia Britannica, Chicago, IL, 1952).

13  See Plato's dismissal of rhetoric in *Gorgias*.

14  See Plato, *The Republic*, in *The Dialogues of Plato*, books 2–3, 5–7.

15  Plato, *Cratylus*, in *The Dialogues of Plato*, p. 113.

16  Plato, *Phaedrus*, in *The Dialogues of Plato*, p. 139.

17  Plato, *The Seventh Letter*, in *The Dialogues of Plato*, p. 810. The student's name was Dionysius II, a ruler of Sicily whom Plato attempted to train as a philosopher-king. The attempt, however, failed.

18  See Mark Johnson, *The Body in the Mind: The Bodily Basis of Meaning, Imagination, and Reason* (University of Chicago Press, Chicago, IL, 1987), pp. xxii–xxiv, for a similar analysis of the assumptions behind contemporary semantic theory and cognitive science.

19  Plato, *Republic*, book 7. Compare expressions such as "illumination," "enlightenment," "I see what you're saying," "I'm in the dark about that," "It was a murky explanation," and so on.

20  René Descartes, *Discourse on Method*, in *Descartes, Spinoza*, Great Books of the Western World, vol. 31 (Encyclopedia Britannica, Chicago, IL, 1952), p. 52. In the early part of this century, John Dewey launched a major broadside against this criterion in *The Quest for Certainty: A Study of the Relation of Knowledge and Action* (Capricorn Books, New York, 1929).

21  Ludwig Wittgenstein, *Tractatus Logico-Philosophicus*, trans. D.F. Pears and B.F. McGuinness, intro. Bertrand Russell (Routledge & Kegan Paul, London, 1961), 4.116 (refers to the numbering of the paragraphs of the text, not the page numbers).

22  Plato, *Republic*, book 6.

23  A classical passage is the *Nicomachean Ethics*, trans. W. Rhys Roberts, in *The Works of Aristotle*, Great Books of the Western World, vol. 9 (Encyclopedia Britannica, Chicago, IL, 1952), vol. 2, book 6, sections 3–7. See also Aristotle, *Metaphysics*, trans. W.D. Ross, in *The Works of Aristotle*, Great Books of the Western World, vol. 9 (Encyclopedia Britannica, Chicago, IL, 1952), vol. 1, book 1, section 1:

> My purpose in embarking on this discussion is to show that everyone regards what he calls wisdom as being concerned with first causes and principles. Thus . . . the man with experience is regarded as wiser than those who have just sensations, of whatever kind; the man who possesses an art as wiser than those who just have experience; the master craftsman as wiser than the manual worker;

and the theoretical sciences as more important than the productive ones. It is, then, clear that wisdom is a science that is concerned with certain principles and causes.

24    See Thomas Aquinas, *The Summa Theologica of Saint Thomas Aquinas*, trans. Fathers of the English Dominican Province, rev. Daniel J. Sullivan, Great Books of the Western World, vols. 19–20 (Encyclopedia Britannica, Chicago, IL, 1952), Ia, 1, 1–8; Ia, 12, 12–13; 1a2ae, 57, 1–2; 2a2ae, 1, 1–6. A concise statement of Aquinas's views is in 2a2ae, 1, 4:

> Faith implies assent of the intellect to that which is believed. Now the intellect assents to a thing in two ways. First, through being moved to assent by its very object, which is known either by itself (as in the case of first principles, which are held by the habit of understanding), or through something else already known (as in the case of conclusions which are held by the habit of science). Secondly the intellect assents to something, not because it is sufficiently moved to this assent by its proper object, but through an act of choice, by which it turns voluntarily to one side rather than to the other. And if this be accompanied by doubt and fear of the opposite side, there will be opinion, while, if there be certainty and no fear of the other side, there will be faith.
>
> Now those things are said to be seen which, of themselves, move the intellect or the senses to knowledge of them. Hence it is evident that neither faith nor opinion can be of things seen either by the senses or by the intellect.

25    A host of books deal with this epistemological paradigm and a possible "postmodern" paradigm shift. The later work of Wittgenstein that we will consider in chapter 4 is significant along with the thought of Hans–Georg Gadamer (chapter 5), Paul Ricœur (chapters 5–8), and the poststructuralist movement (chapter 8). A few other helpful works are Richard J. Bernstein, *Beyond Objectivism and Relativism: Science, Hermeneutics, and Praxis* (University of Pennsylvania Press, Philadelphia, PA, 1985); Alasdair MacIntyre, *Whose Justice? Which Rationality?* (University of Notre Dame Press, Notre Dame, IN, 1988); Alvin Plantinga, "Reason and belief in God," in *Faith and Rationality: Reason and Belief in God*, ed. A. Plantinga and Nicholas Wolterstorff (University of Notre Dame Press, Notre Dame, IN, 1983), pp. 16–93; and Stephen Toulmin, *Cosmopolis: The Hidden Agenda of Modernity* (Free Press, New York, 1990). For a briefer attempt to sort through the various dimensions of this dimension in terms of faith and reason, see my "Much ado about Athens and Jerusalem: the implications of postmodernism for faith," *Review and Expositor*, 91 (Winter 1994), pp. 87–90.

## Chapter 2   Historical Approaches to Religious Language

1   Augustine, *The Trinity*, trans. Stephen McKenna, The Fathers of the Church, vol. 45 (Catholic University of America Press, Washington, DC, 1963), 5.9.10.

2   The allusion is to Friedrich Nietzsche, *Human, All Too Human: A Book for Free Spirits*, trans. Marion Faber, with Stephen Lehmann (University of Nebraska Press, Lincoln, NB, 1984).

3   See especially Walter T. Stace, *The Teachings of the Mystics* (Mentor, New York, 1960), and *Mysticism and Philosophy* (Macmillan, London, 1961).

4   For further treatment of this and other forms of spirituality, see Urban T. Holmes III, *A History of Christian Spirituality: An Analytical Introduction* (Seabury Press, Minneapolis, MN, 1980).

5   Plotinus, *Enneads*, ed. and trans. A.H. Armstrong (Macmillan, New York, 1953), 6.9.11.

6   For a summary account, see the introduction by the translator in Pseudo-Dionysius Areopagite, *The Divine Names and Mystical Theology*, ed. and trans. John D. Jones, Medieval Philosophical Texts in Translation, vol. 21 (Marquette University Press, Milwaukee, WI, 1980), pp. 5–9.

7   Ibid., p. 3.

8   The translation is from Pseudo-Dionysius, *Dionysius the Areopagite on the Divine Names and the Mystical Theology*, trans. C.E. Rolt (Macmillan, New York, 1940), p. 5.

9   Compare Stace, *Mysticism and Philosophy*, p. 290.

10   Moses Maimonides, *The Guide for the Perplexed*, trans. M. Friedlander, 2nd edn (Routledge & Kegan Paul, London, 1904), 1.60.

11   Ibid.

12   For example, Brian Davies, *An Introduction to the Philosophy of Religion* (Oxford University Press, Oxford, 1982), pp. 12–13.

13   Maimonides, *Guide*, 1.53, 1.68. See also David Burrell, *Knowing the Unknowable God: Ibn-Sina, Maimonides, Aquinas* (University of Notre Dame Press, Notre Dame, IN, 1986).

14   See, for example, Stace, *Teachings of the Mystics*, chapter 3.

15   John Duns Scotus, *The Oxford Commentary on the Four Books of the Sentences*, trans. James J. Walsh, in *Philosophy in the Middle Ages: The Christian, Islamic, and Jewish Traditions*, ed. Arthur Hyman and James J. Walsh, 2nd edn (Hackett, Indianapolis, IN, 1983), p. 604.

16   Carl F.H. Henry, *God, Revelation, and Authority* (Word Books, Waco, TX, 1979), vol. 3, p. 364.

17   Ibid.

18   For an interpretation of Tillich in terms of religious language as instrumental only, see Richard Grigg, *Symbol and Empowerment: Paul Tillich's Post-Theistic System* (Mercer University Press, Macon, GA, 1985).

19  Paul Tillich, *Systematic Theology* (University of Chicago Press, Chicago, IL, 1951), vol. 1, p. 239.

20  For Tillich's own account, see Charles W. Kegley and Robert W. Bretall, eds., *The Theology of Paul Tillich*, The Library of Living Theology, vol. 1 (Macmillan, New York, 1959), p. 334.

21  Paul Tillich, *Systematic Theology* (University of Chicago Press, Chicage, IL, 1957), vol. 1, p. 10.

22  Schubert M. Ogden, *The Point of Christology* (Harper & Row, San Francisco, CA, 1982), p. 146.

23  Thomas Aquinas, *The Summa Theologica of Saint Thomas Aquinas*, trans. Fathers of the English Dominican Province, rev. Daniel J. Sullivan, Great Books of the Western World, vols. 19–20 (Encyclopedia Britannica, Chicago, IL, 1952), 1.1.9; 1.13.2 (hereafter this work will be abbreviated as *ST*).

24  *ST*, 1.4.3.

25  *ST*, 1.1.9.

26  Thomas Aquinas, *On the Truth of the Catholic Faith: Summa contra Gentiles*, 1.33.5.

27  *ST*, 1.13.5.

28  *ST*, 1.13.5.

29  See David Burrell, *Analogy and Philosophical Language* (Yale University Press, New Haven, CT, 1973), pp. 119–24, for an account of contemporary revised accounts of Aquinas that see him as less systematic than heretofore.

30  *ST*, 1.13.5.

31  *ST*, 1.12.12.

32  Frederick Ferré, *Language, Logic, and God* (University of Chicago Press, Chicago, IL, 1961), p. 74.

33  *ST*, 1.5.3.

34  *ST*, 1.13.3.

35  *ST*, 1.13.2.

36  Elizabeth A. Johnson, while pointing to analogy as primarily a *via negativa*, stresses this circularity: "Analogical predication rests on an interpretation of the doctrine of creation that sees all things brought into being and sustained by God who is cause of the world, causality itself being an analogical notion." *She Who Is: The Mystery of God in Feminist Discourse* (Crossroad, New York, 1993), pp. 113f. Burrell also notes the problem of circularity and suggests that Aquinas leans to the side of circularity. He then suggests that contemporary linguistic philosophy offers resources for evading this dilemma. *Analogy*, pp. 132–3.

37  Richard Swinburne, *Revelation: From Metaphor to Analogy* (Clarendon Press, Oxford, 1992), p. 42.

38  Eric L. Mascall, *Existence and Analogy: A Sequel to "He Who Is"*

(Longmans, Green, London, 1949), pp. 108–15. Of course, Mascall points towards what he calls a "contuition" of the world's dependence upon God (the cosmological relation), an intuitive insight that goes beyond strict logical inference and the strict literal meanings of words: pp. 69, 89–90. See also Eric L. Mascall *He Who Is: A Study in Traditional Theism* (Archon Books, n.p., 1966), pp. 74ff. Cf. the discussion of Ian T. Ramsey's "discernment" in chapter 4.

39  *ST*, 1.4.3.

40  Karl Barth, *Church Dogmatics* (Attic Press, Greenwood, SC, 1975), vol. 1.1, p. x.

41  Mascall, *Existence*, p. 124.

42  Burrell, *Knowing the Unknowable God*, pp. 31, 46, 57; and *Analogy*, pp. 123, 146, 155. See chapter 6.

43  As James F. Ross says, "In fact, the key assumptions and metaphors of the classical story about analogy were exhausted, as far as fruitful theoretical elaboration is concerned, by the time Cajetan produced *De Nominum Analogia* in 1498, the last systematic explanation of analogy of meaning since the middle ages." *Portraying Analogy*, Cambridge Studies in Philosophy (Cambridge University Press, Cambridge, 1981), p. ix.

44  See for a concise account "The problem of universals," by Frederick Copleston, *A History of Philosophy* (Image Books, Garden City, NY, 1950), vol. 2, pp. 136–55, and also the section on William of Ockham's treatment of universals, vol. 3, chapter 4, pp. 49–61.

45  For a concise introduction to exegesis in the early church, see Karlfried Froehlich, ed. and trans., *Biblical Interpretation in the Early Church*, Sources of Early Christian Thought (Fortress Press, Philadelphia, PA, 1984). For an introduction to the history of exegesis, see Robert Grant and David Tracy, *A Short History of the Interpretation of the Bible*, 2nd edn (Fortress Press, Philadelphia, PA, 1984), and the briefer account of Werner G. Jeanrond, *Theological Hermeneutics: Development and Significance* (Crossroad, New York, 1991).

46  Froehlich, *Biblical Interpretation*, p. 17.

47  Augustine, *The Confessions*, Christian Classics (Broadman, Nashville, TN, 1979), 3.5, 5.14.

48  Froehlich, *Biblical Interpretation*, p. 28.

49  See Grant and Tracy, *Short History*, p. 59.

50  Ibid., p. 66.

51  *ST*, 1.1.10.

52  Martin Luther, *The Babylonian Captivity of the Church*, Works of Martin Luther (Baker Book House, Grand Rapids, MI, 1982), vol. 2, pp. 189f.

53  See Anthony C. Thiselton, *New Horizons in Hermeneutics* (Zondervan, Grand Rapids, MI, 1992), pp. 179–85, for a helpful treatment of the emphasis on the perspicuity of Scripture in the Reformers.

54 See Timothy George, *Theology of the Reformers* (Broadman Press, Nashville, TN, 1988), for helpful discussions of these issues among the major reformers.

55 This is the way Jeffrey Stout has characterized modernity: *The Flight from Authority: Religion, Morality, and the Quest for Autonomy, Revisions* (University of Notre Dame Press, Notre Dame, IN, 1981).

## Chapter 3   The Falsification Challenge

1 Bertrand Russell, *Portraits from Memory* (Allen & Unwin, London, 1957), pp. 26–7. This account may be exaggerated. Russell did not always report the incident in such dramatic fashion.

2 Quoted in Brian McGuinness, *Wittgenstein: A Life* (University of California Press, Berkeley, CA, 1988), p. 99.

3 Ludwig Wittgenstein, *Tractatus Logico-Philosophicus*, trans. D.F. Pears and B.F. McGuinness, intro. Bertrand Russell (Routledge & Kegan Paul, London, 1961). (Originally published in English in 1922.)

4 Ibid., 4.01, 4.014.

5 Ray Monk, *Ludwig Wittgenstein: The Duty of Genius* (Free Press, New York, 1990), p. 118.

6 Wittgenstein, *Tractatus*, 1.1.

7 Ibid., 3.3.

8 Ibid., 4.024.

9 For discussion of this point, see chapters 2 and 3 of Joachim Schulte, *Wittgenstein: An Introduction*, trans. William H. Brenner and John F. Holley, SUNY Series in Philosophy (State University of New York, Albany, NY, 1992).

10 Wittgenstein, *Tractatus*, 4.001, 4.0031.

11 Ibid., 6.1.

12 Ibid., 4.0312.

13 Ibid., 6.124.

14 Ibid., 4.116.

15 Ibid., 7.

16 Ibid., 5.6.

17 Ibid., 6.52.

18 Ibid., 6.522.

19 Ibid., 4.121.

20 Monk, *Ludwig Wittgenstein*, p. 243.

21 Besides the biographies by Monk and McGuinness, see Allen Janik and Stephen Toulmin, *Wittgenstein's Vienna* (Touchstone, New York, 1973), especially the account of Toulmin's own misunderstanding as a student, pp. 21–6.

22  Wittgenstein, *Tractatus*, p. 4.
23  For concise introductions, see John Passmore, "Logical positivism," *The Encyclopedia of Philosophy*, 5 (1967), and A.J. Ayer, editor's introduction, in *Logical Positivism*, ed. A.J. Ayer (Free Press, Glencoe, IL, 1959), pp. 3–10.
24  Peter Achinstein and Stephen F. Barker, eds., *The Legacy of Logical Positivism: Studies in the Philosophy of Science* (Johns Hopkins, Baltimore, MD, 1969), p. v.
25  Wentzel van Huyssteen, *Theology and the Justification of Faith: Constructing Theories in Systematic Theology*, trans. H.F. Snijders (William B. Eerdmans, Grand Rapids, MI, 1989), p. 4. Originally published in 1986.
26  See Moritz Schlick, "Meaning and verification," in *Essential Readings in Logical Positivism*, ed. Oswald Hanfling (Basil Blackwell, Oxford, 1981), p. 34.
27  Karl R. Popper, *The Logic of Scientific Discovery* (Basic Books, New York, 1959), p. 40. Originally published in 1934.
28  See for a discussion Rudolf Carnap, "Intellectual biography,' in *The Philosophy of Rudolf Carnap*, The Library of Living Philosophers, vol. 11 (Open Court, LaSalle, IL, 1963), pp. 51f.
29  Moritz Schlick, "The foundation of knowledge," trans. David Rynn, in *Logical Positivism*, pp. 209f.
30  See, for example, Rudolf Carnap, "Languages," in *Essential Readings*, pp. 150–60 (originally published in 1932). It is common to distinguish between "propositions," which refer to the content of statements, and "statements," which may be expressed in different forms. "There is a table," and "Es gibt einen Tisch," are different statements that express the same proposition.
31  See, for example, Rudolf Carnap, "Intellectual biography," pp. 52, 67–8. Neurath planned a twenty-six-volume international encyclopedia of unified science, which was never completed, that was supposed to compare to Diderot's *Encyclopédie* in the eighteenth century. Carnap allowed a "principle of tolerance" for different constructed languages, which may vary in their strengths. He was also interested in carefully designed international languages like Esperanto. Ibid., pp. 69–71.
32  Rudolf Carnap, "The elimination of metaphysics," in *Logical Positivism*, p. 80.
33  For this point, see Norman Martin, "Rudolf Carnap," in *Encyclopedia of Philosophy*, 2 (1967), p. 28. An example is Rudolf Carnap, *The Logical Syntax of Language*, trans. Amethe Smeaton (Routledge & Kegan Paul, London, 1937).
34  A.J. Ayer, *Language, Truth, and Logic*, 2nd edn (Dover Publications, New York, 1946), p. 32.
35  Ibid., pp. 107–9. C.E.M. Joad launched a prominent attack on Ayer at

this point, arguing that such an approach left one defenseless against those who felt differently, such as Fascists. *A Critique of Logical Positivism* (University of Chicago Press, Chicago, IL, 1950), chapter 9, p. 9.

36 Ayer, editor's introduction, p. 15.
37 Ayer, *Language*, pp. 40, 97–9.
38 Ibid., p. 36–7. Ayer further scaled down his claims in the preface to the second edition a decade later. On Carnap's shift, see Norman Martin, "Rudolf Carnap," in *Encyclopedia of Philosophy*, 2 (1967), p. 26.
39 See especially Popper, *Logic of Scientific Discovery*.
40 Ibid., p. 42.
41 Ibid, p. 41. See also A.J. Ayer, *Philosophy in the Twentieth Century* (Vintage Books, New York, 1982), pp. 131–4.
42 Popper, *Logic of Scientific Discovery*, p. 42.
43 Ibid., p. 37.
44 Antony Flew, "Theology and falsification," in *New Essays in Philosophical Theology*, ed. Antony Flew and Alasdair MacIntyre (SCM Press, London, 1955), pp. 96–7.
45 Ibid., p. 99.
46 See John Wisdom, "Gods," in *Contemporary Analytic and Linguistic Philosophies*, ed. E.D. Klemke (Prometheus Books, Buffalo, NY, 1983), p. 342–51 (originally published in *Proceedings of the Aristotelian Society*, 1944–5). Wisdom's position is further developed in the next chapter, chapter 4.
47 Richard M. Hare, "Theology and falsification," in *New Essays*, pp. 99–101.
48 Ibid., pp. 102–3.
49 Basil Mitchell, 'Theology and falsification," in *New Essays*, pp. 103–4.
50 See chapter 4 for further discussion.
51 John Hick, "Theology and verification," *Theology Today*, 17 (1960), pp. 18–19. All four parables can be found in Basil Mitchell, ed., *The Philosophy of Religion*, Oxford Readings in Philosophy (Oxford University Press, Oxford, 1971).
52 Pascal, *Pensées*, trans. W.F. Trotter, Great Books of the Western World, vol. 33 (Encyclopedia Britannica, Chicago, IL, 1952).

## Chapter 4   Language Games

1 Ludwig Wittgenstein, *Philosophical Investigations*, trans. G.E.M. Anscombe (Macmillan, New York, 1958), 1 (references are to the numbered paragraphs, not to the page numbers).
2 Ibid., 257.
3 Ibid., 107.
4 Ibid., 309. The reference to the "stream of life" is found in Ludwig Wittgenstein, *Zettel*, ed. G.E.M. Anscombe and G.H. von Wright, trans.

Anscombe (Blackwell, Oxford, 1967), 173: "Only in the stream of thought and life do words have meaning."

5 Wittgenstein, *Philosophical Investigations*, 38.

6 Ibid., 124.

7 Ibid., 11.

8 See, for example, ibid., 7, 23.

9 There are only five references in the *Philosophical Investigations*: 19, 23, 241, pp. 174, 226.

10. Ibid., 23.

11 Ludwig Wittgenstein, *On Certainty*, ed. G.E.M. Anscombe and G.H. von Wright, trans. Denis Paul and G.E.M. Anscombe (Harper Torchbooks, New York, 1969), 105.

12 Ibid., 115.

13 Ibid., 247.

14 Ibid., 192.

15 For example, ibid., 116, 125, 144.

16 Wittgenstein, *Philosophical Investigations*, 217, p. 226.

17 Wittgenstein, *On Certainty*, 248.

18 W.V.O. Quine and J.S. Ullian, *The Web of Belief* (Random House, New York, 1970).

19 Wittgenstein, *On Certainty*, 96, 97.

20 Ibid., 94.

21 Ibid., 204.

22 Wittgenstein, *Philosophical Investigations*, 66.

23 Ibid., 67.

24 Jerry H. Gill, *On Knowing God: New Directions for the Future of Theology* (Westminster Press, Philadelphia, 1981), pp. 83–6.

25 Wittgenstein, *Philosophical Investigations*, 71.

26 Ibid. The reference to leaving ragged what is ragged comes from an aphorism of Wittgenstein in *Culture and Value*, ed. G.H. von Wright, trans. Peter Winch (University of Chicago Press, Chicago, IL, 1980), p. 45.

27 Wittgenstein, *Philosophical Investigations*, 109.

28 See, for example, ibid., 256–69. Fergus Kerr notes, "The private language fantasy has been explored in order to bring out that there is nothing that I can find in myself, which I cannot show other people, at least in principle." Fergus Kerr, *Theology after Wittgenstein* (Basil Blackwell, Oxford, 1986), p. 91. Kerr then explores the significance of this publicness of language in general for religious language as more of a public than a private affair.

29 Ibid., 151.

30 Ibid., 199, 202.

31 See, for example, ibid., 68, 84.

32  Ludwig Wittgenstein, *Lectures and Conversations on Aesthetics, Psychology, and Religious Belief*, ed. Cyril Barrett (University of California Press, Berkeley, CA, 1978). See also Norman Malcolm, who contributed to the perception of Wittgenstein as antagonistic to religion, with a response by Peter Winch in Norman Malcolm, *Wittgenstein: A Religious Point of View?*, ed. Peter Winch (Cornell University Press, Ithaca, NY, 1994).

33  Wittgenstein, *Lectures and Conversations*, p. 62.

34  Ibid., p. 55.

35  Ibid., p. 56.

36  Ibid., p. 55.

37  For a helpful treatment of this matter, see Alan Keightley, *Wittgenstein, Grammar, and God* (Epworth Press, London, 1976), pp. 73–80.

38  Wittgenstein, *Philosophical Investigations*, 373.

39  Kai Nielson, "Wittgensteinian fideism," *Philosophy*, 42 (July 1967), pp. 192–3. Nielson actually offers eight descriptions; I have given numbers 5, 6, and 8, which adequately represent the issue for our purposes. For further discussion, see also Kai Nielson, *An Introduction to the Philosophy of Religion* (Macmillan, London, 1982), chapters 3–5, and John Hick, "Sceptics and believers," in *Faith and the Philosophers*, ed. John Hick (Macmillan, London, 1964), pp. 239–40, and a reply by D.Z. Phillips, *Belief, Change, and Forms of Life* (Humanities Press International, Atlantic Highlands, NJ, 1986), chapter 1.

40  Phillips, *Belief*, p. 1.

41  D.Z. Phillips, "Religious beliefs and language games," in *The Philosophy of Religion*, ed. Basil Mitchell, Oxford Readings in Philosophy (Oxford University Press, Oxford, 1971), p. 142.

42  D.Z. Phillips, *Death and Immortality*, New Studies in the Philosophy of Religion (St Martin's Press, London, 1970), p. 38.

43  D.Z. Phillips, "Religious beliefs," p. 139.

44  John Hick, "Reply," in *Reason and Religion*, ed. Stuart C. Brown (Cornell University Press, Ithaca, NY, 1977), p. 122.

45  See Phillips, "Religious beliefs," pp. 120–42, and Phillips, *Belief*.

46  Richard B. Braithwaite, "An empiricist's view of the nature of religious belief," in *The Philosophy of Religion*, ed. Basil Mitchell, Oxford Readings in Philosophy (Oxford University Press, Oxford, 1971), p. 77.

47  Ibid., pp. 82, 84.

48  Antony Flew, "Theology and falsification," in *New Essays in Philosophical Theology*, ed. Antony Flew and Alasdair MacIntyre (SCM Press, London, 1955), p. 96.

49  John Wisdom, "Gods," in *Contemporary Analytic and Linguistic Philosophies*, ed. E.D. Klemke (Prometheus Books, Buffalo, NY, 1983), p. 338. Originally published in *Proceedings of the Aristotelian Society*, 1944–5.

50  Ibid., p. 351.

51  Ibid., p. 342.

52  Ibid., p. 343.

53  Ibid., pp. 343f. Later, the Oxford philosopher Basil Mitchell took up Wisdom's suggestion and showed how such "cumulative case" reasoning is prominently used in many areas of life such as law, literary criticism, and religion. Basil Mitchell, *The Justification of Religious Belief* (Oxford University Press, New York, 1973).

54  Ibid., p. 346.

55  John Macquarrie, "Review of models for divine activity," *The Expository Times*, 85 (May 1974), pp. 251–2. Ramsey was also for many years (1951–66) Nolloth Professor of Philosophy of the Christian Religion and was succeeded in that position by Basil Mitchell.

56  Ian T. Ramsey, *Religious Language* (SCM Press, London, 1957), pp. 19–21.

57  See, for example, ibid., pp. 42–3.

58  Ian T. Ramsey, *Christian Empiricism*, ed. Jerry H. Gill (William B. Eerdmans, Grand Rapids, MI, 1974), p. 130.

59  Ramsey, *Religious Language*, pp. 17–18.

60  Ibid., pp. 53–4.

61  Ibid., p. 59.

62  Ibid., p. 60.

63  Ian T. Ramsey, *Models and Mystery* (Oxford University Press, London, 1964), pp. 2–10. Ramsey was drawing on the analysis of Max Black, which we treat in chapter 6 in connection with metaphor.

64  Ibid., pp. 103–74.

65  Ibid., p. 17.

66  For example, see Frederick Ferré, *Language, Logic, and God*, 2nd edn (University of Chicago Press, Chicago, IL, 1981), p. 141.

67  Of course, the criteria for being biblical, just, or authentic may vary widely between communities. What is startling is how precise these judgments may be within a community.

68  Ian M. Crombie, "The possibility of theological statements," in *The Philosophy of Religion*, ed. Basil Mitchell, Oxford Readings in Philosophy (Oxford University Press, Oxford, 1971), p. 40.

69  Ibid., p. 29.

70  Ibid., pp. 25, 31.

71  Ibid., p. 45.

72  Ibid., pp. 39, 47. See Gilbert Ryle's conception of category mistakes, which are akin to Wittgenstein's notion of confusing language games, for example, applying straightforward scientific analysis to beliefs in an afterlife. His example would be taking language about "mind" or "soul" to refer to separate entities with unique properties. Gilbert Ryle, *The Concept of Mind* (Hutchinson, London, 1949).

73 Crombie, "Possibility," p. 48.
74 See ibid. An example of someone who is dissatisfied with such vague notions of a "reference range" in favor of univocal language is Nielson, *Introduction*, chapter 6.
75 This work is based on the William James Lectures delivered at Harvard University in 1955. John L. Austin, *How to Do Things with Words*, ed. J.O. Urmson and Marina Sbisà, 2nd edn (Harvard University Press, Cambridge, MA, 1975), p. 1.
76 Ibid., p. 31.
77 Ibid., p. 98.
78 These examples are taken from Austin in ibid., pp. 98f.
79 Ibid., pp. 121–22. For further analysis, see John R. Searle, *Speech Acts: An Essay in the Philosophy of Language* (Cambridge University Press, Cambridge, 1969).
80 Ibid., pp. 133–49.
81 Ibid., p. 137.
82 James Wm McClendon Jr, and James M. Smith, *Convictions: Defusing Religious Relativism*, revised edn (Trinity Press International, Valley Forge, PA, 1994; originally published in 1975), esp. chapters 3 and 4. They actually indicate a fourth condition, called "preconditions" (p. 57). However, they do not emphasize it as much as the others, and it can easily be collapsed into the category of "representative" conditions, treated below.
83 Ibid., pp. 58ff.
84 This condition, following Austin, is called "uptake." Ibid., p. 61. It is not the same as the perlocutionary effect because it is the expected and conventional response to the speech act. The perlocutionary effect is not so routine and predictable. For Austin's discussion, see Austin, *How to Do Things*, pp. 117–18.
85 McClendon and Smith, *Convictions*, p. 87.
86 Ibid., p. 64.
87 The remainder of McClendon's and Smith's book largely deals with the question of how this cognitive dimension can be justified.

## Chapter 5  Hermeneutical Philosophy

1 I am following Ricœur's language of "regional" and "general" hermeneutics in Paul Ricœur, "The task of hermeneutics," in *Hermeneutics and the Human Sciences: Essays on Language, Action, and Interpretation*, ed. and trans. John B. Thompson (Cambridge University Press, Cambridge 1981), pp. 44–54. For background to this discussion of the modern history of hermeneutics, in addition to Ricœur's work see

Hans-Georg Gadamer, *Truth and Method*, translation revised by Joel Weinsheimer and Donald G. Marshall, revised edn (Crossroad, New York, 1991), part 2; Richard E. Palmer, *Hermeneutics: Interpretation Theory in Schleiermacher, Dilthey, Heidegger, and Gadamer*, Northwestern University Studies in Phenomenology and Existential Philosophy (Northwestern University Press, Evanston, IL, 1969); and Anthony C. Thiselton, *The Two Horizons: New Testament Hermeneutics and Philosophical Description with Special Reference to Heidegger, Bultmann, Gadamer, and Wittgenstein* (Paternoster Press, Exeter, 1980).

2   A neither full edition of Schleiermacher's notes on hermeneutics nor an English translation of any of them were available until midway through this century. See Friedrich D.E. Schleiermacher, *Hermeneutics: The Handwritten Manuscripts*, ed. Heinz Kimmerle, trans. James Duke and Jack Forstman, American Academy of Religion Texts and Translation Series, vol. 1 (Scholars Press, Atlanta, GA, 1986). In addition, Schleiermacher's views on hermeneutics were mediated largely through Wilhelm Dilthey's account, which does not do justice to the development and balance of his views. See Kimmerle's introduction in ibid., pp. 21–40. Cf. Ricœur, "Task," pp. 45–8.

3   Van A. Harvey, *The Historian and the Believer: The Morality of Historical Knowledge* (SCM Press, London, 1967).

4   Schleiermacher, *Hermeneutics*, p. 188.

5   For example, see ibid., pp. 195–6.

6   Ibid., pp. 190–5.

7   These are typical continental divisions. In Anglo-American education, the subdivisions tend to be three-fold: the natural sciences, the social sciences, and the humanities. The *Geisteswissenschaften* are nearest to our humanities.

8   Martin Heidegger, *Being and Time*, trans. John Macquarrie and Edward Robinson (SCM Press, London, 1962), pp. 183, 193.

9   The key sections in *Being and Time* are paragraphs 31–2.

10  Rudolf Bultmann emphasized the importance of preunderstanding in interpretation as well as many other of Heidegger's themes. He is noted for appropriating Heidegger's existential analysis as laying out the condition of fallen human existence that is met with trust in the gracious acceptance of God. On this basis, the Bible could be "demythologized" and interpreted existentially. For a helpful account of Bultmann's relation to Heidegger, see Thiselton, *Two Horizons*.

11  Ibid., p. 189.

12  Ibid.

13  Ibid., p. 207.

14  See, for example, Gadamer, *Truth and Method*, pp. 258–61. Gadamer summarizes Heidegger's achievement by saying, "[Hermeneutical] Un-

derstanding is the original characteristic of the being of human life itself," p. 259.

15　He especially clarified this purpose in response to critics in his foreword to the second edition of *Truth and Method*, pp. xxvii–xxxviii.

16　Ibid., part 1.

17　Ibid., pp. 101–10.

18　For example, Ricœur, "Task", p. 60.

19　We will return to the issue of authorial intent in treating Ricœur and reader-response theory below. See E.D. Hirsch Jr, *Validity in Interpretation* (Yale University Press, New Haven, CT, 1967), esp. appendix 2, for a well-known critique of Gadamer on this point and a nuanced defense of authorial intent as the determinant of meaning.

20　Gadamer, *Truth and Method*, p. 110: "A complete change takes place when play as such becomes a play. It puts the spectator in the place of the player. He – and not the player – is the person for and in whom the play is played."

21　Ibid., p. 296.

22　Ibid., p. 270. See the whole of part 2 of *Truth and Method* for the entire argument.

23　Ibid., pp. 300–7. Weinsheimer and Marshall translate the phrase as "historically effected consciousness," and in the first edition of *Truth and Method* it was translated as "effective-historical consciousness." See the translator's discussion in *Truth and Method*, p. xv. Gadamer means it to include both the effect or shaping dimension as well as the awareness of the effect of history, p. xxxiv.

24　Ibid., p. 306.

25　Ibid., p. 306.

26　Ibid., p. 297.

27　Ibid., pp. 362–79. See also Gadamer, *Dialogue and Dialectic: Eight Hermeneutical Studies on Plato*, trans. P. Christopher Smith (Yale University Press, New Haven, CT, 1980).

28　Gadamer, *Truth and Method*, pp. 378–9.

29　See ibid., pp. 307–11.

30　These were called the three "subtleties" or capacities: the *subtilitas intelligendi* (understanding), the *subtilitas applicandi* (interpretation or explanation), and the *subtilitas applicandi* (application). Gadamer points out that the pietists added the third, and the Romantics saw the unity of the first two. Gadamer desires to see the unity of all three. Ibid., p. 307.

31　See Krister Stendahl, "Biblical theology, contemporary," *Interpreter's Dictionary of the Bible* (Abingdon Press, New York, 1962), vol. I, pp. 419–20.

32　Gadamer, *Truth and Method*, pp. 324–41.

33　Ibid., p. 308.

34 Ibid., p. 309.

35 Ibid., p. 378.

36 Ibid., p. 474.

37 Ibid.

38 For specific discussion of the universality of hermeneutics, see Hans-Georg Gadamer, "The hermeneutical universality of the hermeneutical problem," in *Philosophical Hermeneutics*, trans. and ed. David E. Linge (University of California Press, Berkeley, CA, 1976), pp. 3–17.

39 See especially Jürgen Habermas, "The hermeneutic claim to universality," in *Contemporary Hermeneutics: Hermeneutics as Method, Philosophy, and Critique*, Josef Bleicher (Routledge & Kegan Paul, London, 1980, originally published in 1971), pp. 181–211. For a concise account of this dialogue, see David Couzens Hoy, *The Critical Circle: Literature, History, and Philosophical Hermeneutics* (University of California Press, Berkeley, CA, 1978), pp. 117–30.

40 On his development of an emancipatory cognitive interest along with a technical and a practical cognitive interest, see Jürgen Habermas, *Knowledge and Human Interests*, trans. Jeremy J. Shapiro (Beacon Press, Boston, MA, 1971; originally published in 1968).

41 Habermas draws upon Austin's speech-act theory to argue for the illocutionary force of arguments as persuading through a better argument.

42 Habermas, "Hermeneutic claim to universality," p. 191.

43 See Jürgen Habermas, "Modernity vs. post-modernity," trans. Seyla Benhabib, *New German Critique*, 22 (Winter 1981), pp. 3–14. Ironically, Habermas's roots are in the neo-Marxist tradition of the Frankfurt School of critical social theory, which is known for its severe attack of the Enlightenment. Even though Habermas is known as the foremost current representative of that school, he is as much of a neo-Enlightenment thinker as a neo-Marxist. For a major account of Habermas's role in the Frankfurt School, see David Held, *Introduction to Critical Theory: Horkheimer to Habermas* (University of California Press, Berkeley, CA, 1980).

44 Habermas has increasingly qualified his transcendentalism, as have some of his followers, so that his thought has moved closer to Gadamer's contextualism. John B. Thompson argues that Habermas has moved in a direction much closer to that of Gadamer: *Critical Hermeneutics: A Study in the Thought of Paul and Jürgen Habermas* (Cambridge University Press, Cambridge, 1981). Anthony C. Thiselton, on the other hand, argues that despite changes, Habermas is still superior to Gadamer because of the continuing transcendental nature of his approach. Oddly, however, he sees an affinity between Habermas and the later Wittgenstein, but not between Habermas and Gadamer. *New Horizons in Hermeneutics: The*

*Theory and Practice of Transforming Biblical Reading* (Zondervan, Grand Rapids, MI, 1992), chapter 11. See Seyla Benhabib, *Situating the Self: Gender, Community, and Postmodernism in Contemporary Ethics* (Routledge, New York, 1992), for an extended argument that Habermas's approach can be contextualized to avoid his transcendental, unhistorical elements. Because of these continuing modifications, the criticisms indicated below apply more strictly to Habermas's earlier work.

45  See Thompson, *Critical Hermeneutics*, pp. 171–3, for a review of these difficulties.

46  See for a pointed critique of this point, William C. Placher, *Unapologetic Theology: A Christian Voice in a Pluralistic Conversation* (Westminster/John Knox, Louisville, KY, 1989), chapter 5.

47  Gadamer, *Truth and Method*, p. xxxviii.

48  Ibid., p. 295.

49  Ibid.

50  Ibid., p. 268.

51  Ibid., p. 269.

52  Ibid., p. 299.

53  Ibid., p. 281.

54  Ibid., p. 279.

55  Ibid., p. 280.

56  See his reply to Habermas's critique, especially the response to Habermas' appeal to Freud: Hans-Georg Gadamer, "On the scope and function of hermeneutical reflection (1967)," in *Philosophical Hermeneutics*, trans. and ed. David E. Linge (University of California Press, Berkeley, CA, 1976), pp. 18–43.

57  A landmark book questioning whether the patriarchal nature of Christianity can speak to women was Mary Daly, *Beyond God the Father: Towards a Philosophy of Women's Liberation*, 2nd edn (Beacon Press, Boston, MA, 1985).

58  Benhabib, *Situating the Self*, p. 151.

59  Two prominent examples are Rosemary Radford Ruether, *Sexism and God-Talk: Toward a Feminist Theology* (Beacon Press, Boston, MA, 1983), and Elisabeth Schüssler Fiorenza, *In Memory of Her: A Feminist Theological Reconstruction of Christian Origins* (Crossroad, New York, 1983). For a broader set of essays dealing with these hermeneutical issues with respect to biblical studies, see Adela Yarbro Collins, ed., *Feminist Perspectives on Biblical Scholarship*, Biblical Scholarship in North America, vol. 10 (Scholars Press, Chico, CA, 1985).

60  Ricœur translated Gadamer's *Truth and Method* into French. For his debt to Gadamer, see Ricœur, "Task."

61  Ricœur, "The hermeneutical function of distantiation," in *Hermeneutics*, p. 143.

62  Paul Ricœur, "The hermeneutics of symbols: I," in *The Conflict of Interpretations: Essays in Hermeneutics*, ed. Don Ihde, Northwestern University Studies in Phenomenology and Existential Philosophy (Northwestern University Press, Evanston, IL, 1974), pp. 287–8.

63  See, for example, Paul Ricœur, "The model of the text: meaningful action considered as a text," in *Hermeneutics*, pp. 197–221, and Paul Ricœur, *Interpretation Theory: Discourse and the Surplus of Meaning* (Texas Christian University Press, Fort Worth, TX, 1976), pp. 71–88. Ricœur's hermeneutical arc is actually imbedded within a broader "discourse theory," which will better be explicated in the context of our examination of structuralism in chapter 8.

64  Paul Ricœur, *The Symbolism of Evil*, trans. Emerson Buchanan, Religious Perspectives, vol. 17 (Harper & Row, New York, 1967), p. 20. At one point, he also treats the Babylonian creation story: pp. 175–91.

65  Ibid., p. 348.

66  In his initial project of a three-part "philosophy of the will," Ricœur detailed in the first part (1950) a phenomenology of the will: Paul Ricœur, *Freedom and Nature: The Voluntary and the Involuntary*, trans. with an intro. by Erazim V. Kohàk, Northwestern University Studies in Phenomenology and Existential Philosophy (Northwestern University Press, Evanston, IL, 1966). Following Husserl's phenomenological method to a large extent, he sketched out the essence of human action, insofar as that is possible, and found a dynamic relationship between what he called the voluntary and the involuntary, or freedom and nature. Then he published two aspects of the second part in 1960, under the rubric of "finitude and guilt." The first was Paul Ricœur, *Fallible Man: Philosophy of the Will*, rev. and trans. Charles A. Kelbley (Fordham University Press, Bronx, NY, 1986), in which he located the potential for the evil use of the will in the tension between freedom and bondage, which he called "the servile will." *The Symbolism of Evil* was the second aspect where he moved to consider actual evil actions, which because of both the freedom and incoherence involved could not be reduced to a phenomenological or essential description but could only be portrayed indirectly via symbolic language. The projected third aspect of this second volume was intended to be a study of symbolic language *per se*, of which the introduction was to be a study of the interpretation of symbols in Freud's psychoanalysis. As was often the case with Ricœur, that grew into a major work on Freud, Paul Ricœur, *Freud and Philosophy: An Essay on Interpretation*, trans. Denis Savage, The Terry Lectures (Yale University Press, New Haven, CT, 1970), which then led him into major studies of metaphor and narrative. The projected third part, a "poetics of the will," has never been completed.

223

67  In addition to *Symbolism*, see Paul Ricœur, "The hermeneutics of sym-
    bols: II," in *Conflict*, p. 315.
68  Ricœur, "Model of the text," p. 211. Although he disagrees with
    Hirsch's emphasis on authorial intent as the determinant of meaning,
    Ricœur employs Hirsch's terminology here.
69  See, for example, ibid., pp. 216–19. We will examine Ricœur's particu-
    lar appropriation of structuralism more closely in the context of chapter
    8, which treats structuralism and poststructuralism.
70  See especially Ricœur, "The hermeneutical function of distanciation," in
    *Hermeneutics*, pp. 131–44.
71  Ricœur refers to the three "masters of suspicion," Marx, Nietzsche, and
    Freud, in this context. Ricœur, *Freud and Philosophy*, pp. 32–6.
72  Ricœur, "Metaphor and the central problem of hermeneutics," in
    *Hermeneutics*, p. 176. Ricœur is drawing on the work of Monroe
    Beardsley here.
73  Ricœur, *Symbolism*, p. 352. See James W. Fowler, *Stages of Faith: The
    Psychology of Human Development and the Quest for Meaning* (Harper, San
    Francisco, CA, 1981), for an influential appropriation of Ricœur's arc in
    terms of stages of spiritual development.
74  Ibid., p. 351.
75  Ibid., p. 349.
76  Ibid., p. 355.
77  In *Hermeneutics*, Ricœur spoke of this third stage as the "reference" of the
    text as distinct from the "sense" of the text uncovered by structuralist
    analysis, borrowing the distinction from Gottlob Frege's distinction be-
    tween the sense and the reference of a word. In his later trilogy on
    narrative, Ricœur prefers the terminology of "configuration," which
    pertains to the fictional world of a story, and "refiguration," which
    pertains to the way that world is appropriated in one's life *à la* Gadamer's
    fusion of horizons. See Paul Ricœur, *Time and Narrative*, trans. Kathleen
    Blamey and David Pellauer (University of Chicago Press, Chicago, IL,
    1984), vol. 3, pp. 5, 100, 158.
78  Ricœur, "The hermeneutical function of distantiation," p. 142.
79  See William C. Placher, "Revisionist and postliberal theologies and the
    public character of theology," *The Thomist*, 49 (1985), pp. 392–416; and
    Kevin J. Vanhoozer, *Biblical Narrative in the Philosophy of Paul Ricœur: A
    Study in Hermeneutics and Theology* (Cambridge University Press, Cam-
    bridge, 1990).
80  Paul Ricœur, *Essays on Biblical Interpretation*, ed. Lewis S. Mudge (For-
    tress Press, Philadelphia, PA, 1980). See especially "The hermeneutics of
    testimony," pp. 119–54, and also "Toward a hermeneutic of the idea of
    revelation," pp. 73–118.

81  Paul Ricœur, *Oneself as Another*, trans. Kathleen Blamey (University of Chicago Press, Chicago, 1992), p. 23.

82  See especially Ricœur, "Model of the text."

83  For an idea of how his approach is fruitful in the sociological context, see Susan J. Hekman, *Hermeneutics and the Sociology of Knowledge* (University of Notre Dame Press, Notre Dame, IN, 1968).

84  Ricœur himself uses the word "spiral" in "Metaphor and the central problem of hermeneutics," p. 171.

85  See Hekman, *Hermeneutics*, pp. 141–4.

86  Paul Ricœur, "Hermeneutics and the critique of ideology," *Hermeneutics*, p. 97.

87  Ibid., p. 99.

88  David Tracy, *The Analogical Imagination: Christian Theology and the Culture of Pluralism* (Crossroad, New York, 1981), p. 119.

89  Ibid., p. 155.

90  Ibid., p. 154.

91  Ibid., p. 100.

92  Ibid.

93  For Iser's work, see *The Implied Reader: Patterns of Communication in Prose Fiction from Bunyan to Beckett* (Johns Hopkins University Press, Baltimore, MD, 1974), and *The Act of Reading: A Theory of Aesthetic Response* (Johns Hopkins University Press, Baltimore, MD, 1978). See also the excellent summary essay by Iser, "Interaction between text and reader," in *The Reader in the Text: Essays on Audience and Interpretation*, ed. Susan R. Suleiman and Inge Crosman (Princeton University Press, Princeton, NJ, 1980), pp. 106–19. For an account of the breadth of reader-response approaches, see the collections by Suleiman and Crosman and by Jane Tompkins, ed., *Reader-Response Criticism: From Formalism to Post-Structuralism* (Johns Hopkins University Press, Baltimore, MD, 1980). For an extended account, see Elizabeth Freund, *The Return of the Reader: Reader-Response Criticism*, New Accents (Methuen, London, 1987). For a Christian perspective, see Michael Vander Weele, "Reader-response theories," in *Contemporary Literary Theory: A Christian Appraisal* (William B. Eerdmans, Grand Rapids, MI, 1991), pp. 125–48.

94  For example, Iser was influenced by the work of Roman Ingarden, who specifically attempted to work out Husserl's phenomenology in terms of reading.

95  Iser, *Implied Reader*, p. 274.

96  Ibid., p. 276.

97  For an example of the application of reader response theory to exegesis, see the entire issue of Robert Detweiler, ed., "Reader response approaches to biblical and secular texts," *Semeia*, 31 (1985).

225

98  Iser, "Interaction," p. 111.
99  See for example, J.C. Ransom, *The New Criticism* (New Directions, Norfolk, CT, 1941). For a brief critical account, see Freund, *Return of the Reader*, pp. 2–6, 40–65.
100  For both "fallacies," see W.K. Wimsatt, *The Verbal Icon: Studies in the Meaning of Poetry* (Methuen, London, 1970; first published 1954).
101  R. Alan Culpepper, *Anatomy of the Fourth Gospel: A Study in Literary Design*, foreword by Frank Kermode, New Testament Foundations and Facets (Fortress Press, Philadelphia, PA, 1983). Culpepper draws heavily upon Iser, but he identifies his work more broadly with literary approaches to the New Testament with their focus upon the text and its readers, rather than on traditional historical-critical studies with their prime emphasis upon the writers and prehistory of the text. See chapter 8 for further discussion of the role of historical-critical approaches to biblical studies.
102  Ibid., pp. 3–4.
103  Notably Stanley E. Fish, "Why no one's afraid of Wolfgang Iser," *Diacritics*, 11, 2–13.
104  Iser, "Interaction," p. 108.
105  We will also return to these issues in chapter 8 where structuralist and poststructuralist approaches present challenges to this view, the former in a conservative and the latter in a radical direction.

## Chapter 6  Metaphor, Symbol, and Analogy

1  Mark Johnson, ed., *Philosophical Perspectives on Metaphor* (University of Minnesota Press, Minneapolis, MN, 1981), p. ix.
2  A concise overview can be found Mark Johnson's introduction, ibid., pp. 3–47. Johnson's oversimplification at times is corrected by Janet Martin Soskice, *Metaphor and Religious Language* (Clarendon Press, Oxford, 1985), chapter 1. Paul Ricœur gives a fuller account in *The Rule of Metaphor: Multi-disciplinary Studies of the Creation of Meaning in Language*, trans. Robert Czerny (University of Toronto Press, Toronto, 1977), pp. 8–64.
3  Aristotle, *Poetics*, in Great Books of the Western World, vol. 9 (Encyclopedia Britannica, Chicago, 1952), p. 1459a.
4  See the way Aristotle used an example like this to show the similarity of metaphor to simile, thus giving rise to the standard view of a metaphor as an elliptical simile. Aristotle, *Rhetoric*, in Great Books of the Western World, vol. 9 (Encyclopedia Britannica, Chicago, IL, 1952), p. 1406b.
5  Ricœur, *Rule of Metaphor*, p. 45. There were some exceptions such as Samuel Taylor Coleridge in the Romantic movement who suggested a more robust view of metaphor over against the limitations of purely

scientific thought, but their denigration of science may have harmed the philosophical respectability of metaphor. Johnson, *Philosophical Perspectives*, pp. 14–16.

6   Thomas Hobbes, *Leviathan* (Clarendon Press, Oxford, 1909), part 1, chapter 4 (p. 25). See also John Locke, *An Essay Concerning Human Understanding*, in Great Books of the Western World, vol. 35 (Encyclopedia Britannica, Chicago, 1952), 3.10.34.

7   These crucial essays are included in Johnson, *Philosophical Perspectives on Metaphor*. Richards's essay is "The philosophy of rhetoric," pp. 48–62 (originally Lecture V of *The Philosophy of Rhetoric* [Oxford University Press, Oxford, 1936], pp. 87–112). Black's essay is "Metaphor," pp. 63–82 (originally "Metaphor," *Proceedings of the Aristotelian Society*, N.S. 55 [1954–55], pp. 273–94). See also Max Black, "More about metaphor," in *Metaphor and Thought*, ed. Andrew Ortony (Cambridge University Press, Cambrigde, 1979), pp. 19–43.

8   Soskice, *Metaphor*, p. 15.

9   Black, "Metaphor," p. 75.

10  See Ricœur, *Rule of Metaphor*, for a preference of Black's terminology and Soskice, *Metaphor*, for a preference of Richards's. Ironically, they both tend to favor their author for the same reason, namely, that they allow for stress on one term but do not put exclusive emphasis on a single word as the bearer of all "the associated commonplaces."

11  Ricœur's views are scattered throughout *The Rule of Metaphor* as he dialogues with many other approaches. More concise presentations can be found in "The metaphorical process as cognition, imagination, and feeling," in Johnson, ed., *Philosophical Perspectives on Metaphor*, pp. 228–47; in Ricœur, "Metaphor and the central problem of hermeneutics," in *Hermeneutics and the Human Sciences: Essays on Language, Action, and Interpretation*, ed. and trans. John B. Thompson (Cambridge University Press, Cambridge, 1981), pp. 165–81; and in Ricœur, "Biblical hermeneutics," *Semeia*, 4 (1975), pp. 29–148.

12  Mary Gerhart and Allan Melvin Russell, *Metaphoric Process: The Creation of Scientific and Religious Understanding*, foreword by Paul Ricœur (Texas Christian University Press, Fort Worth, TX, 1984), pp. 109ff.

13  Monroe Beardsley, "The metaphorical twist," in Johnson, ed., *Philosophical Perspectives on Metaphor*, pp. 111–12. Beardsley puts too much emphasis on these associations being connotations of the words as opposed to more primary meanings. Nevertheless, some incongruity must be seen in terms of common associations in order for a metaphor to be recognized.

14  Black, "Metaphor," p. 75.

15  Ricœur, "Biblical hermeneutics," p. 87.

16  Ricœur, *The Rule of Metaphor*, pp. 299, 245. A related implication for philosophy is that in the philosophical tradition, metaphor's proclivity for

stimulating the feelings and the imagination was a strike against its cognitive reliability. The reason has been seen as threatened by the passions, and the mind by the body. The turn to metaphor is allied with recent attempts to emphasize the way reason is inherently embodied. Thus, the imagination, the feelings, the body, are all means by which we know rather than obstacles to transcend. Unfortunately, there is not space to follow up on this connection in this work. Some books, however, that relate metaphor and this emphasis on embodied knowing are the above-cited works by Ricoeur, "Metaphorical process" and *The Rule of Metaphor*. Also see Mark Johnson, *Body in the Mind: The Bodily Basis of Meaning, Imagination, and Reason* (University of Chicago Press, Chicago, IL, 1987); Jerry H. Gill, *Merleau-Ponty and Metaphor* (Humanities Press, New Jersey, 1991); and Garret Green, *Imagining God: Theology and the Religious Imagination* (Harper & Row, New York, 1989).

17 Donald Davidson, "What metaphors mean," in Johnson, ed., *Philosophical Perspectives on Metaphor*, pp. 200–20.

18 Eva Feder Kittay, *Metaphor: Its Cognitive Force and Linguistic Structure* (Clarendon Press, Oxford, 1987), p. 24.

19 See Mary Hesse, *Revolutions and Reconstructions in the Philosophy of Science* (Harvester Press, Brighton, Sussex, 1980), esp. p. 173, and Ian Barbour, *Religion in an Age of Science*, vol. 1, Gifford Lectures (Harper & Row, San Francisco, CA, 1990), chapter 2. The latter volume is essentially an update of what Barbour had written years before in *Issues in Science and Religion* (Harper & Row, New York, 1966) and *Myths, Models, and Paradigms* (Harper & Row, New York, 1974).

20 Max Black, *Models and Metaphors: Studies in Language and Philosophy* (Cornell University Press, Ithaca, NY, 1962), chapters 3, 13.

21 Ricœur, *The Rule of Metaphor*, study 8, pp. 257–322, esp. p. 302.

22 A very helpful book in this regard is Gill, *Merleau-Ponty and Metaphor*.

23 George Lakoff and Mark Johnson, *Metaphors We Live By* (University of Chicago Press, Chicago, IL, 1980).

24 Soskice, *Metaphor*, p. 51.

25 Ibid., p. 63.

26 Ricœur, "Biblical hermeneutics," p. 94.

27 The French title of Ricœur, *The Rule of Metaphor*, *La métaphore vive*, could be translated as "living metaphor."

28 See Soskice, *Metaphor*, pp. 74–83, for a helpful critique of this view.

29 Paul Tillich, *Dynamics of Faith*, World Perspectives Series, vol. 10 (Harper Torchbooks, New York, 1958), pp. 41, 44. See the entire chapter 3 for the background to the following discussion, pp. 41–54.

30 Ibid., p. 42.

31 Ibid., p. 43.

32 A concise summary of Gilkey's theology, with his treatment of symbol-

ism, is *Message and Existence: An Introduction to Christian Theology* (Seabury Press, New York, 1979), esp. chapters 2–3. For more in-depth treatment, see *Naming the Whirlwind: The Renewal of God-Language* (Bobbs-Merrill, Indianapolis, IN, 1969), and *Religion and the Scientific Future: Reflections on Myth, Science, and Theology*, The Deem Lectures (Harper & Row, New York, 1970).

33 Gilkey, *Message and Existence*, p. 26.

34 See especially Paul Ricœur, *The Symbolism of Evil*, trans. Emerson Buchanan, Religious Perspectives (Harper and Row, New York, 1967) (originally published in 1960). See also Ricœur, *The Conflict of Interpretations*, ed. Don Ihde, Northwestern University Studies in Phenomenology and Existential Philosophy (Northwestern University Press, Evanston, IL, 1974), esp. "Structure and hermeneutics," trans. Kathleen McLaughlin, pp. 27–61, and "The hermeneutics of symbols and philosophical reflections: I," trans. Denis Savage, pp. 287–314.

35 Ricœur, "Hermeneutics of symbols: I," pp. 289–90.

36 See Ricœur, *Symbolism of Evil*, pp. 347–57, and the previous chapter's discussion of Ricœur.

37 Soskice, *Metaphor*, p. 55.

38 Paul Ricœur, *Interpretation Theory: Discourse and the Surplus of Meaning* (Texas Christian University Press, Fort Worth, TX, 1976), p. 61. In a major work, Ricœur explored the use of symbol in Sigmund Freud's dream theory. *Paul Ricœur, Freud and Philosophy: An Essay on Interpretation*, trans. Denis Savage (Yale University Press, New Haven, CT, 1970). Concerning sacred symbols, he is drawing on the work of Mircea Eliade. See especially Ricœur, *Symbolism of Evil*, and Mircea Eliade, *The Sacred and the Profane: The Nature of Religion,* trans. Willard R. Trask (Harcourt, Brace, and Jovanovich, New York, Harvest/HBJ Book, 1959).

39 David Burrell, *Analogy and Philosophical Language* (Yale University Press, New Haven, CT, 1973), p. 162.

40 Ibid., pp. 259f.

41 Ibid., pp. 21f.

42 David Tracy, *The Analogical Imagination: Christian Theology and the Culture of Pluralism* (Crossroad, New York, 1981), p. 410.

43 Soskice, *Metaphor*, p. 64.

44 Sallie McFague, *Metaphorical Theology: Models of God in Religious Language* (Fortress Press, Philadelphia, PA, 1982), p. 13. Interestingly, she, too, notes that Burrell and Tracy's use of analogy is similar to her usage of metaphor, ibid., pp. 198–99, note 16.

45 A good, concise account of the turns in the history of parable interpretation with special attention to the shift towards metaphor is Norman Perrin, *Jesus and the Language of the Kingdom: Symbol and Metaphor in New Testament Interpretation* (Fortress Press, Philadelphia, PA, 1976), chapter 3.

For a more recent perspective that continues to affirm, however, the basic paradigm of metaphor for parable interpretation, see Bernard Brandon Scott, *Hear Then the Parable: A Commentary on the Parables of Jesus* (Fortress Press, Minneapolis, MN, 1989).

46 A similar judgment could be given to Rudolf Bultmann's influential "demythologizing" program. He was correct to see the limitations of a literal approach to myths, but he tended to reduce the meaning of New Testament myths to existential conclusions, leaving the myths behind. This problematic approach was followed in parable interpretation by Dan Otto Via Jr., *The Parables: Their Literary and Existential Dimension* (Fortress Press, Philadelphia, PA, 1967). Ricœur pointed out that the form of the myth cannot be so easily left behind; in other words, not only demythologizing but remythologizing is important. Paul Ricœur, "Preface to Bultmann," in *Essays on Biblical Interpretation*, ed. with an intro. Lewis S. Mudge (Fortress Press, Philadelphia, PA, 1980), pp. 49–72.

47 For further exploration, see Anthony C. Thiselton, "The new hermeneutic," in *New Testament Interpretation*, ed. I. Howard Marshall (Eerdmans, Grand Rapids, MI, William B, 1977), pp. 308–33.

48 John Dominic Crossan, *In Parables: The Challenge of the Historical Jesus* (Harper & Row, New York, 1973) and *The Dark Interval: Towards a Theology of Story* (Argus Communications, Allen, TX, 1975). See especially the latter, chapter 2.

49 Ricoeur, "Biblical hermeneutics," p. 114.

50 Ibid., 77, 126; and Ricoeur, *Essays on Biblical Interpretation*, ed. Lewis S. Mudge (Fortress Press, Philadelphia, TX, 1980), pp. 163–4.

51 Eberhard Jüngel, "Metaphorische Wahrheit," in *Metapher: Zur Hermeneutik religiöser Sprache*, by Paul Ricœur and Eberhard Jüngel (Chr. Kaiser Verlag, Munich, 1974), pp. 112–14.

52 Soskice, *Metaphor*, p. x.

53 Ibid., chapters 6–8. She unfairly characterizes Tracy as a non-realist since Tracy is one of the few theologians who is willing to make transcendental truth claims, but his language sometimes lends itself to an existentialist or subjectivist reading.

54 Ibid., p. 141.

55 Ibid., p. 136.

56 The primary work is McFague, *Metaphorical Theology*, but see also Sallie McFague TeSelle, *Speaking in Parables: A Study in Metaphor and Theology* (Fortress Press, Philadelphia, 1975), Sallie McFague, *Models of God: Theology for an Ecological, Nuclear Age* (Fortress Press, Philadelphia, 1987) and Sallie McFague, *The Body of God: An Ecological Theology* (Fortress Press, Minneapolis, 1993).

57 See particularly McFague, *Models of God*. As a counterpoint, some argue that God as father has privileged status as God's proper name, that is, it is

God's own self-designation, and thus other names in its place are disal-
lowed. See for example, Alvin F. Kimel Jr, "The God who likes His
Name: Holy Trinity, feminism, and the language of faith," in *Speaking the
Christian God: The Holy Trinity and the Challenge of Feminism*, ed. Alvin F.
Kimel Jr (William B. Eerdmans, Grand Rapids, MI, 1992), pp. 188–208
(the whole book contains essays that address this question). This important
discussion deserves longer discussion, but I would mention a few consid-
erations. First, the canonical status of God as father suggests that it indeed
has an irreplaceable status. Second, McFague's position, however, does
not necessarily imply the replacement of one metaphor by another so
much as the interpretation of one metaphor by another – or many others.
Father could thus be seen as an irreplaceable root metaphor in Scripture
that nevertheless licenses many other interpretive metaphors. Moreover,
the main issue is therefore not so much the word as the meaning. (If the
"word-sound" was so crucial, why would a translation into another
language be allowed, for example, the Greek *pater* to the English "father"
or German *Vater* or French *père*?) Third, we must add to the first point,
however, that a multitude of names and metaphors for God appear in the
canon, including numerous feminine allusions. Fourth, God as father
sometimes has a prominent status in the creeds of the church that it does
not have in Scripture. Fifth, its canonical status should not make us
unwary of the way the term has developed patriarchal connotations in
Christian history that are not necessarily present in Scripture and in fact in
our time often contradict its use in Scripture. Sixth, the sharp distinction
between father as a proper name or designator and father as a metaphorical
descriptor is debatable. Can we draw an easy line between this characteri-
zation of God and so many others, which Kimel sees as descriptive and
not as names? The merit of McFague's proposal, seventh, is that the
meaning of the biblical language, including God as father, can be discovered not only through prosaic explanation but through the profusion of
other metaphors that illuminate the biblical meaning for our time. In
Christian worship, prayer, and hymnody, God has been addressed by
many "metaphorical names," we might say, that do not necessarily con-
travene biblical terms but rather express and augment them. Soskice draws
on Ricœur to argue that over against rejection of father-language (and
Christianity) all together on the one hand and absolutizing this one term
over all others: "The other possibility that we have only begun to explore
is that while the paternal imagery remains in place in the historic literature
at least, it be seen not as a figure "well-known" and "invariable" but, as
Ricœur suggests, as an incomplete figure that traverses a number of
semantic levels. It is not a model there from eternity . . . but a mobile
symbol." Janet Martin Soskice, "Can a feminist call God "'Father?'",
*Speaking the Christian God*, p. 92. The treatment of the symbolic or

metaphorical use of the fatherhood of God by Ricœur to which she refers is "Fatherhood: from phantasm to symbol," in *Conflict of Interpretations*, pp. 468–97.

## Chapter 7    Narrative Theology

1   Gary L. Comstock, "Two types of narrative theology," *Journal of the American Academy of Religion*, 55 (Winter 1986), pp. 687–717. Other figures who are significant in narrative theology on the Continent are Eberhard Jüngel and Edward Schillebeeckx. In the Anglo-American world, Stanley Hauerwas is a significant narrativist who is difficult to categorize. His emphasis on the sufficiency of the Christian story draws him close to the Yale School. Alasdair MacIntyre is another extremely significant narrativist whose narrative anthropology draws him nearer to the Chicago School. Carol Christ and Mary McClintock Fulkerson among feminist thinkers, and James Cone among African-American thinkers, have also especially emphasized narrative. To treat others specifically like Sam Keen, Harvey Cox, and David Burrell would be to attempt in a chapter what full-length books have not done.

2   Paul Ricœur, "Metaphor and the central problem of hermeneutics," in *Hermeneutics and the Human Sciences: Essays on Language, Action, and Interpretation*, ed. and trans. John B. Thompson (Cambridge University Press, Cambridge, 1981), p. 175.

3   Ibid., p. 176.

4   Ibid., p. 177.

5   Paul Ricœur, *Time and Narrative*, trans. Kathleen Blamey and David Pellauer, 3 vols. (University of Chicago Press, Chicago, 1984–8).

6   Stephen Crites, "The narrative quality of experience," *Journal of the American Academy of Religion*, 34 (September 1971), pp. 291–311. This and other important essays on narrative theology are included in Stanley Hauerwas and L. Gregory Jones, eds., *Why Narrative? Readings in Narrative Theology* (William B. Eerdmans, Grand Rapids, MI, 1989).

7   Ricœur, *Time and Narrative*, vol. 1, p. xi.

8   Ibid., p. 3. Cf. p. 52.

9   Ricœur, "Metaphor," p. 180.

10   Ricœur, *Time and Narrative*, vol. 1, p. 53.

11   Ibid. Ricœur develops in the various volumes the way in which both historiography (vol. 1) and fiction (vol. 2) are fundamentally "mimetic" and that human identity is more particularly constituted by a continual "interweaving" between the two (vol. 3). "We identified the problem of refiguration with that of the interweaving reference between history and fiction, and said that human time stems from this interweaving in

the milieu of acting and suffering." Ricœur, *Time and Narrative*, vol. 3, p. 99.

12  Paul Ricœur, *Oneself as Another*, trans. Kathleen Blamey (University of Chicago Press, Chicago, IL, 1992).

13  Paul Ricœur, *Interpretation Theory: Discourse and the Surplus of Meaning* (Texas Christian University Press, Fort Worth, TX, 1976), p. 37. Ricœur repeats himself in *Time and Narrative*, vol. 1, p. 80, and makes similar remarks elsewhere.

14  See especially Langdon Gilkey, *Religion and the Scientific Future: Reflections on Myth, Science, and Theology*, The Deem Lectures (Harper & Row, New York, 1970). This approach to myth, which includes Paul Tillich and Ricœur as well as Gilkey, is critical of Rudolf Bultmann's demythologizing program, not in that it is critical of a literal approach to myth but in the way it leaves myth behind and fails to see the need for remythologizing.

15  David Tracy, *The Analogical Imagination: Christian Theology and the Culture of Pluralism* (Crossroad, New York, 1981).

16  Charles Wood is another of Frei's students who has carried the basic ideas forward in significant ways.

17  Hans W. Frei, *The Eclipse of Biblical Narrative: A Study in Eighteenth and Nineteenth Century Hermeneutics* (Yale University Press, New Haven, CT, 1974).

18  Ibid., p. 130.

19  Frei suggests fairly simply that in England where the realistic novel developed, there was no developed tradition of biblical criticism; in Germany there was a tradition of criticism and hermeneutics but no development of realistic prose narrative. Ibid., p. 142.

20  Ibid., p. 13.

21  Ibid., p. 27.

22  Ibid., p. 24.

23  Hans W. Frei, *The Identity of Jesus Christ: The Hermeneutical Bases of Dogmatic Theology* (Fortress Press, Philadelphia, PA, 1967), pp. 44–7.

24  Ibid., pp. vii, 6, 36.

25  Hans W. Frei, *Types of Christian Theology*, ed. George Hunsinger and William C. Placher (Yale University Press, New Haven, CT, 1992), p. 2.

26  Ibid.

27  Ibid., p. x. See also William C. Placher, *Unapologetic Theology: A Christian Voice in a Pluralistic Conversation* (Westminster/John Knox, Louisville, KY, 1989), Chapter 5; and "Paul Ricœur and postliberal theology: a conflict of interpretations?," *Modern Theology*, 4 (1987), pp. 35–52. Two other works that bring them closer together are Mark I. Wallace, *The Second Naiveté: Barth, Ricœur, and the New Yale Theology*, Studies in American Biblical Hermeneutics, vol. 6 (Mercer University Press, Macon, GA,

1990); and Charles J. Scalise, *Hermeneutics as Theological Prolegomena: A Canonical Approach*, Studies in American Biblical Hermeneutics, vol. 8 (Mercer University Press, Macon, GA, 1994). Scalise especially brings into the discussion the distinctive role of the scriptural canon that is an emphasis of Brevard Childs of Yale.

28 See particularly Hans W. Frei, "The 'Literal reading' of biblical narrative in the Christian tradition: does it stretch or will it break?" in *The Bible and Narrative Tradition*, ed. Frank McConnell (Oxford University Press, New York, 1986), pp. 36–77. In this influential essay, Frei takes on Ricœur, Gadamer, and Tracy on this point as well as being too subjective and "existential." As Placher, and I hope chapter 5, have pointed out, this is a one-sided reading of these thinkers. On the other hand, it is a pertinent critique of much in the hermeneutical tradition. What the ongoing discussion has shown is, ironically, how much the two schools are engaged in a common venture, although starting from different traditions.

29 Frei, *Eclipse*, pp. 34–5.

30 Kathryn E. Tanner, "Theology and the plain sense," in *Scriptural Authority and Narrative Interpretation*, ed. Garrett Green (Fortress Press, Philadelphia, PA, 1987), pp. 62–3. All of the essays in this book are devoted to critical reflection upon Frei's work.

31 Hans W. Frei, "An afterword: Eberhard Busch's biography of Karl Barth," in *Karl Barth in Re-View: Posthumous Works Reviewed and Assessed*, ed. H.-Martin Rumscheidt (Pickwick Press, Pittsburgh, PA, 1981), p. 104. This essay in general clearly reveals the importance of Barth to Frei.

32 George Lindbeck, *The Nature of Doctrine: Religion and Theology in a Postliberal Age* (Westminster Press, Philadelphia, PA, 1984).

33 Ibid., p. 16.

34 Ibid., p. 17.

35 Lindbeck therefore rejects Ricœur's intertextuality and also calls into question the emphasis on intertextuality among the poststructuralists, which we will examine in chapter 8. See ibid., p. 136, note 5. Frei, on the other hand, sees more similarity between his project and the poststructuralists. See his qualified approval in "The 'literal reading' of biblical narrative," pp. 55–60.

36 Lindbeck, *Nature of Doctrine*, p. 118.

37 Ibid., p. 121. Cf. David Kelsey, *The Uses of Scripture in Recent Theology* (Fortress Press, Philadelphia, PA, 1975), p. 48.

38 Lindbeck, *Nature of Doctrine*, p. 35.

39 Ibid., p. 39.

40 David Tracy says of *Nature of Doctrine*, "It is an especially welcome contribution from George Lindbeck, the major theological contributor in North America to genuine ecumenical dialogue among the major confes-

sions." "Lindbeck's new program for theology: a reflection," *The Thomist*, 49:3 (1985), p. 461.

41 Lindbeck, *Nature of Doctrine*, p. 55.

42 Ibid., pp. 80–1. Lindbeck and others have drawn heavily on this concept and other work by Clifford Geertz, a cultural anthropologist. See Clifford Geertz, "Thick description," in *The Interpretation of Cultures: Selected Essays* (Basic Books, New York, 1973), pp. 3–30. Geertz borrowed the term from Gilbert Ryle (see chapter 4 of this work).

43 See the entire issue of *Modern Theology*, 4 (January 1988), for critical consideration of this and other aspects of Lindbeck's proposal.

44 Lindbeck, *Nature of Doctrine*, p. 51.

45 Tracy sees Lindbeck as susceptible to the charges of relativism, confessionalism, and fideism – just as Lindbeck sees Tracy as susceptible to charges of foundationalism and reductionism. Tracy ties this tendency in both Frei and Linbeck back to Barth: "As his frequent references to Barth and his colleagues at Yale, H. Frei and P. Holmer, make clear, Lindbeck's substantive theological position is a methodologically sophisticated version of Barthian confessionalism. The hands may be the hands of Wittgenstein and Geertz but the voice is the voice of Karl Barth." Tracy, "Lindbeck's new program," p. 465.

46 For Gilkey, see especially *Naming the Whirlwind: The Renewal of God-Language* (Bobbs-Merrill, Indianapolis, IN, 1969). See David Tracy, *Blessed Rage for Order: The New Pluralism in Theology*, The Seabury Library of Contemporary Theology (Crossroad, New York, 1979), pp. 6–8; and *Analogical Imagination*, pp. 9, 64. Tracy qualified his strong transcendental claims to some extent in *Analogical Imagination* with its hermeneutical emphasis. He backed away even more so in *Plurality and Ambiguity: Hermeneutics, Religion, and Hope* (Harper & Row, San Francisco, CA, 1987). For a clear account of the differences on this score, see William C. Placher (before he began to see more continuity between the two schools), "Revisionist and postliberal theologies and the public character of theology," *The Thomist*, 49 (1985), pp. 392–416.

47 Tracy, "Lindbeck's new program," p. 463.

48 Thiemann characteristically cites Tracy's early work as an example of foundationalist theology. Ronald F. Thiemann, *Revelation and Theology: The Gospel as Narrated Promise* (University of Notre Dame Press, Notre Dame, IN, 1985), pp. 186–7, note 9.

49 Ibid., p. 74.

50 Ibid., p. 75.

51 A key essay on the Yale school's approach to apologetics is William Werpehowski, "Ad hoc apologetics," *Journal of Religion*, 66 (July 1986), pp. 282–301.

52  Thiemann, *Revelation and Theology*, chapters 6–7. See chapter 4 on speech-act theory for the category of "illocutionary force."

53  Ibid., p. 77.

54  Ibid., p. 75. He draws heavily in this section on the thought of W.V.O. Quine and J.S. Ullian, *The Web of Belief* (Random House, New York, 1970). Quine in turn was heavily influenced by the later Wittgenstein.

55  Thiemann, *Revelation and Theology*, p. 77.

56  Ibid., pp. 147–8.

57  Ronald F. Thiemann, *Constructing a Public Theology: The Church in a Pluralistic Culture* (Westminster/John Knox Press, Louisville, KY, 1991).

58  Ibid., pp. 21–5, 153.

59  Ibid., p. 82. He is in fact drawing here upon a more positive assessment of Barth as a model of *ad hoc* apologetics.

60  James Wm McClendon Jr, *Biography as Theology* (Abingdon Press, Nashville, TN, 1974).

61  As of this writing, two volumes have appeared: James Wm McClendon Jr, *Ethics: Systematic Theology* (Abingdon Press, Nashville, TN, 1986), vol. 1; and *Doctrine: Systematic Theology* (Abingdon Press, Nashville, TN, 1994), vol. 2.

62  McClendon, *Biography*, p. 37.

63  See particularly Michael Goldberg, *Theology and Narrative: A Critical Introduction* (Abingdon, Nashville, TN, 1982), chapter 6.

64  Ibid., p. 39. We might compare Ricœur's essay in which he considers several forms of "originary discourse" – prophetic, narrative, prescriptive, wisdom, and hymnic – upon which theology reflects. Paul Ricœur, "Toward a hermeneutic of the idea of revelation," in *Essays on Biblical Interpretation*, ed. with an intro. Lewish S. Mudge (Fortress Press, Philadelphia, PA, 1980), pp. 73–118.

65  Ibid., p. 204.

66  Michael Goldberg, "God, action, and narrative: which narrative? Which action? Which god?" in *Why Narrative*, p. 360.

67  George W. Stroup, *The Promise of Narrative Theology: Recovering the Gospel in the Church* (John Knox, Atlanta, GA, 1981), pp. 236f.

68  Goldberg, *Theology*, p. 214.

69  Ibid., p. 217.

70  Ibid., p. 220.

71  Ibid.

72  Goldberg, *Theology*, p. 240.

73  Terrence W. Tilley, *Story Theology*, preface by Robert McAfee Brown, Theology and Life Series, vol. 12 (Michael Glazier, Wilmington, DE, 1985), p. 211.

74  Ibid., p. 212.

75  Terrence W. Tilley, "Incommensurability, intratextuality, and fideism," *Modern Theology*, 5: 2 (January 1989), p. 94.

76  Ibid., pp. 94f.

77  Ibid., p. 102.

78  Ibid., p. 105. Cf. Comstock who referred to the two basic types as "pure" and "impure." "Two types," p. 688.

79  Tilley, "Incommensurability," p. 102.

## Chapter 8  Strucuralism and Poststructuralism

1  Ferdinand de Saussure, *Course in General Linguistics*, ed. Charles Bally and Albert Sechehave in collaboration with Albert Reidlinger, trans. Wade Baskin (Philosophical Library, New York, 1959). Other key linguists were L. Hjelmslev, Roman Jakobson, and Emile Benveniste.

2  The North American structural linguist Noam Chomsky distinguished similarly between linguistic "competence," which is the theory of language we possess, and linguistic "performance," which is the use we make of the theory.

3  De Saussure, *Course*, pp. 23f.

4  Roland Barthes, *Elements of Semiology*, trans. Annette Lavers and Colin Smith (Hill and Wang, New York, 1967). Originally published in 1964.

5  De Saussure had called for such a science, *Course*, p. 16. In Europe, following de Saussure, this approach tends to be called "semiology," whereas the US tradition, influenced by the work of C.S. Peirce, tends to call it "semiotics."

6  See Dan Sperber, "Claude Lévi-Strauss," in *Structuralism and Since: From Lévi-Strauss to Derrida*, ed. John Sturrock (Oxford University Press, Oxford, 1979), p. 49.

7  See, for example, John Sturrock, ed., Introduction, in *Structuralism and Since*, pp. 1–18.

8  Claude Lévi-Strauss, *Structural Anthropology*, trans. Claire Jacobson and Brooke Grundfest Schoepf (Basic Books, New York, 1963), vol. I, p. 46. Originally published in 1958.

9  Claude Lévi-Strauss, *The Elementary Structures of Kinship* (Beacon Press, Boston, MA, 1969).

10  Claude Lévi-Strauss, *The Raw and the Cooked*, trans. John and Doreen Weightman (Harper & Row, New York, 1969), p. 10. Originally published in 1964.

11  Ibid., p. 1.

12  See Lévi-Strauss, *Structural Anthropology*, trans. Monique Layton (Basic Books, New York, 1976), vol. 2, chapter 2, and *The Savage Mind* (University of Chicago Press, Chicago, IL, 1966; originally published in 1962).

13  Sperber, *Structuralism and Since*, pp. 20–1.

14  For the connection of these three, see Terence Hawkes, *Structuralism and Semiotics* (University of California Press, Berkeley, CA, 1977), chapter 3.

15  A.-J. Greimas, *Structural Semantics: An Attempt at a Method*, trans. Daniele McDowell, Ronald Schleifer, and Alan Velie (University of Nebraska Press, Lincoln, NB, 1983), p. 207. Originally published in 1966.

16  For a helpful account of the use of Greimas's work in parable analysis, see Norman Perrin, *Jesus and the Language of the Kingdom: Symbol and Metaphor in New Testament Interpretation* (Fortress Press, Philadelphia, PA, 1976), pp. 171–4. For more detail, see the discussion of the appropriation of structuralism in biblical studies by John Dominic Crossan and Dan Via Jr later in the text.

17  See Michel Foucault, *The Archeology of Knowledge and The Discourse on Language*, trans. A.M. Sheridan Smith (Pantheon Books, New York, 1972), especially the introduction, for an account of his early work. The accuracy of this self-assessment has been questioned, but he himself said at the time that his work was only "slowly taking shape in a discourse that I still feel to be so precarious and unsure," p. 17. To complicate matters, right after this book, he turned in a more poststructuralist direction. See Hubert L. Dreyfus and Paul Rabinow, *Michel Foucault: Beyond Structuralism and Hermeneutics*, 2nd edn (University of Chicago Press, Chicago, IL, 1983), for a detailed analysis of Foucault's movement from a position dominated more by structuralist conceptions to a position that they prefer not to call poststructuralist but "interpretive analytics." Most of the structuralists (and the poststructuralists), like the existentialists, were uncomfortable with labels, even though the family resemblance, at least, is readily apparent.

18  We can note the appearance of "archeology" in the titles and subtitles of his books in this period, a term which drops out afterwards. For an argument for the continuing value of Foucault's archeological approach, see Gary Gutting, *Michel Foucault: Archaeology of Scientific Reason*, Modern European Philosophy (Cambridge University Press, Cambridge, 1989).

19  Michel Foucault, *Madness and Civilization: A History of Insanity in the Age of Reason*, trans. Richard Howard (Vintage Books, New York, 1988; originally published in 1961).

20  Michel Foucault, *The Birth of the Clinic: An Archeology of Medical Perception*, trans. A.M. Sheridan Smith, World of Man (Vintage Books, New York, 1975; originally published in 1963).

21  Michel Foucault, *The Order of Things: An Archeology of the Human Sciences*, World of Man (Vintage Books, New York, 1973; originally published in 1966), pp. xxi–xxii. Foucault's sweeping historical claims have been severely challenged. See, for example, J.G. Merquior, *Foucault* (University of California Press, Berkeley, CA, 1985), pp. 56–75. His later recognition

(see below) of the pluralism of particular discourses and his acknowledged interest in non-historical issues mitigate somewhat the complaint.

22  See James Miller, *The Passion of Michel Foucault* (Simon and Schuster, New York, 1993), pp. 137–44, for an account of the close relationship that Foucault bore to Kant. Foucault was the first to translate Kant's *Anthropology from a Pragmatic Point of View* into French, and Miller points out how Foucault's work, though quite different in obvious respects, bears an uncanny resemblance to this book by Kant. The difference is that Foucault stressed the historical contingency of the a priori, making his work a kind of "critique of impure reason," p. 150.

23  Miller relates the sensation caused by the book and the way Foucault was catapulted into the public mind, ibid., pp. 148–64.

24  Foucault, *The Order of Things*, pp. 386–7.

25  See, for example, Lévi-Strauss, *Structural Anthropology*, chapter 11.

26  Ibid., p. 50.

27  See Hawkes, *Structuralism and Semiotics*, p. 95.

28  Jonathan Culler, *The Pursuit of Signs: Semiotics, Literature, Deconstruction* (Cornell University Press, Ithaca, NY, 1981), p. 33.

29  Ibid., p. 37.

30  This example is rather simplistic and avoids the challenge of logical positivism that "God exists" may in fact be nonsensical or the emphasis of many others we have considered, including the structuralists, that such a statement has to be considered within the larger structures, forms of life, or horizons in which it occurs. If we do not accept the positivistic strictures, however, the judgment of such a statement's truth value still goes far beyond awareness of the conditions that are set by these larger contexts.

31  Note the issues of *Semeia* that related to structuralist studies: "A structuralist approach to the parables," *Semeia*, 1 (1974); "The Good Samaritan," *Semeia*, 2 (1974); "Narrative discourse in structural exegesis: 1 John 6 and 1 Thessalonians," *Semeia*, 26 (1983).

32  Paul Ricœur, "The hermeneutical function of distantiation," in *Hermeneutics and the Human Sciences: Essays on Language, Action, and Interpretation*, ed. and trans. John B. Thompson (Cambridge University Press, Cambridge, 1981), p. 140.

33  Ibid.

34  Ibid., p. 134.

35  Ibid.

36  Paul Ricœur, "The model of the text: meaningful action considered as a text," in *Hermeneutics*, p. 198.

37  Ricœur, "Hermeneutical function," pp. 139, 143.

38  Ricœur, "Model of the text," pp. 216f.

39  Ibid., pp. 217f.

40 Anthony C. Thiselton, "Semantics and New Testament interpretation," in *New Testament Interpretation: Essays on Principles and Methods*, ed. I. Howard Marshall (Paternoster Press, Exeter, 1979), p. 76.

41 Ibid., p. 81 (his use of Greek has been transliterated for consistency's sake).

42 Ibid., pp. 87f.

43 Thiselton refers in this connection to the similar point made by Bertrand Russell's theory of descriptions, ibid., p. 85. See chapter 3 above.

44 On these last two points, see also the critique of the early Wittgenstein by the later Wittgenstein and the emphasis on the pervasiveness of "linguisticality" by Gadamer.

45 Daniel Patte, *What Is Structural Exegesis?* (Fortress Press, Philadelphia, PA, 1976), p. 1.

46 Ibid., p. 14.

47 John Dominic Crossan, *The Dark Interval: Towards a Theology of Story* (Argus Communications, Allen, TX, 1975).

48 Ibid., p. 49.

49 Ibid., p. 57. Similar kinds of reversals occur in Jesus's aphorisms such as "Blessed are the poor."

50 John Dominic Crossan, *In Parables: The Challenge of the Historical Jesus* (Harper & Row, New York, 1973).

51 See Crossan, *Dark Interval*, chapter 3; and the essays by Crossan and Dan Otto Via Jr in *Semeia*, 1 (1974), which is devoted entirely to structuralist approaches to the Parable of the Good Samaritan. See also the essay by Daniel Patte that is included.

52 Miller's biography of Foucault, *Michel Foucault*, points out that the articles in the late sixties in the main journal devoted to structuralism, *Tel Quel*, had so many diagrams and equations that it took on the appearance of a mathematics journal (p. 134). And Foucault himself confessed to bafflement at Lacan's "impenetrable prose" (p. 135).

53 This is Perrin's conclusion after lengthy consideration of the value of structuralism for parable research. *Jesus*, pp. 175–81.

54 Note the account of Derrida's North American reception initially as a structuralist in Alan Jacobs, "Deconstruction," in *Contemporary Literary Theory: A Christian Appraisal*, ed. Clarence Walhout and Leland Ryken (William B. Eerdmans, Grand Rapids, MI, 1991), pp. 172–3.

55 Modernity is variously defined, as the period from modern philosophy beginning with Descartes in the seventeenth century (which I favor), as the Enlightenment period in the eighteenth century, as the period from the French Revolution (roughly since the nineteenth century), and as the first half of the twentieth century.

56 See Jacques Derrida, *Margins of Philosophy*, trans. Alan Bass (University of Chicago Press, Chicago, IL, 1982), pp. 3–27. Originally published in 1972.

57  Ibid., p. 247.

58  On Rousseau, de Saussure, Heidegger, and Lévi-Strauss, see Jacques Derrida, *Of Grammatology*, trans. Gayatri Chakravorty Spivak (Johns Hopkins University Press, Baltimore, MD, 1974; originally published in 1967). On Edmund Husserl, see *Speech and Phenomena, and Other Essays on Husserl's Theory of Signs*, trans. David B. Allison (Northwestern University Press, Evanston, IL, 1973; originally published in 1967). On Plato, see *Dissemination*, trans. with an intro. Barbara Johnson (University of Chicago Press, Chicago, IL, 1981; originally published in 1972), pp. 62–171.

59  On the last point, see Derrida's meditation on the pervasiveness of metaphor in "White mythology: metaphor in the text of philosophy," in *Margins of Philosophy*, pp. 207–71. It compares with the emphasis on metaphor in chapter 6, albeit in a more radicalized version.

60  Derrida, *Of Grammatology*, p. 158.

61  Christopher Norris, *Deconstruction: Theory and Practice*, New Accents (Methuen, London, 1982), p. 19.

62  For example, see Derrida, *Dissemination*, pp. 62–171.

63  Jacques Derrida, *Aporias*, trans. Thomas Dutoit, *Meridian: Crossing Aesthetics* (Stanford: Stanford University Press, originally published in 1993), p. 16.

64  In fact, Derrida's influence in the English-speaking world has been more in literature and religion departments than in philosophy *per se*.

65  See Christopher Norris, *Derrida* (Harvard University Press, Cambridge, MA, 1987), pp. 228–30.

66  We may contrast his intertextuality with the "intratextuality" of Lindbeck (chapter 7) and Ricœur's notion that our identity is framed by all the texts that we have read. Derrida again is more chaotic and anarchic.

67  Perhaps the most dramatic example is Jacques Derrida, *Glas*, trans. John P. Leavey Jr, and Richard Rand (University of Nebraska Press, Lincoln, NB, 1986; originally published in 1974). Philosophic commentary on Hegel and literary commentary on Genet begin in midstream and are aligned in separate columns on the same page, in different size type, with no obvious connection other than the "structural" one.

68  Diane P. Michelfelder, and Richard E. Palmer, eds., *Dialogue and Deconstruction: The Gadamer–Derrida Encounter* (State University of New York Press, New York, 1989).

69  Jacques Derrida, *Spurs: Nietzsche's Styles*, trans. Barbara Harlow (University of Chicago Press, Chicago, IL, 1979), p. 101.

70  See Michel Foucault, *Discipline and Punish: The Birth of the Prison*, trans. Alan Sheridan (Vintage Books, New York, 1979; originally published in 1975); *Power/Knowledge: Selected Interviews and Other Writings 1972–1977*, ed. Colin Gordon, trans. Colin Gordon, Leo Marshall, John Mepham, and Kate Soper (Pantheon Books, New York, 1980); and *The History of*

*Sexuality,* trans. Robert Hurley, 3 vols. (Vintage Books, New York, 1980–86).

71 Foucault, *Discipline and Punish,* p. 26. Derrida had criticized Foucault's earlier penchant for seeming to write outside of history in favor of his deconstructive working from within. Derrida, "Cogito and the history of madness," in *Writing and Difference,* pp. 31–63. Foucault in his later work moves more in Derrida's direction, although he responded severely to Derrida's critique by rejecting Derrida's project as naive, apolitical game playing. See Miller, *Michel Foucault,* pp. 118–20. Both in fact have been charged with irresponsible frivolity, yet it is not difficult to show that they are much more politically concerned than they are given credit for.

72 See an account of his unpublished Howison lectures, given at the University of California at Berkeley in 1980, which explore the Roman philosopher Seneca and the Christian monk John Cassian in Miller, *Michel Foucault,* pp. 321–4.

73 Gutting emphasizes the moral concern of Foucault's work, as well as the more constructive possibilities: *Archeology,* pp. 1–4. For details of his active political involvement, see Didier Eribon, *Michel Foucault,* trans. Betsy Wing (Harvard University Press, Cambridge, MA, 1991), chapters 16–20. See Miller, *Michel Foucault,* pp. 315–16, for an account of the way he turned from a more anarchic to a more neo-liberal concern for individual freedoms.

74 On the ethical and political dimensions of Derrida, see Norris, *Derrida,* chapter 8.

75 For example, see the critique by Seyla Benhabib, the Habermasian mentioned in chapter 5, Seyla Benhabib, *Situating the Self: Gender, Community, and Postmodernism in Contemporary Ethics* (Routledge, New York, 1992), pp. 16, 224–5; and the essays in Linda Nicholson, ed., *Feminism/Postmodernism,* Thinking Gender (Routledge, New York, 1990).

76 Susan J. Hekman, *Gender and Knowledge: Elements of a Postmodern Feminism,* Northeastern Series in Feminist Theory (Northeastern University Press, Boston, MA, 1990), p. 189. Cf. Chris Weedon, *Feminist Practice and Poststructuralist Theory* (Basil Blackwell, Oxford, 1987).

77 Cf. the discussion of Ricœur in particular in chapter 5, who sees selfhood as a task and goal of interpretation, not as innately given.

78 For an example of this kind of appropriation of poststructuralism in a constructive way for theology, see Mary McClintock Fulkerson, *Changing the Subject: Women's Discourses and Feminist Theology* (Fortress Press, Minneapolis, MN, 1994).

79 See the discussions in Hekman, *Gender and Knowledge,* pp. 82–94, 145–51; and Weedon, *Feminist Practice,* pp. 63–73, 88–91, 165–6. For individual works, see Hélène Cixous and Catherine Clement, *The Newly Born Woman,* trans. Betsy Wing (University of Minnesota Press, Minneapolis,

MN, 1986); Luce Irigaray, *Speculum of the Other Woman*, trans. Gillian C. Gill (Cornell University Press, Ithaca, NY, 1985), and *This Sex Which Is Not One*, trans. Catherine Porter (Cornell University Press, Ithaca, NY, 1985); and Julia Kristeva, *Revolution in Poetic Language*, trans. Margaret Waller (Columbia University Press, New York, 1984; originally published in 1979); and *In the Beginning Was Love: Psychoanalysis and Faith* (Columbia University Press, New York, 1987).

80  For example, see Kristeva, *Revolution in Poetic Language*.

81  Julia Kristeva, "Women's time," in *The Kristeva Reader*, ed. Toril Moi (Columbia University Press, New York, 1986; originally published in 1979), pp. 187–213.

82  Hekman, *Gender and Knowledge*, pp. 90–1.

83  Anthony C. Thiselton, *New Horizons in Hermeneutics: The Theory and Practice of Transforming Biblical Reading* (Zondervan, Grand Rapids, MI, 1992), p. 21. As I mention in the preface, this is a magisterial, detailed work on the interface of contemporary hermeneutics and biblical studies. I find much affinity with his work, but this is a point where I think he fails to see a less radical reading of the poststructuralists and the similarity of their work with the work of Gadamer, Ricœur, and the later Wittgenstein, whom Thiselton affirms to a great extent. He is not alone in his negative reading, however, for several in philosophy read them similarly. Similar criticisms come from the critical theorists Jürgen Habermas, *The Philosophical Discourse of Modernity: Twelve Lectures*, trans. Frederick Lawrence, Studies in Contemporary German Social Thought (MIT Press, Cambridge, MA, 1987; originally published in 1985); David Harvey, *The Condition of Postmodernity: An Enquiry into the Origins of Cultural Change* (Basil Blackwell, Oxford, 1989); and Christopher Norris, *What's Wrong with Postmodernism? Critical Theory and the Ends of Philosophy* (Johns Hopkins University Press, Baltimore, MD, 1990). See also Allan Megill, *Prophets of Extremity: Nietzsche, Heidegger, Foucault, Derrida* (University of California Press, Berkeley, CA, 1985).

84  Thiselton, *New Horizons*, p. 113.

85  Mark C. Taylor, *Deconstructing Theology*, American Academy of Religion Studies in Religion, vol. 28 (Crossroad and Scholars Press, New York, 1982), p. 90.

86  Ibid., p. 91.

87  See for example in "Gnicart, tracing: inter alios", in ibid., pp. 107–29.

88  Ibid., p. 89. See his discussion of negative theology as an intertextual interpretation of Derrida's discussion of negative theology in "nO nOt nO," in *nOts*, Religion and Postmodernism (University of Chicago Press, Chicago, IL, 1993), pp. 28–54.

89  John D. Caputo, "The good news about alterity: Derrida and theology," *Faith and Philosophy*, 10 (October 1993), pp. 453–4.

90 Jacques Derrida, "Jacques Derrida," in *Dialogues with Contemporary Continental Thinkers: The Phenomenological Heritage*, ed. Richard Kearney (Manchester University Press, Manchester, 1984), pp. 123–4.

91 While there is merit in Caputo's observation, I would add two cautions: we should be careful about overdrawing a distinction in Jewish thought between justice and law, and the Western tradition of law to which Derrida refers is more Roman than Greek. Caputo rightly points out that Derrida's ethical emphasis on the significance of the other is rooted on the work of Emmanuel Levinas, a Jewish rabbi-philosopher. For a helpful critical discussion of Derrida's connection with Levinas and the Jewish tradition, see Megill, *Prophets of Extremity*, pp. 305–20.

92 The same theme of doing justice to the "other" over against the "same" is found in Levinas's work and in Paul Ricœur's Gifford Lectures, *Oneself as Another* (see above, chapter 5).

93 Caputo, "Alterity," p. 459. See also Harold Coward and Toby Foshay, eds., *Derrida and Negative Theology* (State University of New York Press, Albany, 1992).

94 Stephen D. Moore, *Poststructuralism and the New Testament: Derrida and Foucault at the Foot of the Cross* (Fortress Press, Minneapolis, MN, 1994).

95 Note his reading of the Samaritan woman story in John 4; ibid., chapter 2.

96 See the articles in *Semeia*: "Derrida and biblical studies," *Semeia*, 23 (1982); "Text and textuality," 40 (1987); "Poststructuralism, criticism, and the Bible: text/history/discourse," *Semeia*, 51 (1990); "Poststructuralism as exegesis," *Semeia*, 54 (1991); and "Ideological criticism of biblical texts," *Semeia*, 59 (1992).

97 An intriguing example of the way they could be appropriated in this regard is Merold Westphal's appropriation of the three masters of suspicion, Marx, Freud, and Nietzsche, as "reading for Lent" in order to unmask the sin in the very chambers of religion. *Suspicion and Faith: The Religious Uses of Modern Atheism* (William B. Eerdmans, Grand Rapids, MI, 1993).

## Chapter 9  Conclusion: A Changing Paradigm

1 Ludwig Wittgenstein, *Philosophical Investigations*, trans. G.E.M. Anscombe, 3rd edn (Macmillan, New York, 1958), paragraph 18.

2 Ibid., p. 107.

3 Ibid., p. 38.

4 Alasdair MacIntyre, *Whose Justice? Which Rationality?* (University of Notre Dame Press, Notre Dame, IN, 1988), pp. 335, 346.

5  Jean-François Lyotard, *The Postmodern Condition: A Report on Knowledge*, trans. Geoff Bennington and Frian Massumi, Theory and History of Literature, vol. 10 (University of Minnesota Press, Minneapolis, MN, 1984), p. xxiv.

# Recommended Reading

John L. Austin, *How to Do Things with Words*, ed. J.O. Urmson and Marina Sbisà, 2nd edn (Harvard University Press, Cambridge, MA, 1975). One of the most influential essays in this century, which develops the argument for speech-act theory.

A.J. Ayer, *Language, Truth, and Logic*, 2nd edn (Dover Publications, New York, 1946). This is the classic English introduction to logical positivism.

Adela Yarbro Collins, ed., *Feminist Perspectives on Biblical Scholarship*, Biblical Scholarship in North America, vol. 10 (Scholars Press, Chico, CA, 1985). Contains essays that deal with feminist hermeneutical concerns in biblical studies.

Gary L. Comstock, "Two types of narrative theology," *Journal of the American Academy of Religion*, 55 (Winter 1986), pp. 687–717. The most commonly cited essay on the Chicago and Yale Schools of narrative theology.

Frederick Copleston, *A History of Philosophy*, vols. 1–9 (Image Books, Garden City, NY, 1985), and W.T. Jones, *The Classical Mind: A History of Western Philosophy*, 5 vols., 2nd edn (Harcourt Brace Jovanovich, New York, 1970). These are the standard English introductions to the history of philosophy, and they complement each other well. The first three volumes of Copleston, which treat ancient and medieval philosophy, are especially helpful for the purposes of this book.

Frederick Ferré, *Language, Logic, and God* (University of Chicago Press, Chicago, IL, 1961). This is still probably the best treatment of the philosophy of religious language, but it obviously does not deal with later movements. It treats Anglo-American language philosophy and some of the hermeneutical issues in neo-orthodox theology.

Antony Flew and Alasdair MacIntyre, eds., *New Essays in Philosophical Theology* (SCM Press, London, 1955). This books contains the valuable texts of the original *University* discussion as well as several others involved in analytical philosophy's challenge to religion.

Michel Foucault, *Discipline and Punish: The Birth of the Prison*, trans. Alan Sheridan (Vintage Books, New York, 1979). A representative work by one of the key structurallist/poststructuralist thinkers, particularly exemplifying Foucault's genealogical approach.

Hans W. Frei, *The Eclipse of Biblical Narrative: A Study in Eighteenth and Nineteenth Century Hermeneutics* (Yale University Press, New Haven, 1974). A ground-breaking work on the subject and the main inspiration for the Yale School of narrative theology.

Mary McClintock Fulkerson, *Changing the Subject: Women's Discourses and Feminist Theology* (Fortress Press, Minneapolis, 1994). An intriguing appropriation of poststructuralist thought for feminist theology.

Hans-Georg Gadamer, *Truth and Method*, translation revised by Joel Weinsheimer and Donald G. Marshall, rev. edn (Crossroad, New York, 1991). Gadamer's *magnum opus* and the key work of hermeneutical philosophy.

Michael Goldberg, *Theology and Narrative: A Critical Introduction* (Abingdon, Nashville, TN, 1982). A very helpful overview of the field along with an insightful correlation with speech-act theory.

Robert Grant and David Tracy, *A Short History of the Interpretation of the Bible*, 2nd edn (Fortress Press, Philadelphia, 1984). This is an excellent account of the history of hermeneutics of biblical interpretation.

Jürgen Habermas, "The hermeneutic claim to universality," in *Contemporary Hermeneutics: Hermeneutics as Method, Philosophy, and Critique*, ed. Josef Bleicher (Routledge & Kegan Paul, London, 1980), pp. 181–211. The important essay in which Habermas sets out his alternative to Gadamer from the perspective of critical theory.

Stanley Hauerwas and L. Gregory Jones, eds., *Why Narrative? Readings in Narrative Theology* (William B. Eerdmans, Grand Rapids, MI, 1989). An excellent collection of some of the most significant writing on narrative theology.

Susan J. Hekman, *Gender and Knowledge: Elements of a Postmodern Feminism*, Northeastern Series in Feminist Theory (Northeastern University Press, Boston, 1990). Provides an important synthesis between poststructuralist philosophy, hermeneutical philosophy, and feminist philosophy.

Mark Johnson, ed., *Philosophical Perspectives on Metaphor* (University of Minnesota Press, Minneapolis, 1981). A collection of many key essays on a revised view of metaphor in this century. See especially the introduction by Johnson for a historical overview.

George Lindbeck, *The Nature of Doctrine: Religion and Theology in a Postliberal Age* (Westminister Press, Philadelphia, 1984). One of the most influential theological books in the eighties and probably the key text on narrative theology: clear, concise, provocative.

James Wm McClendon Jr, *Biography as Theology* (Abingdon Press, Nashville, TN, 1974). A clear and pathbreaking presentation of the importance of biography for theology.

James Wm McClendon Jr, and James M. Smith, *Convictions: Defusing Religious Relativism*, rev. edn (Trinity Press International, Valley Forge, PA, 1994). The updated version of their ground-breaking work in applying speech-act theory to religious convictions.

Sallie McFague, *Metaphorical Theology: Models of God in Religious Language* (Fortress Press, Philadelphia, PA, 1982). The key work elaborating the significance of a philosophy of metaphor for systematic theology.

Basil Mitchell, ed., *The Philosophy of Religion*, Oxford Readings in Philosophy (Oxford University Press, Oxford, 1971). This work, too, contains the *University* discussion, along with John Hick's later contribution as well as other related essays.

Ray Monk, *Ludwig Wittgenstein: The Duty of Genius* (Free Press, New York, 1990). This biography of Wittgenstein is a readable introduction to the thicker context of his life and work while providing a helpful introduction to the philosophical issues.

Richard E. Palmer, *Hermeneutics: Interpretation Theory in Schleiermacher, Dilthey, Heidegger, and Gadamer*, Northwestern University Studies in Phenomenology and Existential Philosophy (Northwestern University Press, Evanston, IL, 1969). An important earlier introductory work to the continental tradition of hermeneutical philosophy.

Daniel Patte, *What Is Structural Exegesis?* (Fortress Press, Philadelphia, 1976). Introduces a constructive appropriation of structuralism for biblical studies.

Plato, *The Republic*, books 2–3, 5–7, and *The Seventh Letter*, in *The Dialogues of Plato*, Great Books of the Western World (Encyclopedia Britannica, Chicago, 1952). These are classic examples of the views of language that have molded the Western mind.

Norman Perrin, *Jesus and the Language of the Kingdom: Symbol and Metaphor in New Testament Interpretation* (Fortress Press, Philadelphia, 1976). Introduces recent work on symbol and on parable interpretation in light of newer approaches to metaphor.

Ian T. Ramsey, *Religious Language* (SCM Press, London, 1957). This book contains the gist of Ramsey's creative exploration of the uses of religious language.

Paul Ricœur, *Hermeneutics and the Human Sciences: Essays on Language, Action, and Interpretation*, ed. and trans. John B. Thompson (Cambridge University Press, Cambridge, 1981). One of the best collections of Ricœur's essays for the issue of hermeneutics, which also serves as an introduction to the historical background of hermeneutical philosophy.

Janet Martin Soskice, *Metaphor and Religious Language* (Clarendon Press, Oxford, 1985). A helpful and influential study of metaphor in relation to the philosophy of religious language.

Walter T. Stace, *The Teachings of the Mystics* (Mentor, New York, 1960). A helpful introduction to the mystical tradition.

John Sturrock, ed., *Structuralism and Since: From Lévi-Strauss to Derrida* (Oxford University Press, Oxford, 1979). A valuable introduction to key structuralist and poststructuralist thinkers.

Susan R. Suleiman and Inge Crosman, eds., *The Reader in the Text: Essays on Audience and Interpretation* (Princeton University Press, Princeton, 1980). Contains important material by Wolfgang Iser as well as other important essays on reader–response theory.

Mark C. Taylor, *Deconstructing Theology*, American Academy of Religion Studies in Religion, vol. 28 (Crossroad and Scholars Press, New York, 1982). An important work by one of the most influential theologians who have appropriated deconstructionist or poststructuralist philosophy.

Anthony C. Thiselton, *New Horizons in Hermeneutics* (Zondervan, Grand Rapids, MI, 1992). In chapters 4–6, Thiselton gives a helpful account of historical issues in hermeneutics and relates them to detailed accounts of current philosophical movements impinging on hermeneutics.

Paul Tillich, *Dynamics of Faith*, World Perspectives Series, vol. 10 (Harper & Brothers, New York, 1958), chapter 3. A pivotal essay on symbol.

Stephen Toulmin, *Cosmopolis: The Hidden Agenda of Modernity* (Free Press, New York, 1990). This is a fresh account of the nature of modernity and a possible "postmodernity" with special attention to the role of language.

David Tracy, *The Analogical Imagination: Christian Theology and the Culture of Pluralism* (Crossroad, New York, 1981). One of the primary theological appropriations of the hermeneutical philosophy of Gadamer and Ricœur.

John Wisdom, "Gods," in *Contemporary Analytic and Linguistic Philosophies*, ed. E.D. Klemke (Prometheus Books, Buffalo, NY, 1983), pp. 338–52. This key essay by Wisdom is an insightful and provocative approach to religious and philosophical language, and it contains the parable of the invisible gardener later used by Antony Flew.

Ludwig Wittgenstein, *Tractatus Logico-Philosophicus*, trans. D.F. Pears and B.F. Pears and B.F. McGuinness, intro. Bertrand Russell (Routledge & Kegan Paul, London, 1961; originally published in English in 1922). This is a difficult work in many places, but major parts are also very accessible. It is one of the most significant works of this century and is relatively concise.

Ludwig Wittgenstein, *Philosophical Investigations*, trans. G.E.M. Anscombe

(Macmillan, New York, 1958); Ludwig Wittgenstein, *On Certainty*, ed. G.E.M. Anscombe and G.H. von Wright, trans. Denis Paul and G.E.M. Anscombe (Harper Torchbooks, New York, 1969). These two works from Wittgenstein's later period are indispensable for understanding him and the Anglo-American philosophy of language.

# Index

Abelard, Peter, 30
afterlife: verification, 55–7
Alexandrian school of exegesis, 31, 32, 33, 87
allegory
  allegorical exegesis, 31–3, 34–5
  metaphor and, 113, 114
  parables of Jesus as, 127–8
analogy, 122, 124–7, 133
  analogical way, 7, 15, 23–9, 35, 193, 200
  argument against, 21
  historical-critical approach to, 36, 202
anthropology, 166, 167
Antiochene school of exegesis, 31, 33–4, 87
Aquinas, St Thomas, 112, 160, 194
  and analogy, 15, 23–7, 28, 35, 119, 124–5, 130
  influences on, 19, 33–4
  on knowledge and faith, 12
  and metaphor, 114
  and moderate realism, 30
  and the negative way, 18, 20
Aristotle, 9, 30, 120, 137–8
  and figurative language, 10, 11, 113
  on knowledge and faith, 12
Augustine, St, 1, 12, 29, 137, 160, 193
  and allegory, 32

influences on, 17, 33
  Wittgenstein and, 59–60
Austen, Jane, 108
Austin, John L., 13, 79–82, 83, 197
Ayer, A.J., 44–6

Barbour, Ian, 119
Barth, Karl, 28, 144–5, 160
Barthes, Roland, 163, 166, 180
behaviorism, 66, 166
Being-itself, 90–1
  God as, 21–3
belief, religious, 54, 73–4, 202
  biography and, 154–5
  convictional language, 83–5, 202
  falsification challenge, 47–58
  Wittgenstein and, 63–4, 67–8, 69–72
  see also faith
Benhabib, Seyla, 99
Bible/biblical studies
  figurative language in, 11, 20–1, 113–14
  historical-critical approach to, 33, 35–6, 88, 102–3, 104, 164
  and narrative theology, 7, 134–5, 136, 139–53, 156–9
  reader-response theory and, 107, 109–10
  Reformers and, 34
  structuralism and, 7, 163, 168–9

251

Bible/biblical studies (*cont.*)
  *see also* exegesis;
    hermeneutics; religious
    language; theology
binary oppositions, 167–8
biography, 135, 153, 154–62
Black, Max, 114–16, 119
Braithwaite, Richard, 72, 203
Buddhism, Zen: *koan*, 19–20
Bultmann, Rudolf, 219 n10, 230
  n46, 233 n14
Burrell, David, 28–9, 124–6, 133,
  210 n36

Californian School of narrative
  theology, 135, 153, 154–62
Calvin, John, 34, 141
Caputo, John D., 190–2
Carnap, Rudolf, 42, 44, 45, 46, 213
  n31
Chicago School of narrative
  theology, 134–9, 149, 153, 161
  contrasted with Yale School, 140,
    142, 143, 144, 145, 150
Childs, Brevard, 139
Chomsky, Noam, 237 n2
Christology, 147
Cixous, Hélène, 188
*Cloud of Unknowing, The*, 17
Coleridge, Samuel Taylor, 226 n5
Comstock, Gary, 134
conceptualism, 30
convictional language, 83–5, 202
Crites, Stephen, 137
critical hermeneutics, 96–107
Crombie, Ian, 78–9
Crossan, John Dominic, 128–9, 131,
  178–80
Culler, Jonathan, 6, 172–3
Culpepper, Alan, 109–10
Cunningham, Richard B., ix, xi
Cupitt, Don, 131

*Dasein*, 91
Davidson, Donald, 118

death-of-God movement, 189–90
deconstruction, 5, 7, 180, 182–4,
  186, 188–92
  *see also* poststructuralism
Derrida, Jacques, 121, 180–4, 186,
  198
  readings of, 189–92
Descartes, René, 12, 181, 188
"descriptive fallacy," 13, 80, 197
Dewey, John, 207 n20
Dilthey, Wilhelm, 89–90, 91, 92
Dionysius II, 207 n17
Dionysius the Areopagite, 17–19
discourse ethic, 96–7
Dodd, C. H., 127–8

Ebeling, Gerhard, 128
Eckhart, Meister, 15–16, 17
empiricism
  British, 38, 75
  logical empiricism, 38, 75–6
equivocal language, 195, 200, 203
  negative way, 15–21, 23, 76,
    189–92, 193
Erigena, John Scotus, 29
"eschatological verification," 55–6
etymology, 176, 177–8
evil, 16, 25, 48, 52
  symbolism and, 101, 123
exegesis of Scripture, 14–15, 31–6,
  103, 134
  Alexandrian school of, 31, 32, 33,
    87
  allegorical, 31–2, 34–5
  Antiochene school of, 31, 33–4,
    87
  four-fold, 7, 32–3, 33–4
  metaphor in, 127–9
  structuralism and, 178, 180
  *see also* Bible/biblical studies;
    hermeneutics
existentialism, 4–5, 163, 164,
  166–7
  in hermeneutics, 90–1, 104, 174

faith, 12, 104, 153

*see also* belief, religious; fideism
falsification challenge, 7, 37, 47–58,
    73–4, 200
    falsification principle, 46–7, 56
    responses to, 50–8, 67
    *see also* verification principle
feminist philosophy, xi, 5, 7, 132–3,
    230–2 n57
    feminist hermeneutics, 99, 192
    and poststructuralism, 187–8
Ferré, Frederick, ix, 25, 27
fideism, 160, 162
    Wittgensteinian, 67, 69–72, 73,
    145, 148
figurative language, 9, 11, 20–1
    *see also* allegory; analogy;
    metaphor; symbolism
Flew, Anthony: falsification
    challenge, 37, 47–50, 69, 73,
    76
    responses to, 50–8, 67
Foucault, Michel
    and poststructuralism, 180–1,
    184–6, 192
    and structuralism, 163, 166,
    169–71, 172
foundationalism *see* Yale School
Frankfurt school of critical theory,
    96, 221 n43
Frege, Gottlob, 224 n77
Frei, Hans, 139, 140–4, 146, 147,
    149, 150, 157, 159
Freudian psychoanalysis, 96, 97, 106,
    223 n66
Fuchs, Ernst, 128
functional analysis, 37
Funk, Robert, 128

Gadamer, Hans-Georg, 87, 128,
    142, 149, 198, 199, 201
    Derrida and, 184
    Frei rejects, 143
    Habermas and, 96–9, 105–6
    ontological hermeneutics, 90,
    92–5

metaphor and, 120
Ricœur and, 100–1, 104, 105–6,
    107
Genesis story, 1–2, 156
Gerhart, Mary, 116
Gilkey, Langdon, 2–3, 135, 143,
    149
    religious symbolism and, 122,
    123, 139
Gill, Jerry, 65
Gnosticism, 31–2
God
    as Being-itself, 21–3
    God-talk, 78
    metaphor and, 130–3
    name(s) of, 17, 20
    *see also* belief, religious; evil;
    falsification challenge
Gödel, Kurt, 42
Goldberg, Michael, 80, 154, 155–9,
    160–1
Gospels, 36, 95, 109–10, 151,
    156–7, 158
Grant, Robert, 33
Greek philosophy, 8–12, 32
    *see also* Aristotle; Plato
Greimas, A.J., 166, 167, 168, 179

Habermas, Jürgen, 96–8, 99, 105
Hare, Richard, 50–2, 69, 76
Hegel, G. W. F., 100, 164
Heidegger, Martin, 87, 93–4,
    100–1, 128, 137
    *Being and Time*, 90–2
Hekman, Susan, 187, 188
Henry, Carl, 21
Heraclitus, 8
hermeneutics, 4–5, 7, 87–111, 193,
    197, 201
    critical, 96–107
    deconstruction and, 184, 188–92
    feminist, 99, 192
    general, 87–90, 142
    hermeneutical arc, 101, 104, 105,
    139

hermeneutics (*cont.*):
  hermeneutical circle, 33, 88–9, 92, 136
  legal, 87, 94
  methodology of, 88, 89, 92, 95, 99, 100, 102–3, 110, 111
  narrative and, 134–9, 148–9, 199
  New Hermeneutic movement, 128
  ontological, 90–5, 100
  reader-response theory and, 107–11
  regional, 87, 142
  Ricœur and, 100–7, 173, 174–5
  Romantic, 88, 90, 102, 109, 136–7, 174
  structuralism and, 173–5
  of suspicion, 106, 153, 203
  *see also* Bible/biblical studies; exegesis; narrative theology
Hesse, Mary, 119
Hick, John: parable, 55–8, 76
historical approaches to religious language, 14–36
  literal and allegorical exegesis, 31–6
  three traditional ways, 15–29
  universals controversy, 29–31
historical-critical approach to biblical studies, 33, 35–6, 88, 102–3, 104, 164
Hobbes, Thomas, 114
Holmer, Paul, 139
Hume, David, 4, 26–7, 45
  Hume's fork, 38, 39
Husserl, Edmund, 90–1, 137, 182
Huyssteen, Wentzel van, 42

I-language, 75
ideal speech situation, 96, 97
ideology critique, 96, 102, 105, 106, 143, 153, 203
  feminist, 99
Ingarden, Roman, 225 n94
intratextual theology, 145–6, 160–1

Irenaeus, St, 31–2, 160
Irigaray, Luce, 188
Iser, Wolfgang, 108–9, 110

James, William, 54
Jeremias, Joachim, 127–8
Jesus
  as exegete, 31
  identity of, 141
  parables of, 7, 127–9, 156, 158, 168–9, 178–9, 201
  sayings of, 35, 36, 115
Joad, C. E. M., 213–14 n35
Johnson, Elizabeth A., 210 n36
Johnson, Mark, 5, 112, 120, 121, 126, 195
Jülicher, Adolf, 127–8
Jüngel, Eberhard, 129, 130

Kant, Immanuel, 5, 26–7, 90, 100, 239 n22
Keller, Helen, 3
Kelsey, David, 139, 146
Kierkegaard, Søren, 2
Kimel, Alvin F. Jr, 231 n57
Kittay, Eva Feder, 118
knowledge: need for clarity and certainty in, 11–12
*koan* (Zen Buddhist riddle), 19–20
Koran, 88
Krieger, Murray, 109–10
Kristeva, Julia, 188

Lakoff, George, 120, 121, 126, 195
language, philosophy of, 4–13
  *see also individual movements and philosophers* language games, 59–86, 198
  later Wittgenstein, 59–67
  religious
  language as cognitive, 72–9
  religious language as noncognitive, 67–72
  speech-act theory, 79–86
  *see also* Wittgenstein

legal hermeneutics, 87, 94
Lévi-Strauss, Claude, 163, 166, 179, 180, 182
  on kinship, 167–8, 171
Levinas, Emmanuel, 244 n91
Lindbeck, George, 139, 143, 144, 145–50, 160, 201
literal language *see* univocal language
Locke, John, 114
logic, 38–42, 44, 198
  symbolic logic, 38, 103
logical atomism, 38–9
logical empiricism, 38, 75–6
logical positivism, 4, 6, 42–7, 49–50, 61, 109, 199–200
  and figurative language, 114, 115, 119, 193
  limitations of, 75
  verification principle, 43–6, 47
  Wittgenstein influences, 37, 39, 41, 42
logical symbolism, 45
logocentricism, 182, 183, 191
Luther, Martin, 34, 35, 146, 160
Lyotard, Jean-François, 199

McClendon, James William, 79–80, 82–4, 135, 154–5, 161
McFague, Sallie, 125, 126, 129, 132–3
MacIntyre, Alasdair, 199
Maimonides, Moses, 15–16, 19
Mascall, Eric, 27–8
meaning, 3, 11, 58, 143–4, 156, 195–6
  deconstruction and, 181, 182–3
  structuralism and, 165
  *see also* truth
Merleau-Ponty, Maurice, 3
metaphor, 7, 112–33
  and analogy, 124–7
  as cognitive, 114–22, 133, 195–6, 204
  "dead," 85–6, 121, 126, 130–1

in exegesis, 127–9
and God, 25, 130–3
irreducibility of, 115, 128, 134, 161, 200–1
models as, 119, 120
and narrative theology, 135–6, 137
as ornamental, 112, 113–14
parables of Jesus as, 3, 128–9, 201
philosophy of, 5, 101, 197, 198
in theology, 129–33
*see also* allegory; analogy; symbolism
metaphysics, 5, 6, 25, 28, 60
  logical positivists dismiss, 41, 42, 43, 44–5
Mitchell, Basil, 52–5, 57, 76, 85, 217 n53&55
moderate realism, 30
modernity: defined, 240 n55
Moore, G. E., 38, 39
Moore, Stephen D., 192
mysticism, 2, 7, 15–20, 41
myths, 7, 129, 139, 172, 178–9, 230 n46

narrative structure, 168–9
narrative theology, 5, 7, 134–62, 193, 195, 196, 197, 198–9, 200–1, 202
  Californian School, 154–62
  Chicago School, 135–9
  Yale School, 139–53
negative way, 15–21, 23, 76, 193
  negative theology, 189–92
  *see also* equivocal language
neo-Platonism, 16–17
Neurath, Otto, 42, 213 n31
New Criticism, 109
New Hermeneutic movement, 128
Nielson, Kai, 69
Nietzsche, Friedrich, 121, 184, 185
nominalism, 7, 29–30
Norris, Christopher, 183

Ockham, William of, 29–30
Ogden, Schubert, 22–3
ontological hermeneutics, 90–5, 100
"ordinary language philosophy," 10,
    61, 79
Origen, 32, 34

parables
    in falsification challenge, 47–58
    of Jesus, 7, 127–9, 156, 158,
        168–9, 178–9, 201
Parmenides of Elea, 8
Pascal, Blaise, 57
patriarchy critique *see* feminist
    philosophy
Patte, Daniel, 177–8
Paul, St, 17, 31, 32
Peirce, C. S., 6
Perrin, Norman, 128
phenomenology, 4–5, 43, 90–1,
    99–100, 101, 107–8, 137
Phillips, D. Z., 69, 70–2, 77
Philo, Judaeus, 32
philosophical hermeneutics *see*
    hermeneutics
physicalism, 43
Placher, William, 142
Plato, 8, 9–10, 29
    on knowledge, 12
    neo-Platonism, 16–17
    prefers speech, 9, 181, 182
Plotinus, 16, 17
poetics, 5, 9, 10, 11, 112
Popper, Karl, 46–7, 49
postmodernism, 181
poststructuralism, 110, 162, 163,
    165, 180–92, 193, 197, 199,
    201
    deconstruction, 5, 7, 180, 182–4,
        186, 188–92
    feminism and, 187–8
    in religious studies, 188–92
    *see also* structuralism
pre-Socratics, 8
Propp, Vladimir, 166, 167, 168,
179, 180
Pseudo-Dionysius the Areopagite *see*
    Dionysius the Areopagite
psychoanalysis, 96, 97, 106, 223
    n66
psychologism, 43
Pythagorean School, 9, 16

Quine, Willard, 64

Ramsey, Ian T., 74–8, 112
reader-response theory, 107–11, 143,
    160, 183
realism, 7, 29–31
Reformers, 34
    *see also* Calvin; Luther
regional hermeneutics, 87, 142
relativism, 64–5, 160, 162
religious language, 6–7, 12
    as cognitive, 13, 72–9
    historical approaches to, 14–36
    logical positivism and, 37, 41, 42,
        43–4, 44–5
    as logically odd, 75, 76, 77
    as noncognitive, 7, 15, 51, 67–73,
        203
    philosophy of, 1–3, 6–13
    poststructuralism and, 188–92
    recent approaches to, 193–205
    speech-act theory, and, 79–80,
        82, 83–6
    structuralism and, 173–80
    Wittgenstein and, 41, 67–8,
        69–72
    *see also* analogy; Bible/biblical
        studies; equivocal language;
        exegesis; hermeneutics;
        metaphor; narrative theology;
        symbolism; univocal language
rhetoric, 5, 8–9, 10, 11
    metaphor and, 112, 113, 114
Richards, I. A., 114–16
Ricœur, Paul, 4, 149, 236 n64
    and critical hermeneutics, 99–107,
        142–3, 161, 201

on metaphor, 113, 116, 117, 120, 121, 135–6, 195, 231–2 n57
mimesis, 138
and myth, 230 n46
and narrative theology, 110, 135–9
on parables, 129
and structuralism, 173–5, 180
and symbolism, 123, 124
Romantic hermeneutics, 88, 90, 102, 109, 136–7, 174
Roscellinus, Johannes, 30
Rousseau, Jean-Jacques, 182
Russell, Alan, 116
Russell, Bertrand, 37–9, 40, 41, 91
Ryle, Gilbert, 217 n72

Saussure, Ferdinand de, 163–6, 173, 180, 182
scepticism *see* skepticism
Schleiermacher, Friedrich, 87–9, 90, 145, 160
Schlick, Moritz, 42, 43, 45
science
impact on philosophy, 7, 44
scientific language, 44, 72, 119
Scotus, John Duns, 15, 20–1, 22, 23–4
Scripture *see* Bible/biblical studies; exegesis; hermeneutics
semiotics/signs, 6, 122, 123, 165–6, 172–3
*see also* structuralism; symbolism
skepticism, 8
Skeptical School, 11, 30
Smith, James, 80, 82–4
Socrates, 8, 9, 11
in Plato's dialogues, 10, 182
Sophist movement, 8–9
Soskice, Janet Martin
on analogy, 126
on metaphor, 118, 120, 124, 125, 129, 130, 131, 231–2 n57
speculative philosophy, 8, 9

speech
ideal speech situation, 96, 97
*langue* and *parole*, 163–4, 174–5
versus written word, 9, 181, 182
speech-act theory, 79–86, 154, 155–7, 159, 172, 197
applied to Gospels, 151, 156, 157
in structuralism, 172, 177
Stroup, George, 157
structuralism, 5, 7, 100, 101–2, 163–73, 193, 199, 201
critique, 171–3, 197
in religious studies, 173–80
*see also* poststructuralism
Sturrock, John, 5–6
Swinburne, Richard, 26
symbolism, 3, 10, 21, 110–11, 121, 139, 195, 196
of evil, 101, 123
and metaphor, 126, 127
and religion, 22, 33, 122–4
substitutionary theory of symbolic language, 11
symbolic logic, 38, 45, 103
*see also* metaphor; semiotics

Tanner, Kathryn, 144
Taylor, Mark C., 189–90, 203
Tertullian, 31–2
theology
as grammar, 68, 147
and metaphor, 129–33
narrative theology, 134–62
negative theology, 189–92
and philosophy, 6–7
and symbolism, 123
Thiemann, Ronald, 139, 143, 144, 148, 150–3, 156, 157
Thiselton, Anthony C., x, 175–7, 180, 189, 201
on Habermas, 221–2 n44
Tilley, Terrence, 154, 159–61
Tillich, Paul, 21–2, 52, 121, 122–3, 124, 233 n14
Todorov, Tzvetan, 168, 171

Tracy, David, 131, 135, 139, 142,
    143
  on analogy, 124–6
  on classic texts, 106–7
  and Lindbeck, 149, 234–5 n40,
    235 n45
truth
  elusive nature of, 47, 196
  Gadamer on, 92
  truth claims, 6, 96–7, 151–3
  truth question, 147, 148, 155,
    156, 157–9, 173, 201–5
  *see also* meaning

universals, 14, 15, 29–31
*University* debate, 37, 47–58, 67, 78,
    85
univocal language
  analogy and, 125, 126
  logical positivism and, 37, 41, 43,
    114, 119
  for philosophy, 10, 11, 181–2,
    193–4
  recent attitudes towards, 195–6,
    197, 200, 203–4
  schools of exegesis and, 32, 33–4
  univocal way, 7, 15, 20–3, 26, 28
  Wittgenstein (later) and, 85–6,
    119, 121–2, 125

verification principle, 43–6, 47,

56–7, 201–2
Via, Dan Jr, 128, 129, 179–80
Vienna circle *see* logical positivism

Waismann, Friedrich, 42
Westphal, Merold, 244 n97
Whitehead, Alfred North, 38, 120
Wisdom, John, 47–8, 50, 55, 73–4,
    77–8
Wittgenstein, Ludwig
  early theories, 12, 37–8, 39–42,
    45, 91, 197
  fideism, 67, 69–72, 73, 144–5,
    148
  influence of later theories, 110,
    118, 119, 121–3, 139–40, 142,
    185, 194, 197, 198, 199, 201
  influence on logical positivism,
    37, 39, 41, 42
  language games, 58, 59–72
  and religion, 63–4, 67–8, 69–72,
    202
  written word: limitations, 10, 181,
    182

Yale School of narrative theology,
    134–5, 138–53, 160, 161

Zen Buddhism: *koan*, 19–20
Zwingli, Ulrich, 34